THE SPELL BOOK FOR BEGINNERS

THE COMPLETE GUIDE TO USING CANDLES, CRYSTALS, AND HERBS IN OVER 150 MAGIC SPELLS: 3 BOOKS IN 1

BRIDGET BISHOP

HENTOPAN
PUBLISHING

© COPYRIGHT 2021 BRIDGET BISHOP - ALL RIGHTS RESERVED.

The content contained within this book may not be reproduced, duplicated or transmitted without direct written permission from the author or the publisher.

Under no circumstances will any blame or legal responsibility be held against the publisher, or author, for any damages, reparation, or monetary loss due to the information contained within this book. Either directly or indirectly.

Legal Notice:

This book is copyright protected. This book is only for personal use. You cannot amend, distribute, sell, use, quote or paraphrase any part, or the content within this book, without the consent of the author or publisher.

Disclaimer Notice:

Please note the information contained within this document is for educational and entertainment purposes only. All effort has been executed to present accurate, up to date, and reliable, complete information. No warranties of any kind are declared or implied. Readers acknowledge that the author is not engaging in the rendering of legal, financial, medical or professional advice. The content within this book has been derived from various sources. Please consult a licensed professional before attempting any techniques outlined in this book.

By reading this document, the reader agrees that under no circumstances is the author responsible for any losses, direct or indirect, which are incurred as a result of the use of the information contained within this document, including, but not limited to, — errors, omissions, or inaccuracies.

HENTOPAN
PUBLISHING

CONTENTS

THE CANDLE MAGIC SPELL BOOK

Introduction	3

PART I: UNDERSTANDING CANDLE MAGIC

1. The Magic of Candles	9
2. Candle Basics	16
3. Preparation	28
4. Interpretation	35
5. After the Spell	44

PART II: THE SPELLS

6. Love and Relationship Spells	53
7. Friends and Family Spells	78
8. Money and Prosperity Spells	100
9. Work and Career Spells	118
10. Health and Well-Being Spells	137
11. Protection Spells	157
Final Words	177

THE CRYSTAL MAGIC SPELL BOOK

Introduction — 183

Part I
UNDERSTANDING CRYSTAL MAGIC

1. The Magic of Crystals — 189
2. Crystal Basics — 200
3. Crystals and Chakras — 213
4. Essential Crystals — 226
5. Preparation — 244
6. Crystal Grids — 254
7. Crystal Elixirs — 262

Part II
THE SPELLS

8. Healing Spells — 271
9. Love Spells — 296
10. Prosperity Spells — 316
11. Protection Spells — 338

Conclusion — 357

THE HERB MAGIC SPELL BOOK

Introduction — 361

PART 1:
Understanding Herb Magic

1. The Magic Of Herbs — 367
2. Herb Magic Basics — 374
3. The Wheel Of The Year — 383
4. Essential Herbs — 401
5. Gathering Herbs In Nature — 423

6. Growing Your Own Herbs	431
7. Using Herbs In Your Magic	438

PART 2:
The Spells

8. Love Spells	451
9. Health Spells	476
10. Wealth Spells	499
Final Thoughts	523
Notes	527

SPECIAL OFFER FROM HENTOPAN
PUBLISHING

Get this additional book free just for joining the Hentopan Launch Squad.

If you want insider access, plus this free book, all you have to do is scan the code below with your phone!

THE CANDLE MAGIC SPELL BOOK

A BEGINNER'S GUIDE TO SPELLS TO IMPROVE YOUR LIFE

INTRODUCTION

The mesmerizing flicker of a candle flame contains magical depths that, if we know how to plumb them, can bring us our heart's desires. Candles are used in rituals the world over, from the lighting of candles in the nave of a church to the centering on the flame in meditative practice. They are vessels of pent-up energy, releasing intention into the air as they burn, amplifying the wishes and wants of those who know how to channel that energy. This is why they are central to the practice of magic and to witchcraft in general, featured in numerous rituals, ceremonies, and spells of all kinds.

When I first started practicing witchcraft about a decade ago, I was facing a difficult time in my life: I was let go from my first real job, anxious about my finances and concerned that I wouldn't be able to keep my apartment (would I have to go back to live with my parents?). The anxiety was crushing. My boyfriend at the time and I had been bickering constantly and decided to take a break; when I lost my job, all I could focus on was how awful my life was, which led to our eventual break-up. It seemed as if nothing in my life was going right. In fact, I started to wonder if I even had the ability to live a good, stable life as a functioning adult. Things were pretty bleak.

Then, a friend of mine introduced me to witchcraft, and it seemed like something that I could at least pass the time with, letting go of my constant worry in the comfort of the rituals. The simple spells that my friend taught me actually seemed to help things—not only did I get another, *better* job, but I also started dating again. In fact, for the last three years, I have been in a happy, exciting, committed relationship. The changes were gradual at first, but as I became more comfortable and skilled with the spells, the stronger my magic seemed to be. Perhaps this is because the most important benefit I gained from the witchcraft was an overwhelming sense of self-confidence. I knew that I was good enough, worthy of love and success, and that I had the power to put my life back in order, not just to live but to *thrive*.

Now that I'm in my early 30s, I can look back on that period of my life and feel certain that I won't ever have to go through that again. Over the years, I have learned many, many spells and introduced many, many people to these rituals. It's deeply satisfying to help others through the rough patches in their lives, which is why I want to help you as well! I find that candle magic is an excellent place to start: it's simple and straightforward, and you don't need a lot of esoteric accessories or widespread knowledge to get started and to *see results*.

If you are curious about the wide world of magic, and the casting of spells in particular, then you can get started with this introduction to some simple candle spells, the practical application of magic at its best.

In this book, you will discover the ancient art of candle magic; learning how to prepare rituals for specific spells, interpret your results, and clear up afterwards with ceremonial success. Here you will find spells for love and relationships, friends and family, money and prosperity, work and career, health and well-being, and protection. The various spells you will find under these headings are organized into a simple template that will tell you when to perform the spell, what you need to complete it, and a step-by-step set of instructions to carry out the ritual. The spells here will address nearly every aspect of your life, enabling you to take control of your own happiness and overall success.

Many people who are seeking a spiritual outlet for their difficulties and desires are increasingly turning to magic and spells. There is a reason why cultures across the globe and throughout history have celebrated sacred events around the fire. There is a reason why gathering around the hearth is a symbol of comfort and security, of affirming basic human connections and communal spirit. Candles remind us of the power of the flame, of the wisdom resident in fire. We can channel those powers to harness the energies in our own lives to do better, to have better, to live better lives. In this book, you will find opportunities to establish your own practical magic, using these simple spells to improve your situation and enhance your happiness. Once you get into the rhythms of the rituals, you will no doubt find your self-confidence increase as your power grows—and you will find that you have the power to determine the shape and scope of your own life. Burn bright!

PART I: UNDERSTANDING CANDLE MAGIC

How does candle magic work? Basically, candles represent energy, specifically the transformation of energy: when a candle is unlit, the energy is dormant; when the candle is lit, the energy is released, transformed by the flame and affected by the air. If you put intentions behind the release of that energy, then you can channel and shape that energy to fit your own needs and desires. All fire is transformative—think about how fire transforms raw ingredients into satisfactory meals, for example—and if you understand how to apply your intention to fire, then you can shape the process of transformation.

It is also important to note that, while the fire is the central element of energy in candle magic, there are other attributes to be taken into account when setting up your spells: the color of the candle has significance, as do the symbols that may surround it or be carved directly into it. Thus, you can customize each spell to fit your particular needs, demonstrating your intentions in numerous ways so as to increase the possibilities for success each time. In the following chapters, you will learn more about the history of candles and the use of fire in ritual events, as well as become familiar with the basic properties of candles and how to use them. There are specific steps to take when preparing to cast a candle spell, and ways in which you can determine how successful a spell is, thus ultimately improving your rate of success. You will also learn how to complete the spell and close out the ritual by cleansing your space, by utilizing elements from the spell to enhance results, and/or by disposing of items properly, depending on the spell.

Finally, you must be aware that fire is also transformative in terribly destructive ways—the ashes left after a house fire are nothing short of devastating—so you must strive to be responsible with your candle magic, not only in your intentions but also in your applications. That is, magic (some spell it "magick") in its purest sense is not about wishing ill on others, or even exercising any will over others, but rather it is about *personal* transformation and the fulfilment of *personal* (positive) goals. Witchcraft is not the work of harm or hate or control. In addition, candle magic should always be practiced with safety in mind, so always be cautious when using live fire in any ritual or spell. With these precautions in mind, you can move on to a greater understanding of how candles work and how to perform some basic magic.

1

THE MAGIC OF CANDLES

Candles are a common element in ritual practices around the world, not just in witchcraft. Their centrality to rituals and magic is easy to understand when you are aware of how the powerful element of fire has been viewed throughout history, both mythological and actual. We are also well aware of the practical nature of fire and of candles: fire both warms and provides food, while candles provide light and scent. For centuries, humankind depended on candles specifically to light their rooms after dark, while fires warmed our dwellings before electricity. It is no surprise then that the element of fire and its vessel of the candle have become important symbols and conductors of magical power well into the modern age. There is something ancient and mysterious about fire, and without it, human civilization could not exist. The candle, therefore, is also infused with the mystery and potency of this tempestuous element, its ability to cleanse and transform, to destroy and renew.

Mythological tales about fire abound throughout history and across cultures. There is, for example, the famous story about Prometheus, the Titan of Greek mythology who gifted fire to humans and was therefore punished by Zeus: he was to be chained to a rock, where his liver would be eaten each day by Zeus's eagle (only to regrow afresh for another meal the next) for eternity. Why was he punished? Because giving humans the gift of fire was to grant them a civilization, an opportunity to become more like the gods. Fire is forever associated with the civilizing impulse: we gather around the hearth, and with this burning light we signal to others that this is a place of warmth and civil society. It is to that light, in the great Hall of Heorot, that the monster Grendel is drawn in the ancient epic, *Beowulf.* The light represents the beacon of civilization, from which Grendel has been exiled, and he enacts his revenge by ravaging the hall night after night until the hero Beowulf is sent to dispatch him. In both tales, fire is the element that forges civilized culture.

In many places, fire is also often associated with divinity: think of the Biblical tale of the burning bush, wherein Moses is given a message from God that he is the one to lead the Israelites out of Egypt. This fiery message of divine intervention also crops up when the pillar of fire serves to guide the Israelites through the dark wilderness on their gruelling trek. There is also fiery retribution to be found in the Bible, as in the burning of the wicked cities of Sodom and Gomorrah.

In both Eastern and Western cultures, fire has been used to divine the future and to decode messages, to understand prophecies and interpret events. Animal bones would be thrown into fires, and the cracks that appeared under the pressure of heat would be interpreted, guiding decisions and uncovering divine intentions. Indeed, for much of Western cultural history, fire has been seen as a god in and of itself, ascribed with anthropomorphic abilities; it could *feed* and *devour*, or *breathe* and *grow*, finally decaying into death. Fire was so instrumental to supporting human existence that it became viewed as nearly human itself.

It is also considered to be an agent of purification: after a forest is burned in a fire, it is able to spring back to life out of the ashes. Disney's original *Fantasia* displayed this in its "Night on Bald Mountain" sequence set to the crashing music of Wagner; the fire appears as a demonic force, devouring everything in its path until nothing is left. And yet, new life magically appears once the spring rains replenish the earth, renewing the world. This is the myth of the phoenix, of course: as the ancient symbol of rebirth, the phoenix grows old and feeble, but instead of dying, it bursts into flames and rises anew from the ashes in a cycle of hope and reanimation. Like funeral pyres in many religions, the fire represents a purification in death and a releasing of the spirit into more divine realms.

More practically, fire allows us to cook food in an act that definitively separates humans from other animals; only humans cook food and create elaborate cuisines. Again, fire is fundamental to the process of constructing a civilization, a culture. It also expands our ability to be productive, providing light after dark so we can study or work; many inventions originated by the light of the fire after a day's work is done. It has also been crucial to our ability to survive and thrive throughout the seasons, keeping us warm through the winter in colder climes. Fire made it possible to live in various corners of the globe, and it still serves as a powerful symbolic reminder of the comforts of home and community. It is a beacon shining through the dark.

Fire is also regarded as one of the four fundamental elements, along with earth, water, and air. Each of these elements has a specific role to play: fire itself, as aforementioned, is the symbol of transformation and is represented by the sun and stars, as well as other natural (and forceful) elements, like erupting volcanoes and stark deserts. Because fire is always in motion—dancing or devouring, flickering or slowly being snuffed out—it reads as the most animated of elements, though both water and air (and even earth) move in their own ways, as well. Its connection to the sun and light in general associates it with illumination, not just purely physical illumination but also mental enlightenment, bringing clarity to thought and imagination to ideas. The "aha" moment of invention is said to be one of illumination: when we have a revelation, we are said to have "seen the light." Fire is also associated with great strength and health overall, because its vibrancy is so lifelike, and it aligns closely to passion, as our internal fires/desires burn brightly.

With regard to magic, fire is instrumental in many rituals and ceremonies, often called upon to represent masculine energies and projective powers. This element is particularly conducive to certain intentions, including igniting the passions (and, concomitantly, compassion) within a relationship; increasing your own personal energy ("lighting a fire under you"); and discovering hidden truths, bringing illumination to secretive darkness. Fire is also used in many protection spells and rituals, as you gather those you love closer to the fire, that symbol of hearth and home. It can also help in banishment spells, purging negative thoughts and renewing good habits out of old; this is using fire as in the process of purification and rebirth. It can also improve confidence and self-awareness; again, the illumination of fire to reveal (and cast out) the negative. Fire was also often used to strengthen resolve ("an iron will be forged in the fire")—just as fire can temper the blade so that it is stronger and, paradoxically, more flexible, so can fire forge mental strength and an even temperament. Fire propelled warriors to victory, not only through its ferocious strength and powers of destruction but also via its power to inspire revelation, illuminating the strategies necessary for success. These are all examples that you can begin to apply to your own personal needs as you start to learn certain spells.

There are many ways in which you can connect to the element of fire when implementing magical rituals—candles, of course, will be our primary vessel for the remainder of the book, though you can explore other sources, as well. Building bonfires is one of the central events at many gatherings, including a gathering of like-minded witches: with the right intentions, flames can be read for divination or used to create a meditative state for contemplation. A more contained cousin to the bonfire, the hearth fire is central to home and family, or friends and community; spells cast here cement bonds and create protective boundaries. Lanterns and (especially) fire torches can be symbolic of lighting the way in spells that ask for guidance, as well as those that illuminate the truth of complicated circumstances. Torches are often lit to initiate a ceremony, and ceremonially snuffed as the magic is completed. As in most magical practice, the more connected to nature your tools are, the stronger their magical powers; thus, wood fires are particularly potent. Different woods indicate different symbolic associations; for example, cherry wood is used to create good fortune and foster love, while apple wood nurtures youthful health and general happiness. Even the ashes (and wax), the leftover by-products of ritual fires, can be used for magical purposes: you can include these in amulets and charms to increase their potency.

Candles, in particular, are central to most modern witchcraft practice: they are symbolic of all of the powers of the element of fire, and they can be procured easily and utilized in a controlled fashion. These all-purpose magical tools not only help to generate magic from intention, but they are also key to marking sacred space. Instead of emphasizing the destructive aspects of fire, candles symbolize the warmer, gentler, comforting aspects, and thus are commonly used in personal wish spells. The magic of candles can bring about personal transformation and significant regeneration. In secular culture today, we often celebrate our birthday by blowing out candles, signifying the ineluctable movement from one state to another, from this age to that age, the ongoing process of transformation.

Basically, all spell work is about transforming an intention—your wish, your desire, your request—into a reality. Candles work as some of the most effective communicators of those intentions; they are akin to messengers, carrying your messages of intent out into the spiritual realm where they can be heard. As a candle burns, it is transformed, seeming to dissipate from the material form (the candle slowly disappears) as it carries in its flame your intentions to the ethereal plane. This process helps beginners to clearly visualize what they wish their magic to do: inculcating the candle with your intention allows you to envision its manifestation. While the candle is primarily associated with the element of fire, it is particularly potent in spell work because it contains or relies on all of the other elements, as well: the candle itself, the wick and the base, represent the earth, grounding the candle to that subtle strength; the wax represents the element of water as it melts and runs while the candle burns, working to reshape the form of things; and the flame itself relies on air to keep it burning and dancing (fire needs oxygen to survive, just as we do). Thus, using candles in magical practice is both easy and powerful. In fact, the very act of lighting a candle—even if you don't intend to perform magic—can alter the very atmosphere of a space. We become more alert to the presence of unseen energies surrounding us when we focus on the flicker of a lit candle.

As you can clearly see, the element of fire is central to our understanding of human civilization in general. Its magical potency has been recognized throughout the centuries and utilized for both conquest and comfort, destruction and regeneration. We still employ fire, particularly in the form of candles, for many rituals, both sacred and secular, and modern witchcraft relies heavily on their power. In the next chapter, you will be introduced to the many types of candles that can be used for different forms of magic, as well as the many correspondences that are used in conjunction with candle flames to create formidable magical spells.

2

CANDLE BASICS

When using candle magic, you must consider not only the appropriate candle to use but also other factors that influence the potency of your intention. Basically, the candle that you choose, and how you choose to enhance its power, is paramount to the success of your spells. Here you will find advice on what kinds of candles to choose and how to interpret various correspondences, as well as how to incorporate additional elements into your candle magic to increase the efficacy of your spells.

First, as you are almost certainly aware, candles come in a variety of shapes and sizes, which impact how you will use them in your spell work. Below I list which kinds of candles are best for the various spells that follow in the second part of the book--at least the ones that have provided the best results for me over the years. This list describes the main varieties of candles and when to use them:

Tea candles: tea, or tealight, candles are very small, round candles usually ensconced in their own metal or plastic container. They are quick burning because they are so small, and they are generally used in groups, often within special holders. These can be used for short spells that invoke a quick intention. I like to use these when I need a mid-week boost of energy or focus; a quick good fortune or prosperity spell before payday or the completion of a big project is also great for short-lived spell work.

Votive candles: these medium-sized candles are short and squat and take longer to burn than tea candles. Because of their shape, they burn quite slowly as the wick sinks into the candle. They often leave a significant amount of wax behind after burning their cores hollow. See below for more on when and how to use them.

Pillar candles: similar to votive candles in shape, pillar candles are quite large, tall and broad, and take quite a long time to burn out. Again, like votives, pillar candles will leave behind a hefty amount of wax. Thus, when using both votive and pillar candles, consider the spell: if the spell requires the candle to burn all the way out before the intention is invoked—as most spells do—then these candles, particularly the pillar, might not be well-suited (unless you have the time and/or strength of intention to wait). However, there are some spells wherein you burn a candle in stages, depending on the phases of the moon or days of the week (among other factors), which would mean that either of these choices would be pertinent: I use pillar candles when casting spells that have to do with long-term goals, regardless of the category. Finally, there are some spells for which you want to have leftover wax to create other magical objects (amulets, talismans) or to perform completion rituals. These candles would be good choices for those purposes.

Taper candles: the taper candle is the all-purpose candle for spell work: tall and slim, these burn steadily and fairly quickly, though not as fast as the tea candle. They also typically produce the tallest and brightest flames (the chunky shape of the votive and pillar candles tend to obscure the flame after a few moments of burning), and the wax melts away as the candle burns down. These are my preferred candle: they last long enough to fully convey intentions, and have enough surface area on which to carve symbols (to be discussed in the following chapter) when I need a boost of power.

Special "spell" candles: you can also find numerous varieties of special candles, made specifically for certain kinds of spells, on the market (they are easy to find online). These are candles that have been made with other magically tuned materials, such as herbs, crystals or essential oils, and/or endowed with particular magical symbols to enhance their power. Certainly, these can be a part of your spell work, if you like, though these special spell candles are more expensive than ordinary candles (which can be used for magical purposes) and they are not imbued by *you* with your specific intentions. That is, they aren't customized to your particular needs. Thus, save these for very special occasions or complicated spells wherein you may need a boost. See below, however, for ways in which you can endow your ordinary candles with greater magical potency.

Figure candles: like the special spell candles, these figure candles have particular functions and are often also imbued with essential oils and other enhancements to increase their power. These include not only male and female representations, often used for love and romance spells, but other powerful symbols within the world of witchcraft, including the skull, the cross, and the cat. There are also figure candles for specific body parts, which are used both for healing rituals and for enhancement spells. Again, these can increase the potency of your candle magic, though you can also manipulate an ordinary pillar candle to create the same effect by carving symbols into it. See below for some specific suggestions.

Other considerations: finally, you should also consider the material from which your candle is made: many mass-produced candles are made of paraffin, which can produce faintly toxic chemicals (paraffin is a by-product of petroleum); thus, most witches prefer to use candles made of natural materials, such as beeswax (most popular) and soy. You should also note that only new candles should be used for spell work; as with any potentially magical object, candles pick up energy and resonate with vibrations from previous uses. Thus, your spells will likely not be as effective unless you use a new candle for each one. If you are concerned about waste, consider recycling leftover candle wax for household use: you can melt together leftover bits of wax and pour into a simple mold (cleaned out can, for example), inserting a new wick. These leftover candles won't be effective for spell work but they are quite adequate for the dinner table or living room.

In addition to the type of candle used, there are additional factors to consider when choosing your candles for particular spells. There are magical correspondences inherent to specific features: for example, the color red corresponds to passion and strength, and is also associated with the fire element; the herb thyme corresponds to purification and is often used in cleansing or banishment spells. This also applies to timing. When you cast your spell has an impact on its efficacy, and to the seasons and natural cycles. You can find elaborate tables of correspondences across the magical spectrum. Below are some simple lists of basic correspondences that will improve the focus of your intention and thus the potency of your spell, along with the reliability of your results:

Color Correspondences: when choosing your candle for spells, you want to pay close attention to color; colors are associated with various elements and characteristics. Choosing the right color for your intention will increase the efficacy of your spell. Here are some basic correspondences:

- *Green* is associated with nature and fertility, as well as money and good fortune.
- *Red* is associated with power and passion, as well vitality and courage.
- *Pink* is associated with friendship and romance, as well as compassion and innocence.
- *Yellow* is associated with success and happiness, as well as travel and imagination.
- *Blue* is associated with truth and communication, as well as fidelity and patience.
- *Orange* is associated with creativity and joy, as well as ambition and justice.

- *Purple* is associated with wisdom and spiritual power, as well as warding off evil.
- *Silver* is associated with intuition and dreams.
- *White* is associated with purity and cleansing, as well as peacefulness and balance.
- *Black* is associated with grounding and learning, as well as protection and banishment.

Phases of the Moon: The moon is considered a powerful symbol of feminine energy, mysterious in its nature and full of quiet strength. Different spells work differently during the various phases of the moon. For example, some spells use the growing power of the waxing moon to increase the potency of a spell, while other spells require that you cast it during a full moon for maximum effect. Fewer spells call for casting during a waning moon, though there are various spells that require you to track the phases of the moon in order to complete the full spell.

Days of the Week: in addition to the cycles of the moon, each day of the week has its own corresponding set of powers and characteristics, making spellcasting more or less effective on certain days. With most magic, the phase of the moon takes precedence over the day of the week. For example, if a full moon falls on a Wednesday, but your spell suggests a Sunday would be a better corresponding day, the full moon trumps the day of the week. Still, when it is possible to apply the correspondence of a particular day to your intentions, here is a simple guide:

- *Sunday* is named for the sun, so it radiates masculine energy and works well with red, gold, and yellow colors.
- *Monday* is named for the moon, so it, in contrast, radiates feminine energy and works well with blue, white, and silver colors.
- *Tuesday* corresponds to the planet Mars, so it brings with it masculine attributes and is associated with courage and strength.
- *Wednesday* comes from "Woden's Day," which associates it with the Norse god Odin, and is also connected to the planet Mercury. Mercury was the messenger of the gods, so this indicates that Wednesday is an excellent day for communications, as well as divination.
- *Thursday* is associated with Thor and the planet Jupiter, both gods in different pantheons, again signalling a masculine energy. It is frequently associated with the harvest, thus with abundance and wealth.
- *Friday* brings with it a feminine energy, associated with the planet Venus as well as the Norse goddess Frigga, and thus the powers of romance and love, and the colors of pink and white. It is also ripe for fertility energy.
- *Saturday* ends the week with more masculine energy, in particular the power of wisdom and self-restraint, contrary to what our modern-day weekends might entail. It is also an opportune time to confront issues of death.

Symbol Enhancements: you can also enhance the power of your candle by using various symbols along with the candle; these can clarify your intentions in visible ways that will both help you focus and increase the likelihood of specific results. These symbols can be carved directly into candles, drawn on paper that rests underneath your candle's base (protected from the flame, of course), or simply drawn with your hand or a wand into the air to signify your intentions. More on this will be addressed in the following chapter. There are any number of magical symbols that you can use in your spells, from the pentacle, which represents the four fundamental elements (fire, water, air, earth) in harmony with the divine, to the witches' knot, which represents the unbreakable unity among the elements and natural cycles.

Herbal Additions: you can also add herbs, with their magical properties, to your candle magic to make it more potent and to clarify your specific intentions. There are herbs too numerous to count that have been used in magic rituals and spells all across the world, but here are some, with their attendant characteristics, that you can readily find in grocery stores, markets, and home gardens:

- *Basil* is a common kitchen herb, a potent potential medicine and an all-purpose protective shield. It is most frequently used in spells for protection and can be used for smudging (ridding a space of negative energy). It is also associated with fertility, partly because of its bright green color and strong aroma.
- *Thyme* is another powerful herb used in a number of applications. Not only does it get rid of negative energy, but it also fosters stronger psychic energy and encourages sleep. It is often used in purification rituals and cleansing baths and can be useful in healing spells, as well.

- *Cinnamon* is technically a spice, but is considered a part of the herbal "magic family," if you will. It is often used in romance or sexual enhancement spells, as well as prosperity spells. Its main function, though, is to keep away bad energies, promoting positive spiritual connections.
- *Sage* is the most common herb used in the practice of smudging, which is to rid a space of negative energy. In addition, it also has associations with fertility and longevity—it is purported to have powerful protective properties.
- *Rosemary* also has healing properties and can be employed to enhance intellectual capacities. Because it is a mild stimulant, rosemary can give you—and your spells—a boost of energy when needed. Burning rosemary and jasmine together is a potent protection against illness, as well as an aid to hard work. Like most herbs, rosemary can also be used for purification purposes.
- *Nutmeg* is purported to bring on psychic visions (indeed, it can cause hallucinations if ingested in large quantities—not recommended for health reasons). It is also used to increase sexual energy and powers of clairvoyance.
- *Lavender* is excellent at promoting good sleep, as it is associated with calmness and serenity. It is also used in spells that help with clarity of thought, and is often used in love potions, as it is thought to be conducive to wishful thinking. Ritual cleansing can be assisted by lavender, as well.
- *Chamomile* is another herb that is thought to produce peacefulness and aid in sleep. The "Sleepytime tea" you see in stores is most often made from chamomile. It can also help in

protection spells; one old wives' tale suggests that if you have chamomile in your garden, you become a guardian of the land.
- *Dandelion* is not merely a pesky weed in your backyard, it is also thought to be a welcoming plant, good for use in friendship or attraction spells, and it can act as a messenger, along with the flame of the candle. It is employed in divination rituals, as well.

Crystal Enrichments: crystals and semi-precious stones are often used in magic, and alongside candles, they can greatly enhance certain kinds of spell work. As with herbs, there are literally thousands of examples found around the world, but here are a few fairly common crystals and stones that have properties conducive for various kinds of magic:

- *Jade* has a beautiful green color that inherently connects it to wealth and good fortune, as well as fertility. It is very common in Asian cultures and thought to bring luck.
- *Amethyst* has a soothing purple color that is often used in spells for pacifying anger and fear because of its calming qualities. Many witches sleep with an amethyst under their pillows.
- *Quartz* in its pure white form is considered a booster of energy: when casting stones for divination, white quartz is usually placed in the middle to amplify the messages. It can do the same work in spells.
- *Rose quartz*, with its lovely pink shade, is often used in spells

related to romance and friendship.
- *Citrine* is nicknamed the "success stone," and is often used in prosperity rituals and spells. It can be various shades of brown with hints of orange, so is also associated with the earth element (groundedness) and with joy.
- *Hematite* is a deep black stone that is used to chase off bad energies and help to break bad habits.
- *Moonstone* comes in a plethora of colors, but is thought to be most potent when it mimics the color of its namesake, the moon (pale grey, light blue). Because of its direct association with the moon, it is used in love spells and to call upon feminine energies.
- *Bloodstone* is actually a dark green, despite its name, though it can have flecks of red within it. Its association with blood makes it useful in spells regarding passion (or the lack thereof), as well as in healing applications.
- *Tiger's Eye* contains within it both the powers of the earth (brown) and the sun (yellow, gold). It can be worn for protection, and its golden eye attracts prosperity.
- *Lapis Lazuli*, with its deep blue color, has been prized the world over. It is thought to promote intuition and psychic connection, and to help soothe and protect.

Essential Oil Boosts: these are infusions of natural plants and herbs into an oil in order to intensify them and make them easy to apply. They are often used in spells to increase the potency of the magic; in candle magic, they can be used to anoint the candle, clarifying and intensifying the intentions. There are commonly used essential oils made of lavender, patchouli, cinnamon, orange and other citrus oils, cedarwood, sandalwood, and juniper, among others.

3

PREPARATION

Now that you have amassed the appropriate candles for your spell work, along with some additional magical boosters as described in the previous chapter, we can turn our attention to how to most effectively cast a spell. Getting results isn't merely about having the right magical aids on hand, it is also about how you prepare your space and how you prepare your materials. These simple steps will give your space a boost of positive energy, allowing your intentions to flow from you through your candle and spell out to the ethereal plane. You are readying yourself to make your message *loud and clear*, guaranteeing good results.

Setting up an Altar

Most spellcasting takes place at an altar that reflects the witch's personal magical style as well as adheres to some basic guidelines to enhance energy flow and magical potency. This is the symbolic centerpiece of your magical practice. While you can set up a makeshift altar each time you decide to cast a spell, most practitioners choose to set up a permanent space somewhere in their home in order to have it ready to go whenever it feels right to cast a spell. You can also make a moveable altar, if you like, so that you can clear the space whenever the altar is not in use. This is also handy should you decide to practice spell work outdoors: many witches find that they can more powerfully connect with the universal energy when they are surrounded by nature and natural objects.

Before you embark upon building your altar, however, you will want to cleanse your space: you can do this by smudging, which is the burning of herbs (such as sage or rosemary) to clear the space of negative vibrations. You might also consider taking a ritual bath to cleanse *yourself* of negative energy, if you feel that this would be beneficial to your goals. Putting quartz crystals around the bath, along with some purifying (white) candles and perhaps some lavender essential oil in the water, will refresh your spirit and clarify your mind. I always smudge before I tend to my altar, even after it's set up, and I usually smudge before the casting of any spell: it not only helps to clear my mind, it also gives me time to focus on my intentions. In terms of the ritual bath, I do that as a matter of routine about once a week, not merely for specific spells. It keeps my energy up and my magic flowing!

While there aren't any specific rules as to what your altar should look like, there are some common features that many witches utilize. You must have a flat (ideally, non-flammable) surface upon which to place your candles and other objects of ritual significance; many witches like a round or oval shape, because it is both representative of egalitarian communion (as with the witch's knot symbol) and associated with femininity. It is also common for the base of the altar to be made of natural material, such as wood or stone, rather than artificial or "cold" materials, such as plastic or steel. You can use what you have around the house, if you like, such as an unused end table or small desk—whatever suits your purposes and feels right to you. Part of the practice of magic is to start trusting in your intuitions—you'll know it's right for your purposes when you feel it is.

Once you have the base of your altar ready to go, begin to adorn it with whatever magical materials you feel are appropriate for your needs. The point of setting up an altar is to turn an ordinary space into a magical, conducive one. This extraordinary place is where your intentions will be heard, and your spells will yield results. Thus, think about what kinds of crystals and stones, symbols and colors you wish to represent your magical intentions would be best suited to making your altar a sacred space. These amplifications can change with the seasons, of course, and should also be customized for each spell. For example, think about green stones to reflect the fertility of the spring season, while fall hues of gold and orange can usher in prosperity and strength for the colder months. Another key component of practicing successful spell work is to connect with nature, tuning into natural cycles and phases.

In my case, I find that there are all sorts of natural objects that *speak* to me when I am paying attention. For example, I am drawn to stones and crystals of all kinds, so whenever I travel, I look for something that vibrates with the power of the place I'm in. This then goes on my altar, pulling in the magic from all over. (There are exceptions to this, of course: *never* take stones from sacred places, like volcanic rock from Hawaii: I can attest that the goddess Pele will hound you until you return it.) On my altar, I have a rock encrusted with sulfur that I found in the northeast; it brings me joy and good fortune; I have some geodes that I picked up out west that open up my space and mind to greater possibilities; and I keep a crystal of andalusite that I found in Morocco, which radiates psychic power alongside a Buddha figurine of jade that I procured in China. These things remind me not only of my travels, but of the spirit in which I opened up to the various energies and cultural touchstones that can be found everywhere. I also keep in the center of my altar a small, smoothed branch that I took from my childhood home. It centers my magic and keeps me grounded overall. You can clearly see that whatever you find that speaks to your energy and rights your mind will be welcome on your altar.

The primary function of your altar, ultimately, is to keep your magical materials arranged in a thoughtful and energy-boosting way that makes clear your intentions for a particular spell. This, of course, varies according to the spell, the intention, and the spell-caster's individual preferences; however, there are a handful of guidelines that will help you successfully get started. Keep any symbols or tools that are associated with the earth or water elements to the left of center, while arranging objects associated with air and fire elements to the right of center. The central part of the altar is for what you consider to be your most powerful magical symbols, and is also the space in which you set up your specific candle for a particular spell. To maximize the flow of energy, you can be even more elaborate, setting up earth elements facing north, fire elements facing south, water elements facing west, and air elements facing east: these are the cardinal directions that correspond to each fundamental element. Many altars keep a candle to the south for fire, a small bowl of salt to the north for earth, a chalice of water to the west for water, and a feather to the east for air. Still, arrange your altar according to your own intuitive feeling: this is undoubtedly the best way you will glean the maximum power from your space.

Remember that your altar is endowed with a sense of life: you must tend to it as you would tend to a houseplant or pet. Without upkeep, the altar becomes drained of energy, stagnant and cold. Make sure that your altar is meaningful enough that you do tend to it; it should feel a part of you and your magical energy. This is a sacred space, full of power, intention, and serenity—but it should also be conducive to practical usage. If it becomes so crowded that casting spells becomes difficult, or if your spell work isn't getting the best results, then it's time to rethink and rearrange the space. You can also "re-charge" your altar on occasion, if you feel it's losing potency, by using some of the following methods for charging candles.

Cleansing and Charging Candles

Once you have an altar set up, and a spell picked out, it's time to tend to your main magical object: the candle. Choose an appropriate color for your spell, of course, and then be sure to cleanse the candle well. This can be done in a couple of different ways: if you are confident in your spell work and clear in your message, you can cleanse a candle using intentions alone. You might also consider smudging the candle, using burning sage or rosemary to clear out any negative energies that might yet hover. This is to lift away the industrial and commercial associations from the candle; the process of packaging and shipping surely strips a candle of its positive energy. I myself usually smudge the space itself before doing spell work, making sure my candles are charged beforehand.

"Charging" candles before you utilize them grants them even more potency when used in spell work and this can also be done in different ways. One of the most effective ways to charge any magical object is to allow it to bathe in moonlight: one night under a full moon can fully charge a candle or other item, while a week under a waxing moon also works. You can also charge a candle by aligning it with a quartz stone, a booster of energy, for a full day. Or you can arrange stones around it, according to the correspondences assigned to the four elements and four cardinal directions: this invites all the available energies to converge onto your candle. You create a flow of spiritual energy that is open to your intentions. This kind of charging can also be done with your altar.

Carving and Anointing Candles

You can prepare your candles for spell work by carving them. This means that you should literally carve your intentions into the candle using words or phrases or magical runes that encapsulate what you intend the spell to manifest. Or you can carve particular magical symbols into the candle in order to boost its connections to the natural and/or spiritual world, creating a stronger flow of energy. If you aren't achieving the results you'd like from your initial spells, try different methods to see which works best for your magic. If words and phrases aren't working, try symbols, and vice versa.

You can also increase your success rate by anointing or "dressing" your candles before spell work. This involves rubbing the candle with essential oils appropriate to your intention (or, in some instances, adding a drop or two to where the wax will pool). If your spell involves bringing something to you (love, friendship, prosperity, and so on), anoint the candle from the top, moving down to the middle, then from the bottom moving up to the middle. If your spell intends to cast something away (as in banishment or protection spells), then start in the middle working upwards to the top and downward to the bottom.

Finally, you can boost a candle's energy even further by first anointing it, then rolling it in herbs that correspond to the intentions behind your spell. These are among the many ways in which you can increase the potency of your spells. When we move into the second section of the book, you will find instructions for ways to use certain energy-enhancing methods in particular spells.

4

INTERPRETATION

As you begin to practice your brilliant candle magic, you will want to learn how to interpret what your candles are trying to tell you with their mysterious dance. Why does a flame sometimes seem to flicker, sometimes to grow tall and insistent, sometimes to sway gently? Why does the wax sometimes drip, sometimes pool, sometimes create geometric designs of fascinating complexity? Part of developing your magical skill is about gaining the knowledge necessary to analyze the messages that you are receiving. While you are, indeed, the arbiter of the intentions, the candle itself is a vessel (linked to all of the elements, as discussed in previous chapters) for responses to your inquiries. For me, this is one of the most fascinating parts of practicing candle magic: learning to interpret how your intentions are being received and understanding how and why your spells are ultimately successful or not. The candle's response gives you crucial insight into why your intentions are realized or why your spell has faltered.

Now that you are able to choose the perfect candle for the spell, parsing out its shape and size and color, adorning it with whatever symbols or potency boosts you deem relevant to your intentions, you can begin to delve into the art of interpretation. A candle is communicating something important to you, but what it is trying to say is only revealed through an understanding of certain symbols, and is reliant on your own intuition. In other words, the following explanations for particular signals are enhanced by your own personal intentions, feelings, and powers. You may develop your own candle symbology over time, as you become more well-versed in how your spells interact with the candles themselves. In any event, there are three branches of interpretation that are relevant to practicing candle magic: divination by fire (which some call pyromancy, its own important branch of magic), divination by wax (or, ceromancy), and divination by smoke (or, capromancy). We will explore each in turn.

Lest we forget, all of the various ways in which a candle reacts to our ministrations can be explained by science and logic, through the knowledge of physical and chemical reactions. However, because we have brought the candle into a magical space—prepared as described in the previous chapter—we have imbued it with a power greater than the sum of its explicable parts. It now exists in our magical realm, and one of the constants of magic is that *everything* means something. We just have to figure out what those signals mean to *us*.

DIVINATION BY FIRE:

Clean Burn: typically speaking, if a candle flame doesn't actually do much, then that is a good sign that your message is being heard. Your spell work is likely working, though it may not show itself in a very dramatic or obvious fashion.

Tall or Bright Flame: if your candle burns brightly and stands tall and strong, this indicates that your magic itself is potent and that your intentions are clear. You will most likely achieve excellent results from your spell.

Small but Steady Flame: while this is still a sign that your intentions are being heard, it usually indicates that the power behind them is somewhat feeble. You may need to better focus your energies or clarify your intentions. If you increase your concentration during the spell, you may begin to see results in the flame; if it grows taller, then your stronger focus can be credited. In either case, your spell should reap some results, if not to the degree that you originally hoped for.

Small and Weak Flame: if the flame is both small and weak, seeming to sink into the wax, then this is a sure sign that you are asking for something that is out of reach—at least for the time being. If this weak flame succumbs to the wax, it signals that your request has fallen on deaf ears. Re-evaluate your intentions: are they, in fact, feasible? If so, then the timing is probably wrong. Regroup and check your calendar for a more auspicious time.

Dancing Flame: this mysterious sign often indicates that there are forces at work beyond your intentions. Of course, a dancing flame reveals a lot of energy, but this energy is diffuse and chaotic, so there may be other factors that are impeding your spell work. This is when you must look deeply into the flame to see what its movements might mean to you: gaze into it with eyes open but relaxed. You are looking *into* and even *beyond* the flame to discern what the signs are telling you.

Rapid Flicker Flame: if the flame acts as if it is being switched on and off, flicking rapidly in a noticeable pattern, then this indicates that there are strong energies present. It often means that you are being clearly heard in the present moment, so you should expect quick, decisive results. A flickering flame is also a good opportunity to practice divination in general, as its rhythmic movement can put you into a trance-like state.

Sputtering Flame: if the flame pops and hisses, this can indicate that there is interference; either someone or something is working against your spell. If this flame also burns unevenly, you can almost be certain that some kind of interference is pre-empting your spell. However, if a candle is particularly noisy, it's possible that spirits and ancestors are trying to speak to you, so you might do well to listen.

Blue Flame: if your candle produces the rare blue flame, you can rest assured that you are in the presence of strong and benevolent energies. Sit back and bask in the awe of your potency: a blue flame indicates that you have been able to call upon some of the strongest magic available. The more typical red or yellow flames reveal that your magic is working, but they aren't quite as powerful as the elusive blue flame.

Extinguished Flame: if the flame simply goes out suddenly, without your assistance, then clearly the spell is over. Typically, this indicates that your appeal will not be granted, that something more powerful than your magic opposes your intentions—at least for the time being. In some instances, on the other hand, this can simply mean that your intention has been heard and will be granted. If your request and spell are straightforward and simple, then it may not take much time and focus for your intentions to be heard.

"Eternal" Flame: if the flame refuses to be extinguished, then this clearly tells you that you aren't quite done. Perhaps you've missed an important component along the way or perhaps you need a moment to boost your power or clarity, but sit with it for a minute and try to figure out what you may have missed before trying to put out the candle again. Also be aware that most spells call for allowing the candle to burn out on its own, while those that do call for extinguishing the flame usually require snuffing the candle or pinching the wick. You should never blow out a candle when practicing spell work: this blows the intentions away.

Refusal to Light: if a candle stubbornly resists your attempt to light it, then you best just walk away. Your intentions are either already determined by external forces, or they are simply not within your reach. Take some time to ponder what might be blocking your magic. You might need to cleanse your space again—or yourself—and reconsider your original intentions.

DIVINATION BY SMOKE:

Abundance of Smoke: if your candle puts out a lot of smoke while you are practicing, this is the candle's way of acknowledging the element of air. It doesn't necessarily indicate that the spell is a success or a failure; instead, it invites you to ponder the smoke, to parse out what you see that might lead to a greater understanding of what is at play in your intentions.

Smoke Moves Away: if the candle smoke moves away from you, the meaning is dependent on the spell being cast. In general, smoke that drifts away from you indicates that your energy is diffuse and dissipating, moving away from your intention. However, when you are casting spells that have to do with the actions of others or your intentions to heal or otherwise create influence over things, then this can indicate that your intentions are being heard and are traveling toward their ultimate destination.

Smoke Moves Toward: if the candle smoke moves toward you, this usually means that you are attracting energy and receiving blessing for your requests. This is an especially good sign when casting spells regarding love or money. However, if your intentions are negative—as you were forewarned about in the introduction to Part I—then this can indicate that you will be caught up in the unintended consequences of your negative intentions.

White Smoke: this is nearly always interpreted as a positive sign, that there are beneficial elements listening to your intentions. If a puff of white smoke appears at a particularly opportune time (say, right as you envision the culmination of your intention), then it is almost certain that your request will be granted.

Black Smoke: this is not always a bad sign, though most often it signals that you'll have no luck with this request. It can sometimes be a signal that you need to do more work—more cleansing, more preparation—before you attempt this particular spell again. It basically warns you not to waste the time until you are fully ready.

DIVINATION BY WAX:

Wax Crater: if your candle burns through the middle but leaves tall expanses of wax unburned around the perimeter, this indicates that the spell was probably not powerful enough to work. This is why pillar candles aren't always recommended for candle magic: they don't burn fully, which means the intentions cannot be heard completely. Try improving the potency of your magic with symbols and/or anointments, or clarify and intensify the message of your intentions. Or do as I do and try again with a different candle (such as a taper) that will better channel the flow of your energy. Leave pillar candles for spell work that calls upon you to use a candle over the course of many days and has a plan for leftover wax. I'll explain when pillars or votives are useful in the second part of the book.

Wax Puddle: this is what happens when your candle burns quickly, leaving a puddle of wax in its wake. While not necessarily a negative signal, this does indicate that your level of passion behind your intention is particularly intense (which can impact your magic in unexpected ways, so proceed with caution). In addition, this wax residue gives you the opportunity for more analysis: look to see what it says, how it speaks to you. This kind of divination might give you valuable information for your next spell or your future in general. You can find a whole host of resources that interpret various shapes and forms, should you decide to do some research, but you can also rely on your own intuition and feelings.

Drip-free Wax: if your candle burns steadily without creating any wax trails or drips, this indicates that your spell and your intentions are clear and acceptable. You can expect decisive results.

Wax Drips: if, on the other hand, your candle drips a lot of wax, this could mean that your spell is ill-conceived, messy. If the drips congregate on one side or the other of the candle, this indicates that something—your intentions, yourself, your powers—is out of balance. Drips to the left might mean that your psychic energies need grounding, while drips to the right might mean that you aren't fully invested in the magic. Your own intrusive thoughts or skeptical beliefs are getting in the way.

Candle Detritus: if the wick deposits black flecks into the puddling wax, this indicates that your spell work may create some unintended consequences. Thus, you might have to do some cleanup after the spell is complete. Think about what baggage you might have unintentionally brought to the spell (guilt or sadness, anxiety or fear), then work to tie up those loose ends.

Candle Soot: if you are burning a candle within glass, you might end up with a soot pattern that you can interpret. Typically, if you see soot only around the top of the candle container, then your energies have overcome what might be blocking your magic, but if you soot covers the entire container, then you've probably been stymied in your request for the time being. Take some time and try again when you feel more energized.

Inexplicable End: if your candle does something totally unexpected (e.g., burns through a plastic tea candle container, partially explodes or does something else dramatic), then you should probably consider that your spell was rejected. In this case, you probably want to cleanse your space and think hard about whether this spell is worth pursuing.

As I mentioned at the beginning of the chapter, this aspect of practicing candle magic can be among the most creative parts of spell work. You will tap into your intuition and powers of interpretation to generate your own magical vocabulary that you will rely on to recognize when your work is successful. It will also increase your potency of divination, in general, and help you to be more attuned to the magical flow of energy within your daily life.

5

AFTER THE SPELL

Once you have completed your spell work, it is important to consider how you dispose of any ritual items used. It's unwise to simply chuck a spent candle or other magical tool into the trash can for an unknown end. Indeed, you can increase the potency of your spell, in many cases, by practicing carefully curated post-ritual routines. First, you must know how to complete your spell work by ending the ritual with its own magical script. Second, there are some basic guidelines, depending on the spell, for how to safely dispose of candles or, alternately, how to use the spent materials of your spell for further communication or closure.

First, let's examine what it takes to complete a spell. It's not enough to simply walk away once your intentions have been conveyed and your candle has been burned. As with any ritual of consequence, the conclusion has value as well. Part of this comes in carefully disposing of the ritual items, as will be discussed below, but it is also important to conclude your spell work session with a definitive gesture. For example, I cast a circle when I practice my spells. While this practice is not necessary when you do your candle magic, I find it helps me to focus my intentions and to clear my head so that I can devote all of my energies to my spell. To cast a circle is to prepare your space for your spell work (or any other magical ceremony or ritual in which you wish to engage). Establish a boundary within which your magic will take place by distributing magically conducive materials around your workspace.

I usually cast a small circle around my altar for basic candle magic, though if my intentions are quite important or require lots of energy, I might cast a larger circle around the room in which I work. Occasionally (though rarely), I'll cast a circle around my house for stronger spells at various seasonal events). This just means marking your magical territory by using magical stones or crystals, relevant herbs, or salt (which has cleansing powers) to draw a literal circle. If you want to be even more elaborate, you can place corresponding ritual items to mark the four cardinal directions; I do this when I want to create a particularly strong flow of energy. Thus, the circle is now the repository of all of your intentions, cleansed of counter-energies, and ready for your personal magic to shine. When your spell work is complete, close the circle by removing the items in reverse order of how you initially set them up, thanking the elements and energies that attended to your intentions during that session.

Keep in mind that you do not always have to cast a circle to practice your spell work, though as I said, it helps me to get into the spirit of the spell, focusing my mind and encapsulating my attention. If you don't have the time or inclination, you can simply smudge your space by burning sage or rosemary, cleansing away any negative energies. Or you can cast a circle without extra materials simply by acknowledging the four cardinal directions and the space in which your magic is to occur. The power of thought and intention is central to all magic, so this is oftentimes adequate to the task. It will be up to you to decide what works best for your candle magic. Just remember to acknowledge, with some show of gratitude, the forces that attend to your intention.

After completing your ritual, it's important for a variety of reasons to dispose of ritual items carefully. First, these items once held significant meaning to you, and they are imbued with your magic; throwing them away without ceremony is akin to tossing aside the power you have so carefully cultivated. You don't want these items to languish in landfills or fall into the possession of negative forces. Second, if the leftover detritus from all of your magical workings begin piling up, then not only does it create inconvenient physical clutter, but it can also block your new intentions by creating psychic clutter. Naturally, we all work best when our minds and spaces are clear. Third, most practitioners of magic have an unspoken commitment to the environment and thus wish to dispose of their magical items in ways that both honor nature and nurture an ethical responsibility. So, for all of these reasons, you should skip the trash can in favor of other methods of disposal. There are some spells in Part II for which specific disposal instructions are outlined, but here you will find general guidelines for how to properly and respectfully clear out used ritual items.

Recycle: there are certain magical items that you can re-use, especially if you take the time to recharge them (as explained in Chapter 3). For example, most stones and crystals used in spell work are recharged and reused. The items you have arranged on your altar are also typically there for the duration, though if you find your magic flagging, try some new arrangements. Some items are never re-used, such as herbs and other food items, essential oils and any other organic compounds; their magic is typically used up in the course of one spell. Finally, some ritual items—including candles—are sometimes re-used. Typically, once a candle has been designated for a particular spell, it is considered spent once the spell is complete (you can recycle the wax for making household candles, as mentioned previously), but there are exceptions to this based on your own intuition. If you feel that your candle has not spent its energy, then by all means, re-use it. Much of candle magic is about gaining confidence in your own gut feelings.

Evaluate: if you have a collection of ritual items that you feel are not up for recycling, then take stock of what they are before deciding how to dispose of them. For example, if an item is clearly not biodegradable, then trying to dispose of it in nature is simply harmful. If an item is likely to cause harm should someone accidentally stumble across it (such as broken glass from a candle holder), then ensure that it is disposed of in a safe and responsible manner. If an item is intensely personal (and, especially, identifiable as yours), then you want to take extra care in disposing of it discreetly and respectfully. You most certainly don't want these items to cause you trouble in the future; unresolved personal issues are often buried within these personal items.

Disposal by Earth: many ritual items can be consigned to the earth for proper disposal. This applies to candles, especially candles made of natural materials, as they are environmentally friendly and quickly biodegradable. This method also has the benefit of bestowing respect upon nature, returning the gift that was granted you to its rightful place. While this might seem as simple as putting your spent candle in the trash—it'll end up in a landfill anyway, right?—this misses the point of magic, which is to elevate the everyday to the extraordinary. Thus, finding a place to bury it that feels right to you is more in keeping with the spirit of your spell work. I have a garden in which I consign some of my biodegradable items, fuelling my future magical herbs with the remnants of my magical past.

Disposal by Air: this is impractical for candles themselves (you cannot just toss them into the air and be done with them, and even small remnants of wax are likely too heavy for the wind to carry them away), but it can be done with ashes that remain after the spell. This is especially pertinent when you have been casting spells for healing or for banishment; you want the negative energies to be swiftly carried away by the winds. You can also do this with herbs and salt, if used in the casting of your circle or in the spell itself.

Disposal by Fire: perhaps the most definitive way to dispose of ritual items is through fire, which both consumes the objects completely and consecrates their impurities. Thus, anything with particularly heavy signification might be best disposed of by fire. However, beware of burning anything that contains toxic residues (such as plastic) and make sure that you follow safety protocols and regulations for your area. You certainly don't want to be responsible for producing a destructive wildfire or putting others (or yourself!) in harm's way.

Disposal by Water: sending ritual items off to a watery grave is another way in which to dispose of them with respect and care. Water transforms whatever it touches, so this method of disposal washes away the old and leaves a revitalized energy in its place. If you are so inclined, you can even dispose of items via toilet water: this is not something that I do, as I find it a bit irreverent, but some of my friends find it invigoratingly final (a metaphor for flushing the "crap" out of your life). As with fire disposals, be responsible for any water burials: you don't want to cause plumbing problems, for one, or to litter streams and lakes with non-biodegradable materials. Small spent candles and bits of wax should be fine for this method.

Other: finally, consider whether you want these spent magical items to end up residing near you or scattered far away. In most cases, I like to keep my magical items close: they are personal to me, and I feel their presence adds to and increases my powers over time. However, there are exceptions. If you are freeing yourself from an unwanted energy (person, feeling, event, and so on), then you might find it more appropriate to consign the spent item to a faraway place.

Each element of your candle magic is important, including completing the ritual properly and disposing of magical items with respect and ceremony. While these actions may seem like afterthoughts, they are actually contributing to the constellation of your powers, helping you to increase your potency and improve the strength of your intentions.

PART II: THE SPELLS

In the second part of the book, we move on to the heart of the matter: how to cast spells using our best candle magic. Here you will find that I follow a fairly standard template for my spells—which you can, of course, vary according to your personal intuition, experience, and specific intention, which should help you to get started conjuring up real results. You will also find suggestions for how to increase your potency when necessary and how to deal with the leftover odds and ends of your practice.

In the chapters that follow, you will discover a plethora of spells for love and relationships, including self-love and self-confidence, as well as passion and fidelity; concomitantly, there is also a chapter on friends and family spells, which will focus on communication and trust, ending interference, and bringing new friends into your life, among other issues. You will also find spells for money and prosperity, bringing you opportunity and good fortune, as well as helping you dissipate debt and find lost objects. There are spells specifically geared towards your work and career goals, such as getting a new job or raise and increasing your motivation. Health and well-being spells are also covered, including specific spells on healing, but also some more regularly useful spells, like how to dispel anxiety or conquer fears. This same chapter also contains spells for sleep (oh, how we all could use that!) and creative thinking, among others. Finally, we conclude with the ever-important protection spells, helping us to feel safe and secure —and peaceful—in our own lives.

So, gather your magical materials, set up your altar, and prepare to light your candles: you are primed to embark upon a magical practice that will amplify your powers and intensify your intentions so that you can manifest the life you desire and deserve.

6

LOVE AND RELATIONSHIP SPELLS

Casting love spells, like love itself, is one of the most enduring and mysterious forms of magic you can perform. Because we are so culturally attached to the expansive nature of love—it includes platonic love, passionate love, romantic love, spiritual love—we often invoke the time-worn cliché that "love conquers all." And, indeed, it just might; however, for those of us casting love spells for the first time, be aware that you cannot conjure love out of nothing. I find that many beginners mistake the underlying purpose of love and relationship spells: they are to augment and to refine what already exists, rather than to create something out of nothing. Candle magic is about harnessing energies that are already present, not calling them up from some void. Thus, you cannot *force* a love that is not there, just as you cannot redefine the elemental energies that assist you with your intentions. Having said that, there is nothing wrong with using a spell to nudge along a crush, or to soothe yourself at the end of a relationship.

In fact, this is what the following spells are supposed to do: channel your intentions toward a greater experience of love, in whatever form, while nurturing your soul when love is lost. Surely you will find, among these spells, one or two at least that will re-energize your love life and reignite your happiness, mimicking the flame dancing at the center of your candle magic.

Sustaining Self-love: A Spell for Yourself

Since all love flourishes only when you have self-love, this is the ideal spell to get started in the love department. After my break-up, this was the first spell that worked for me, letting me remember how worthy I was to love myself, which, ultimately, attracted the love of others.

WHEN TO PERFORM THE SPELL:

Any time during a waxing moon

HOW LONG IT TAKES:

As long as it takes the candle to burn down

WHAT YOU'LL NEED:

1 red candle, either taper or tea

Lemon and/or orange essential oil

Amethyst or rose quartz crystal

STEPS:

1. Cleanse yourself: when implementing a spell of self-love, take a long ritual bath, washing away your anxieties and fears, letting go of all your bad energy. When you are ready to begin the spell, cleanse your altar or space. I recommended smudging with sage.
2. Choose your candle: a taper if you need a bigger boost, a tea candle if you need a slight jolt. Anoint your candle with

essential oil: the lemon symbolizes cleansing power and new beginnings, while the orange symbolizes joyfulness and energy.

3. Light your red candle; the red here symbolizes courage and power. As you light it, imagine that you are setting your own self-assurance ablaze.
4. Once the flame is tall and strong, pass your amethyst or rose quartz through the flame (carefully, so as not to burn yourself) while repeating your personal mantra: *"I am powerful and whole. I am worthy and kind. I am loving and loved."* Do this seven times.
5. Lay the crystal in front of the candle and meditate as the candle burns down, repeating your mantra silently to yourself, or visualizing your particular self-worth. Remind yourself of your strengths and passions, your vitality and joy.

Conjuring Confidence

While the previous spell helps you to regain a sense of self-love, this spell will help you reclaim your self-confidence—useful when looking for love, of course, but also good for when you are merely looking to meet new people or try new things. This is another simple spell that should become a go-to anytime you need a pick-me-up.

WHEN TO PERFORM THE SPELL:

Sunday during a waxing or full moon

HOW LONG IT TAKES:

As long as it takes the candle to burn down

WHAT YOU'LL NEED:

1 gold taper candle

Ylang-ylang essential oil

A mirror

Paper and pen

STEPS:

1. Prepare your space: if you're using an altar, cleanse it, and cast a circle for concentration.
2. Anoint your candle with ylang-ylang oil, which boosts both self-confidence and balance. The gold of the candle radiates energy and success.
3. Light your candle, and as the candle burns, write down a list

of accomplishments that you are proud of, characteristics you cultivate with care, and whatever you feel is most worthy about yourself.

4. Once the flame has almost died, turn to your mirror (whether it be a small hand mirror or a full-length mirror) and read aloud to yourself all of the affirmations you put to paper while the candle was burning.

5. Once the candle is completely spent, close your circle and keep your affirmations close by: sleep with them under your pillow for seven days or carry them in your pocket or purse for the following week.

Letting Go of Lost Love

This spell is a combination of a healing spell and a purification spell: you are essentially trying to heal from the end of a relationship as well as purify and strengthen yourself to move forward. While it may seem to require a long time in comparison with most spells you'll see in this book, it is important to note that letting go of failed relationships or great loves that faltered is one of the most difficult endeavours we face as humans. Take the time to allow yourself to mourn; grieving is part of the process that leads us back to the full force of joyfulness ever-present in our lives.

WHEN TO PERFORM THE SPELL:

Start at the beginning of the waning moon

HOW LONG IT TAKES:

Seven days

WHAT YOU'LL NEED:

3 pillar candles: one purple, two white

Sharp tool for carving (optional)

STEPS:

1. Cleanse your space thoroughly and charge your candles before using for best results (see Chapter 3 for details).
2. Arrange your candles in a triangle on your altar, with purple at the top and the two white candles at the base: the purple

represents our spiritual power, the representation of our highest self, while the two white candles represent you and your lost love. You can carve your names in each, if you like, or a symbol that represents each of you in turn. This can help you focus your intention and clarify your potency. The white symbolizes your desire to purify the negative energy that exists between the two of you.

3. Light the candle that represents you first, imagining your best qualities and letting the flame carry away the worst of you. Do the same with the second white candle, remembering the best about your lover and letting the worst be carried away in the wind. Finally, light the purple candle and let it guide you to a peaceful place, visualizing both of you at your best *without expectation*. This is to let go of the bad feelings, of the ill wishes, and of the hurt: you can both be purified and strong separately. If your feelings are especially acrimonious at first, use a sage bundle while the candles burn to further dispel any negative energy amongst the symbolic candles.

4. When you feel calmer and grounded, then snuff the candles out in reverse order, beginning with the purple, then moving to the white candle of your lost love and ending with yourself. Do this for seven days until the new moon begins.

5. With each day, as your candles burn down and grow smaller, you should feel your serenity increasing and your heart less burdened. Once the ritual is complete, take care in disposing of the remains. Some might want to bury the bits of wax in a

comforting place, a remembrance of the relationship gone, while others might want to let them go by water, allowing them to be carried away once and for all.

Discovering Desirability: Another Spell for Yourself

Once you've rid yourself of lost love, you will often want to remind yourself of how absolutely desirable you are to many. Even if you aren't mourning a lost love, rediscovering your desirability is another way in which you open yourself up for love and success, self-confidence and a greater sense of self-worth. In fact, this spell goes well with a makeover: I like to cast it when a new season rolls around, as I change out my wardrobe, get a new hairstyle, and generally invite new and positive energies into my life.

WHEN TO PERFORM THE SPELL:

As close to the full moon as possible

HOW LONG IT TAKES:

As long as it takes the candle to burn down

WHAT YOU'LL NEED:

1 red or orange taper candle

Patchouli incense (optional)

Clear quartz crystal

STEPS:

1. Charge your quartz crystal before using, if possible, and cleanse your space before beginning the spell. Light your patchouli incense before you begin the spell, if you like, to enhance the sexual and spiritual energies at work.

2. Place your crystal at the cardinal direction that most fits the element you wish to respond to your intention: north for earth, if your intention is for general, grounded desirability; south for fire, if your intention is for sexual desirability; west for water, if your intention is romantic desirability; and east for air, if your intention is for fun and frolic.
3. Place your candle at the center of your altar or space and light it—red for passion, orange for joyful—while repeating this simple spell three times over: *May I be seen and seen well today, with no harm to come my way. From this fire, desire I seek, bring to me energy at its high peak.*
4. Imagine the crystal pulling energy from your chosen element, burning up through the flame of your candle, and flowing into you like bright smoke.
5. Once the candle has burned down, show gratitude for the element that responds to your request and carry the crystal with you for seven days.

Alluring Love: The Ultimate "Come-Hither" Spell

This is a very simple but extremely useful spell to have in your repertoire to return to time and again, for various reasons. It is intended to attract your desired intention to you: not only can it conjure up love, but it can bring to you whatever it is that you need at a given time. As you change your magical tools slightly, this all-purpose spell responds in kind.

WHEN TO PERFORM THE SPELL:

Begin during a waxing moon, so that your final spell culminates at the full moon

HOW LONG IT TAKES:

Up to nine days

WHAT YOU'LL NEED:

2 taper or pillar candles

An inscribed intention on a piece of paper

Anointing oils, symbols (optional)

STEPS:

1. Choose your candles according to what you wish to invite into your life: red candles will bring you passion; pink candles will bring you romance or friendship; green candles will introduce good fortune or wealth into your life; blue candles can bring peace and harmony, and so on.

2. You can further enhance the potency of your candle magic by inscribing each candle with a symbol or a word that represents your intentions, or by anointing it with corresponding oils (such as patchouli or cinnamon for passion, rose for romance, basil for fortune, and lavender or chamomile for peace).
3. Cleanse your space, and arrange your candles side by side, with your written intention between them. Be sure your intention is clear and your focus is strong.
4. Light both candles, letting the flame settle into a steady rhythm before passing your intention over the flames of each, letting the fire consume the intention, transmitting it to the ethereal plane. Be sure to practice caution when doing this: use tongs to hold the paper, and have a flameproof container to catch the ashes.
5. When you have finished, scatter the ashes into the wind; thus, you are invoking the element of fire to ignite the intention and the element of wind to deliver that intention. There are two ways to complete this spell: if you find yourself available on the full moon, use its power to cast this spell once—as long as your intention is clear and your potency is flowing—with taper candles that you allow to burn through. On the other hand, if you plan ahead, you can cast this spell on nine consecutive nights using pillar candles that you snuff each night, culminating at the full moon, which can increase the likelihood of a definitive response.

Finding A Faithful Lover

This is a powerful spell that can even bring you a forever soulmate. While the items that you will need are fairly simple, the spell itself is somewhat complicated, requiring an understanding of the four cardinal directions and their corresponding elements. You are trying to harness a free-flowing energy that creates a space for lasting love and fidelity.

WHEN TO PERFORM THE SPELL:

At the full moon (note that it can be more powerful when performed outdoors)

HOW LONG IT TAKES:

20-30 minutes

WHAT YOU'LL NEED:

4 red taper candles

2 white taper candles

STEPS:

1. Carefully cleanse your space: make sure the space is large enough for you to stand or sit in the middle of your candle arrangement. Whether you cast this indoors or outdoors, be sure to take adequate safety precautions: you don't want to start a fire!
2. Orient yourself to the north, and place your four red candles at the four cardinal directions. Light each one in turn,

starting with your candle to the north and invoking the power of the earth, then move to your right in a clockwise pattern: light the candle to the east, symbolizing the air; the candle to the south, symbolizing fire; and the candle to the west, representing water. You are invoking all the elemental powers to aid you in your intentions.

3. Turn back to the north, and light your white candles. Place the first one slightly to the left of you, still oriented north, and place the second one slightly to the right of you. Repeat your intention as you see the flames rise up and remain steady.

4. Now pick up both white candles (again, using caution), and tilt them towards one another so that their flames meld as you hold the intention in your mind.

5. Blow out the flames together, sending the intention out onto the ethereal plane, then close the circle you have created by blowing out each red candle in reverse order (from west to south to east to north). Be sure to bury the white candles in a place of significance, so the earth nurtures the intention to fruition.

Healing Unhappiness: A Relationship Spell

This spell should only be performed on auspicious occasions and not relied upon too much; it's a delicate balance to banish the bad parts of a love relationship without harming the good parts. Thus, you should choose your time wisely, following what is mentioned below but also relying on your sense of energy and working when you feel your powers are at their most potent. Because the spell is rather tricky, it may take a couple of times to get right. Be patient and follow your intuitions.

WHEN TO PERFORM THE SPELL:

During a waxing moon and in spring or fall for the most powerful results

HOW LONG IT TAKES:

As long as it takes the candle to burn down

WHAT YOU'LL NEED:

1 red taper candle

Dried lavender, catnip, and ginger

STEPS:

1. Be sure to cleanse your space thoroughly: I recommend a full sage smudging of the area (even of the whole house, if that feels necessary). This is also a spell for which I would cast a circle before beginning: you want all the energy to gather at the center of your intention.

2. Sit cross-legged, as if for meditation, and place your candle in front of you. Make sure that there are no artificial lights to distract you from the candle and ritual to follow.

3. Light your candle and focus your intentions into your lower abdomen: feel your romantic and sexual energy there and push it up and outward toward your candle, coursing up through the candle and out through its flame. When you feel that your energy has reached its peak, rub the herbs together between your palms and sprinkle them over and around you. These work to purify the negative energies while intensifying the positive.

4. Recite your intention—in fact, writing something personal about the issue or issues to be healed can be quite powerful—as you watch the candle burn down, manifesting your intention.

5. When the candle has burned, and the spell is complete, return the dried herbs to the wind and sleep with the remains of the candle under your pillow until the full moon.

Rekindling Passion: A Candle Flame Spell

This is the kind of spell that can be cast whenever you feel your relationship is in need of a boost (you could also invest in a date night or some new lingerie as you contemplate casting this spell: it certainly can't hurt).

WHEN TO PERFORM THE SPELL:

Right before the full moon

HOW LONG IT TAKES:

15-20 minutes

WHAT YOU'LL NEED:

2 red pillar candles

Rose essential oil

String, preferably red

Written intention

STEPS:

1. Ready your space and prepare your candles: on one, carve a heart (this symbolizes your lover), and on the other, carve a symbol of attraction, such as a moon or a bolt of lightning.
2. Place the candles to your left (your heart side), with the heart candle to the left of the other, tie them together with a string and anoint them each with a couple of drops of rose oil close to the wick.

3. Light both candles, letting the flames grow strong and steady. When you feel their energy is strong, let your written intention burn in the flame of the left candle (the one with the heart).
4. Let the candles burn down to where the string binds them together, taking care not to let the string burn or the candles be severed. Snuff them gently, leaving them bound together.
5. At the full moon, place the still bound candles at a location where they can absorb the light of the full moon, then safely bury them or burn them fully.

Peaceful Parting: Another Relationship Spell

Letting go of the past is another obstacle to our happiness, and yet sometimes it is the healthiest decision we can make—parting with a former lover, in particular. If you have come to the conclusion that your relationship is no longer working, then wishing for an amicable split is the best way to go about damage control. This is a form of a healing spell.

WHEN TO PERFORM THE SPELL:

Any time during a waning moon

HOW LONG IT TAKES:

As long as it takes the candles to burn down

WHAT YOU'LL NEED:

1 white candle, 1 blue candle, 1 red candle

Rosemary and basil (fresh or dried)

Spring water

STEPS:

1. Cleanse your space by smudging: rosemary is good here, as it symbolizes memory; you indicate that you wish to remember the good and make peace with the bad as you move on.
2. Arrange your candles in a triangle, with the white (purifying) candle at the apex, and the blue (peace) and red (love) candles at the base. Before lighting your candles, infuse your spring

water with basil and have it ready to splash on your face as you move through the ritual. This both cleanses you of bad intention and purifies your mindset. I use a natural spring water infused with fresh basil that I put in a small spray bottle, but you can simply use a bowl.

3. Light the candles, starting with the white, and repeat your intention after lighting each candle: *"I am cutting these cords, I am releasing these ties. All that's in this past are peaceful goodbyes."* Spritz or splash your face with basil water each time.

4. Let the candles burn down to complete the spell: the size of the candles dictates the length of the spell, so the size you choose should adequately represent how much energy needs to be expended in creating peace (a pillar should only be used if much acrimonious discord precedes the end, while a tea candle can be used if wistful harmony is already in sight).

Thwarting the Third Wheel: Banishing an Interloper Spell

If your relationship is being interrupted by the intrusive presence of another, then this spell can effectively remove the interloper. This doesn't mean that you are banishing this person from your life—you really don't want to get rid of your mother-in-law or his or her best friend *completely*—just from interfering in your relationship.

WHEN TO PERFORM THE SPELL:

Any time during a waning moon

HOW LONG IT TAKES:

15-20 minutes

WHAT YOU'LL NEED:

2 small white candles, 1 small black candle

Hematite crystal

STEPS:

1. As with any spell that has some element of banishment to it, be sure to smudge your space well. You don't need any more negative energies alongside the ones you wish to be rid of.
2. Place your candles in front of you, with the black candle in between the white candles (you can guess what this symbolizes). Light the white candles first, starting with the one to your left (heart) side. Affirm the purity of the love connection between these two symbolic candles.

3. Then light the black candle, symbolizing the interloper, and state your intention clearly: tell the interloper not just that you want them to "butt out" but also specifically what you wish them to do (or to quit doing). The more specific you are, the better your result.
4. Before allowing the flame to go out, smother the black flame with the hematite crystal, using caution so as to avoid harming yourself. Then let the other two candles burn all the way down naturally.
5. Be sure to dispose of any remains of the black candle in a final way, such as releasing it by water.

Buzz, Buzz Begone: A Spell to Ward off Unwanted Attention

While we crafty folk dedicate most of our time to bringing in positive energies to our lives, there are those times when we just want to be rid of that creepy person at the office or gym who stands a little too close. It's a testament to your growing powers that you will find yourself being a subject of attraction, but you can nudge away the unwanted suitors with this simple spell.

WHEN TO PERFORM THE SPELL:

Any time during a waning moon, Saturday being the best day

HOW LONG IT TAKES:

As long as it takes the candle to burn down

WHAT YOU'LL NEED:

1 small black candle

Salt

Crystal of your choice

STEPS:

1. Cleanse your space as mentioned in the previous spell; you'll want negative energies cleared well
2. Make a circle at the center of your altar and place the black candle in its center. Salt is used in both protection and

banishment spells: here you are containing the one who is assailing you with unwanted attention.

3. Light the candle and state your intention clearly. Again, the more specifically you relay your request, the better your results.

4. Let the candle burn while you focus your energy on your intention, but before it goes out, snuff it with your crystal. Choose a crystal that represents your current state of mind, something positive and carefree. I like citrine because it both grounds me and re-energizes my happier side.

5. After the ritual is complete, scatter the salt to the winds and be sure to release the spent candle far away from you (as with a water burial . . . or a quick flush). Wear or carry your chosen candle with you for the next seven days.

7

FRIENDS AND FAMILY SPELLS

After the ever-popular love spell, spells that assist with friends and family matters are among the most sought-out for practitioners of magic. These are the kinds of spells that can help you forge relationships, mend relationships, and deepen relationships with the most important people in your life. Like love spells, they are not intended to force anyone into behaving or feeling a certain way; rather, they are aimed at further developing the potential that is already there, or at improving an established relationship—even if that means casting a spell to nudge someone away from an interfering role. I make it a habit to work on some of these spells, such as the one on communication, with regularity, because it reminds me of the ways in which we should all nurture and care for our closest relationships. The magic itself creates a positive energy that enhances that understanding, and it does double duty by reminding us to be aware of our role in maintaining strong and caring relationships in general.

As with all candle magic, these spells are simple and straightforward, but powerful and lasting. You will find spells that cover a range of intentions here, from making new friends to ending potentially hurtful gossip to increasing the bond of trust between friends, among others. I am certain you will find some that will make it into your regular rotation of conjuring up happiness and fulfilment!

Forging a Friendship: A Spell to Attract Friends

Just as with a love spell, this isn't meant to bewitch a random stranger into falling into a friendship with you. It's really more about *you*, making yourself open and available to the possibilities for friendship that swirl around you on a daily basis. If you have a particular person in mind, then the clarity of your intention might make the spell more potent, but even if you are just casting about (literally) for some new companions, this spell can enliven the energies around you, increasing the potential connection.

WHEN TO PERFORM THE SPELL:

Any time during a waxing moon

HOW LONG IT TAKES:

As long as it takes the candle to burn down

WHAT YOU'LL NEED:

1 small orange drawstring bag

1 yellow taper candle

1 carnelian stone

1 teaspoon of allspice berries

STEPS:

1. Cleanse your space and make sure your altar has enough room for the objects needed to perform the spell.
2. Place your candle in the center of the altar, its yellow color

symbolizing inspiration and optimism, then place your orange drawstring bag in front of it. The orange indicates attraction and vitality, drawing these energies into your spell. Put the carnelian stone—a symbol of success and smart choices—atop the bag, and encircle these with the allspice berries, which summon good fortune.

3. Light your candle and contemplate the kind of friendship you wish to forge. Make sure your intentions are clear—write them down beforehand if you need some focus—and once you feel your positive energy flowing through you, place your palms upon your friendship objects and chant three times: *"Strong, true friendships, please come to me. As I will it, so make it be."*

4. Allow the candle to burn down while you continue to visualize your future friendships. Close your circle if you have cast one.

5. Gather up the allspice berries and the carnelian stone and place them in your drawstring bag. Carry this friendship pouch with you until the next full moon. It should attract new people and new possibilities to you!

Attracting Appreciation: A Spell for Popularity

There are a variety of spells that one can cast when seeking to increase your popularity. In fact, this kind of spell is similar to any attraction spell (for love, for good fortune, and so on). Here is one I like because it is very simple and a quick way to give your energy a confidence booster.

WHEN TO PERFORM THE SPELL:

Any time during a waxing moon, and a Thursday is a strong day for attraction

HOW LONG IT TAKES:

10-15 minutes

WHAT YOU'LL NEED:

1 gold candle

3 yellow candles

Citronella candle or incense (optional)

STEPS:

1. Cleanse your space before you begin; you could think about burning citronella incense or a candle, as it both energizes and cleanses.
2. Carve your name into the gold candle, for you are the center of this little spell, with your good fortune and powerful attractive potential. Set it on the altar and surround it with

the three yellow candles in a triangular pattern. The idea is that the energy and brightness of the yellow, along with the magical property of three, will be drawn to your even more brilliant gold.

3. Light the gold candle first, then light the three yellow candles in a clockwise fashion. As you light the candles, recite your incantation: *"Look at me here, for all to see. I'm encircled by energies three. With my poise and talents galore, I bring fascination to me forevermore."*

4. With this spell, you may snuff the candles rather than waiting for them to burn down. Wait for three days, and if you feel that your intention hasn't been answered, repeat the spell with the same candles, this time allowing them to burn all the way down.

Dispelling Loneliness: A Spell for Solitary Times

This spell may seem a little odd, in that it's not an attraction spell. When you experience loneliness, there are all sorts of spells to which you can turn, such as the previous spell regarding popularity, or any number of friendship and/or relationship or love spells. Here, though, is a spell especially for those times when you are lonely but don't have a lot of choice in the matter: this is for those times when we are alone (sheltered in place, for example, traveling alone for business, or simply spending some solitary time for healing). Thus, this spell is closer to a balancing or healing spell, designed to help you soothe yourself.

WHEN TO PERFORM THE SPELL:

A full moon is best, but it can be done during the last phase of the waxing moon

HOW LONG IT TAKES:

As long as it takes the candle to burn down

WHAT YOU'LL NEED:

1 purple or blue taper candle

Cypress essential oil

Other crystals or oils (optional)

STEPS:

1. You should always cleanse your space before casting a spell,

of course, but this is a spell wherein it's more important to cleanse the negative energies from the self. Take a ritual bath surrounded by candles (for comfort rather than for magic) as an act of self-care and cleansing. You can add some favorite crystals to your set-up, should you feel lacking in energy, or put a few drops of invigorating or calming essential oil in the bath (try some rosemary for uplift, or some lavender for soothing).

2. Once you feel yourself ready, place your purple or blue candle at the center of your altar. Purple is best if you want to build your psychic protections against loneliness, if you are in a seeking mood. Blue is best if you desire peacefulness and acceptance.
3. Anoint the candle with a few drops of cypress oil, which facilitates balance and inner peace, then light and focus your gaze on the flame.
4. Here there is no specific incantation, rather a reflection on the solidity and wonder of your presence. You might repeat the mantra, *"I am enough"* or some other affirmation that places you directly at the center of your life.
5. Once the candle has burned down, place the wax remnants under your pillow for seven days, feeling yourself grow more peaceful with each passing day.

Getting Rid of Gossip: A Quasi-Banishment Spell

This quirky little spell isn't directly a banishment spell—you're not getting rid of a person but rather a bad habit—but a binding spell. Your intention is to direct some energies toward encouraging discretion. Some spells of this nature call for an actual cow's tongue as a representation of the gossip's oversharing mouth, but we'll just craft a candle for our needs.

WHEN TO PERFORM THE SPELL:

Any time during a waxing moon

HOW LONG IT TAKES:

As long as it takes the candle to burn down

WHAT YOU'LL NEED:

1 black pillar candle

Salt

Pen, paper, and string

STEPS:

1. Smudge your space with sage to get rid of negative energy.
2. Write the name of the offending gossiper on your piece of paper, then tie it to the candle with string (white is fine, as it signifies purification). Sprinkle a circle of salt around the candle, containing the negative energies to that specific location.

3. Light the candle, and as it burns, recite your intention: *"I cast your words far from me, your wicked tongue no longer free. Your words are gone out of my mind, as your wagging tongue I now do bind."*
4. Let the pillar burn all the way through the center, then bury the remains—along with the string, which should still be intact (you want the binding to endure)—somewhere remote and silent.

Conjuring up Clear Communication

This is an excellent spell to perform at the change of the seasons, when you want to clear away old energies and make way for new and clearer vibes, somewhat like a magical spring cleaning. This spell can ease tensions between you and others, preventing miscommunication and promoting openness and tolerance. I make it a point to perform this spell every year before the winter holidays, just to ensure that I'm equipped and ready for a variety of family interactions.

WHEN TO PERFORM THE SPELL:

During a full moon

HOW LONG IT TAKES:

As long as it takes the candle to burn down

WHAT YOU'LL NEED:

1 small glass jar with a tightly fitting lid

Allspice, cinnamon, nutmeg, cloves, and salt

1 brown taper candle

STEPS:

1. Cleanse your kitchen before you make your spell jar. These handy magical tools can be made for a variety of purposes, and their magical energies will last for quite a while if you construct them during a full moon and charge them with a candle and strong intentions.

2. Layer three teaspoons of each dried spice into your jar, finishing with three teaspoons of salt. The allspice brings providence, while the cinnamon provides mental focus, the nutmeg clarity, and the cloves a healing energy. The salt provides a protective barrier to keep any negative energies at bay.
3. Bring your spell jar to your altar and light your brown candle—brown to ground you in the practical, mothering energies of the earth. Pass it over your spell jar three times clockwise, wishing for clarity of communication, then pass it over your spell jar three times counterclockwise, requesting openness and compassion in communication. You are unlocking all of the positive energies available.
4. Snuff the brown candle when you have finished and keep it handy for the next three months to recharge your spell jar as necessary. When the candle is spent, the spell jar should radiate energy for another three months, so keep it somewhere appropriate, like the kitchen or living room, where most conversations take place. (Don't waste the spices when the jar's magical time is done. Throw them into a hearty stew or other savory dish.

Vanquishing a Fight: A Spell to Mend a Friendship

A broken friendship can be one of the most damaging things we experience in our lives. If you have had a fight with a friend, or had a more serious falling out, here is a spell that will help you mend that bond and dispel those negative energies.

WHEN TO PERFORM THE SPELL:

Any time during a waxing moon, Friday being the best day

HOW LONG IT TAKES:

As long as it takes the candles to burn down

WHAT YOU'LL NEED:

2 pink votive candles

A mirror large enough to hold candles

A picture or other representation of you with your friend

STEPS:

1. Cleanse your altar, and if you have time, charge the mirror you will be using in the spell by moonlight: leave it outside under the moonlight for three nights (or, if a full moon is handy, one night under a full moon).
2. Put the mirror in the center of your altar, and place the photo of you with your friend face down on the mirror so that the picture is reflecting itself. If you don't have a physical photo to use, you can write down your names (or draw

symbols that represent the two of you, or both) on a piece of paper, placing it face down as well.

3. Place your candles on the photo or paper and light them from left to right. Make your intention clear: *"There is no stronger bond than we friends two. I relinquish my anger, and embrace you, too. We remain strangers no more, as we bring friendship to the fore."*

4. Let the candles melt onto the photo or paper (though take care not to start a fire), then bury everything except the mirror under a strong tree, preferably close to your home. Apple trees are signifiers of friendship, so if you have one nearby, that would be quite lovely.

Strengthening Bonds: A Spell to Bolster a Friendship

Sometimes, when we have been friends with another person for so long, we begin to take for granted both the little frustrations and the wonderful perks of the relationship (this is true of romantic relationships, as well). But friendships must be nurtured like any other relationship. The following spell can serve as a reminder—and re-binder—of all that makes your friendship remarkable.

WHEN TO PERFORM THE SPELL:

Any time during a waxing moon: if your friend is female, try this on a Friday. If the friend is a male, try a Saturday.

HOW LONG IT TAKES:

As long as it takes the candles to burn down

WHAT YOU'LL NEED:

Pen and paper

1 white taper candle and 1 pink taper candle

Two pieces of string

STEPS:

1. Ready your altar for the spell, cleansing and doing some tidying up. This is a reminder spell, so it's a good time to declutter your space, clearing the way for fresh energies.
2. Now write two separate accounts of your friendship: on one piece of paper, talk about the little annoyances or the few bad

moments, maybe when you have been let down or disappointed. On the other piece of paper, write an account of all of the wonderful parts of your friendship, recounting all the best qualities of your friend and how your friendship has bettered your life.

3. Place your candles side by side, and light the white candle first; this is for purifying and regeneration. Then light your pink candle, symbolizing friendship and platonic love. Reread your first piece of paper, then set it alight with the flames from each candle—use caution here, and have a non-flammable place to let the paper burn to ash. You have let go of whatever negative energy exists between you.

4. Now, reread the second piece of paper while the candles burn down, then take your two pieces of string and make a knot of friendship. Roll up the paper and tie it tightly with your knotted string. Let the candles finish burning down, then take the wax remnants and the letter bundle and bury them at the foot of a strong tree (as suggested in the previous spell, an apple tree is ideal, though oak or ash are also considered magical).

Invoking Trust Between Friends

While you can cast this spell at any time to increase the level of trust you may have with a friend or family member, it is specifically designed to help you to overcome what you considered to be a breach of trust. This is a quirky spell that requires some flexibility, depending on what items are available to you. You can ensure success by fully investing in your intention; be sure that you aren't harboring any guilty secrets yourself or your intentions might backfire.

WHEN TO PERFORM THE SPELL:

Must be done during a full moon

HOW LONG IT TAKES:

As long as it takes the candle to burn down

WHAT YOU'LL NEED:

1 blue taper candle

Dandelion in whatever form you can find

Quartz crystal

STEPS:

1. Like many full moon spells, this is best done outdoors, though use precaution when burning candles outside. Choose a secluded spot, and though it doesn't have to be while the moon is out (that is, at night), it might be more powerful during that time.

2. Cast a circle around you, using stones that you find in your area (or bring salt to demarcate your magical boundary).
3. Place the quartz in the center of the circle, so it enhances the energy you bring with you to the circle.
4. Place the candle at one of the four cardinal directions: north if you want to reinforce trust that is already there; south if you need to heal a breach of trust toward you; west if you need to establish trust; or east if you need to heal a breach of trust you created.
5. Light the candle and repeat your incantation at least three times: *"Let this shine the light of trust, so that this friendship will be more robust. Keep truth in mind at all times, and honesty will prevail in all climes."*
6. As the candle burns down, sprinkle your dandelion root or extract around the inner edge of your circle. If you happen to have access to a common garden dandelion, you can blow the seeds from the head, scattering them throughout the circle, welcoming the energy of trust.
7. When the candle is spent, close your circle, and bury the candle there.

Magic for Meddling: A Spell to End a Family Member's Interference

There are a number of ways to interrupt someone's interference, and this one relies on the old adage that you can catch more flies with honey than with vinegar. It can be a little messy but the end results are usually worth it—and a side effect is that your relationship with the meddler is sweetened. I've used this a couple of times on my own mom, whose love sometimes veers toward the vexing. It helps--in a kind and loving way!

WHEN TO PERFORM THE SPELL:

Any time during a waning moon

HOW LONG IT TAKES:

About 15 minutes for seven days

WHAT YOU'LL NEED:

1 white pillar candle

Honey

Fennel seeds

STEPS:

1. Cleanse your space, and cover your altar with wax paper to protect its surface. Alternately, use a large plate or platter that can be washed after the ritual.
2. Coat the purifying candle in honey—you're intending to

sweeten the relationship, attracting positive interactions—then roll it in fennel seeds. Fennel wards off other's influence, stopping the meddling in its tracks.

3. Light the candle, while you repeat your intentions three times: *"As much as your advice is well-meaning, it really does interfere. So, I ask you to cease repeating, your help does not belong here."* Be sure to state the person's name while reciting the spell.

4. Snuff the candle once you've finished the spell, then repeat each day for seven days. Your candle should be spent at this point, and the best way to send it off is by water or fire.

Reunion Revived: A Spell to Bring Friends Together

This is an excellent spell for when you want to reunite with friends that you haven't seen in a long time. It can even work to reconnect with friends with whom you've lost contact. With a slightly different intention, you can also use it to revitalize the bonds between a circle of friends.

WHEN TO PERFORM THE SPELL:

Best at the full moon, but it can be done during the waxing moon

HOW LONG IT TAKES:

As long as it takes the candle to burn down

WHAT YOU'LL NEED:

1 blue taper candle

Rosemary essential oil

A key, or something symbolic of a key

STEPS:

1. Cleanse your space well. I'd recommend a thorough sage smudging, as this spell needs all the positive potency it can conjure.
2. Anoint your candle with rosemary oil, the herb of remembrance and purification. The blue here represents water, smoothing over the time apart, as well as dreams and wishes.

3. Light your candle and focus your intentions: *"I wish to bring you back to me, my bosom buddy so far and free. My memories remain so fond I wish for us to renew this bond."* Keep repeating your incantation while you pass your key— or, again, something non-flammable that is symbolic of a key —through the flame, moving in a clockwise motion. You are opening up the possibilities for reconnection, unlocking the obstacles.
4. Once your candle has burned down, dispose of it by burying it somewhere near and dear to you. Tie a string around the key so you can wear it until the next full moon. Alternately, fasten it to your clothes or bag with a pin. If possible, keep it close to your heart.

8

MONEY AND PROSPERITY SPELLS

These abundance and banishment spells are quite popular with most candle magic practitioners: they are very practical and fairly simple to perform. Remember, though, as with any magic, there should be ethical limitations to your spell work—your prosperity should not come at the expense of anyone else's good fortune—as well as an assumption of responsibility with regard to money matters. That is, casting spells to rid ourselves of debt or to increase our financial well-being are intended to boost the practical efforts that you are already making in your daily life. The spells are intended to reward good behavior with an extra magical enhancement. They work for you as long as you also work for yourself.

Making Money!: A Spell to Attract Prosperity

Harnessing the power of the moon is one of the most effective ways to attract money and prosperity, in general. The waxing moon always symbolizes the growing of potency, so taking advantage of this crucial resource, not just in timing but in energy itself, is tantamount to success.

WHEN TO PERFORM THE SPELL:

Any time during a waxing moon

HOW LONG IT TAKES:

As long as it takes the candle to burn down

WHAT YOU'LL NEED:

1 green taper candle

Gold-colored coin

Cinnamon, basil, dried orange peel

STEPS:

1. As mentioned in the introduction to the spell, this is best performed outdoors under the light of the waxing moon (or at least at a window that lets in the moonlight). Cleanse your space, cast a circle, and be sure to take precautions when lighting a candle, so as not to cause a fire outside.
2. Have all of your items close at hand as you light your green good fortune candle. Once the candle exhibits a steady flame,

take the coin in your left hand and your herbal accoutrements in the right hand: the cinnamon represents prosperity, while the basil symbolizes both money and protective energy, and the orange peel indicates happiness.

3. Rub your hands together, releasing the scents into the air while infusing yourself and the coin with their essences and state your intention clearly: *"Make the money flow, make my money grow. I ask for wealth, prosperity, and health."* Recite this three times while releasing the scents and watching the candle flame.

4. Once the candle has burned down, bury it in an auspicious spot, sprinkling the remnants of the herbal items over its mound. Carry the coin with you until the next waxing moon begins.

Debt Begone!: A Spell to Decrease Debt

This is essentially a banishing spell, focused particularly on money, but it also contains elements of healing. The sense of relief and release that we feel when our debt burdens are lifted is quite wonderful. I know I performed this spell a lot when I was paying off my student loans: the last time I performed it, I received a wholly unexpected notice that I had paid too much and was getting a hefty refund. How's that for working some crafty magic?

WHEN TO PERFORM THE SPELL:

Any time during a waning moon, though Saturday is best

HOW LONG IT TAKES:

As long as it takes the candle to burn down

WHAT YOU'LL NEED:

1 purple taper candle

Frankincense essential oil

Pen and paper

STEPS:

1. Cleanse your space well. I'd recommend a thorough sage smudging here, as this spell needs all the positive potency it can conjure.
2. Anoint your candle with the frankincense oil, which helps with stress and banishes unwanted ties to the past. Your

purple candle represents your wisdom and helps to ward off the negative.

3. On your paper, write down your debts alongside your intention to get rid of them. If you are so inclined, you can draw a banishing symbol (usually the pentacle) on the back of the paper (you might also choose to carve the banishing symbol into your candle).

4. Place the candle atop your paper, light it and call upon the energies you invoke to assist you in this banishment: *"I ask for some simple relief so I can rid myself of stress and grief."*

5. As the candle burns, focus your intention on how you will feel once you are out from under this burden; let it be an invitation to feel peace. Ideally, the paper will burn as the candle burns down to it (be sure to practice sensible fire safety), but you may need to help it along. Put everything in a flameproof pot or cauldron and let it burn away.

Conquering Hardship: A Spell to Change Your Luck

We could all use some good fortune in our lives and this is a simple spell that can be performed at just about any time. This spell can function as a straightforward luck spell, but it can also be more intensely focused on overcoming a stretch of bad luck.

WHEN TO PERFORM THE SPELL:

Best at the full moon, but it can be done during the waxing moon

HOW LONG IT TAKES:

As long as it takes the paper to burn

WHAT YOU'LL NEED:

1 green taper candle

1 Jade stone

Pen and paper

Flameproof container

STEPS:

1. You might want to consider cleansing not just your altar space where you will perform this spell, but your entire home, or at least the part of your living space where you spend the most time. You want to rid yourself of whatever negative energies are crowding out your good fortune.
2. Before you light your candle, have a flameproof pot or cauldron at the ready and place your jade stone in it—this

will promote your good luck, and strengthen banishment of the bad. Write down what you consider to be your misfortunes as of late and place this list into the cauldron.

3. Light your wealth and good fortune candle, set the paper alight, and recite your incantation seven times: *"Misfortunes of the recent past are burning now; they will not last."*

4. Place the candle back on its base and wait until the paper is turned to ash. Blow the candle out—yes, this is one of the appropriate times to extinguish a candle with gusto; you're blowing away misfortune—and let everything in the cauldron cool. Retrieve your jade stone and sleep with it underneath your pillow for one week. Toss the ashes to the winds, and bury your good fortune candle somewhere auspicious: a garden is excellent for this, but any place where nature grows in abundance is appropriate.

Payback Time: A Spell to Recoup What You're Owed

While your intentions could be specific to one particular situation, this spell can also be used generally to attract money that is due to you (better tax refund, higher wages, and so on).

WHEN TO PERFORM THE SPELL:

Any time during a waxing moon

HOW LONG IT TAKES:

About 10-15 minutes for nine days

WHAT YOU'LL NEED:

1 green pillar candle

1 white pillar candle

Basil essential oil

STEPS:

1. Cleanse your space, and place your candles nine inches apart: the green is for the money you wish to recoup and the white represents yourself. Orient them according to the cardinal directions best for your energy: whichever element seems to be most like you (grounded would be north, passionate would be south, serene would be west, and flighty would be east) is where the white candle should go, and place the green candle at its opposite direction, creating a flow of energy.

2. Anoint the candles with basil oil, and as you light them, recite your intentions: *"Return my money three times three, bring this happiness and wealth to me. Not where others would feel harm, so I wish it with this charm."* Repeat this three times, then snuff your candles.
3. Repeat this ritual—ideally at the same time each day—moving the candles closer together by an inch each day: by the ninth day (three times three), your candles should touch, and your money should come your way!

Opening up Opportunities: A General Luck Spell

This spell involves the wonderful magical mint plant, so I'll take the opportunity to suggest that, if you are interested in growing your magical skills and repertoire, plant an herb garden. Your own home-grown herbs (for cooking, drying, making oils, and so on) are powerful tools: basil, rosemary, sage, and mint are all frequently used and easily grown.

WHEN TO PERFORM THE SPELL:

Any time during a waxing moon, though Thursday is the day most associated with abundance

HOW LONG IT TAKES:

As long as it takes the candles to burn down

WHAT YOU'LL NEED:

1 green tea candle

1 gold tea candle

1 orange tea candle

1 bunch of fresh or dried mint

STEPS:

1. Smudge your altar with sage or rosemary, sending away negative energies. Set up your candles in a triangle, with the green good fortune candle at the point, and the gold luck candle and orange vitality candle forming the base.

2. In the center space of your candles, place your mint: be sure to rub it between your palms to release its scent, emphasizing your intentions (you can also anoint the candles with mint oil, if you have some on hand).

3. Light your candles and cast your spell: *"Here I bring myself good luck, true prosperity, and positive energy. Peace and happiness, fortune and wealth, bring it to me all in good health."*

4. Let the candles burn down as you visualize all that this good luck will bring you. Once they are burned down, be sure to dispose of them properly (however you feel will be best for your energies), and be sure to use the mint for tea or other recipes, literally consuming your good fortune.

Overcoming Obstacles: A Spell to Remove Roadblocks

This magic works as both a banishing spell and an attraction spell: you are banishing whatever roadblocks are preventing you from achieving your goals, while attracting the powerful energies and strength you need to overcome the obstacle.

WHEN TO PERFORM THE SPELL:

Any time during the waning moon, though waiting until the waning moon is at crescent phase is most potent

HOW LONG IT TAKES:

As long as it takes the candle to burn down

WHAT YOU'LL NEED:

1 black taper candle

Essential oil of your choice

Herbal-spice blend of cayenne pepper, ginger, sage, mint, bay leaf (1-2 teaspoons each)

A pinch of coffee grounds (optional)

STEPS:

1. Prepare and cleanse your altar, as per usual.
2. Anoint your black banishment candle with essential oil. Choose one that is appropriate for your particular situation (if it's a financial obstacle, try mint or basil; if it's a

relationship obstacle, try cinnamon or rose; if it's a health obstacle, try eucalyptus oil, and so on).

3. Roll your candle in the herbal-spice blend: cayenne helps to "burn" away the bad energy, while ginger strengthens your resolve; sage helps with cleansing, while mint increases the banishment; and bay leaf serves as protection. The optional coffee grounds work to bolster the strength and speed of the spell.

4. Light your candle, and recite your spell: *"I ask for success with nothing to block my way. Cast aside the obstacles forever and a day."* Repeat this incantation as the candle burns down.

5. Be sure to dispose of the candle remains as you would for a banishment: a watery grave or a fiery destruction.

Mining the Money Tree: A Spell to Lead You to Money

This is a spell to help you find direction and open up the channels of communication that will point you in the right direction for reaping some well-deserved prosperity.

WHEN TO PERFORM THE SPELL:

Best at the full moon, but it can be done during the waxing moon

HOW LONG IT TAKES:

As long as it takes the candles to burn down

WHAT YOU'LL NEED:

2 green votive candles

2 small glass jars

Some rice

6 black peppercorns

STEPS:

1. This is an unusual spell in that it doesn't require your presence at the altar or any specific incantations. Basically, it brings positive energy into your living space that is designed to help you find a prosperous direction. Thus, begin by cleansing your home with a good sage smudging.
2. Next, prepare your prosperity jars. Put a handful of rice in each of your jars for purification and positive energy; add

three black peppercorns to each, as these will bring protection and energy to you and your intentions.

3. Place the jars at the northernmost part and the southernmost part of your home, with a candle next to each. Be sure to exercise safety precautions, as the candles will burn without you being directly present.
4. Light the candles and allow them to burn all the way down: you are summoning energy to your prosperity jars via the flame, channeling it from north to south (or vice versa) to bring grounded security and reborn energy into your life. Open windows, if you can, to increase the flow.
5. Once the candles are burned down, bury them in your garden or under a nearby sturdy tree. Leave the jars in place until the next full moon.

Locating Lost Items

This is an easy spell to quickly find whatever inanimate object you've lost. For more significant losses (such as lost loves and other emotionally charged scenarios), look to spells in Chapters 6 and 7.

WHEN TO PERFORM THE SPELL:

Anytime needed

HOW LONG IT TAKES:

As long as it takes the candle to burn down

WHAT YOU'LL NEED:

1 silver tea candle

STEPS:

1. Cleanse your altar, and clear your mind: oftentimes, our energy becomes occluded with frustration when we lose something.
2. Light your silver candle for mystical guidance and call up the assistance you need: *"Please help me find what I clearly seek, so I can overcome my pique."*
3. As the candle burns, visualize the lost object and see if the flame flickers in any particular direction or takes any impressionistic form. It will often give you clues as to where your object might be.

Brokering the Best Deal: A Spell for Successful Negotiation

Use this spell anytime you need some good luck in achieving the best result from any personal or professional scenario that will impact your overall prosperity (such as a better job or a pay raise—more on these in the following chapter). I'll also mention here that, as with many spells, if you wear some of the colors that correspond to your intentions—for example, orange, gold, or green—it can increase the potency of your message.

WHEN TO PERFORM THE SPELL:

This is a sun spell, so choose a day with maximum sunshine, preferably a Sunday or a Wednesday

HOW LONG IT TAKES:

As long as it takes the candle to burn down

WHAT YOU'LL NEED:

1 gold taper candle

Tiger's eye stones

Orange essential oil

STEPS:

1. Cleanse your space as per usual and orient the candle in between the north and south cardinal directions.
2. Anoint your candle with orange oil, which engenders vitality

and success, and place your tiger's eye stones to the north and to the south of your candle. These stones channel both the masculine energy of the sun (in its golden eye) and the feminine energy of the earth (in its rich brown tones).

3. State your intentions clearly: *"I am worthy of the best possible outcome. I have confidence and clarity, along with purity of intentions. I call upon the powers of the sun and the strength of the earth to assist my request."*
4. Let the candle burn down as you visualize the ideal result, then carry the tiger's eye stones with you for the next seven days (of course, you should have them with you during the actual negotiation!).

9

WORK AND CAREER SPELLS

These spells delve deeply into improving your career path, as well as assisting you with specific workplace dilemmas and desires. We all define success differently, so work on putting your individual intentions into each of the following spells, envisioning your own particular recipe for success. One of the many wonderful things about working candle magic is that it accesses the fundamental energies of the four elements in order to generate more positive energy, with your intentions directing that energy in a certain way. This is why this kind of magical prowess is especially well-suited to bolstering your career and grounding your workday: you are harnessing these powerful energies and channeling them into your overall design for a successful life. For me, these spells were instrumental not only in improving my work situation, but also in helping me to clarify what I wanted and how to get it. Many of these spells are mini-motivational speeches in their own right!

Manifesting Your Dream Job: A Spell for Good Work

This is a simple spell that can be adapted for any number of purposes, but it seems to be especially effective when job seeking.

WHEN TO PERFORM THE SPELL:

Any time during a waxing moon, with Sunday being the ideal symbolic time

HOW LONG IT TAKES:

As long as it takes the candle to burn down

WHAT YOU'LL NEED:

1 gold pillar candle

Basil essential oil

Pen and paper

Orange pouch

STEPS:

1. Smudge your space before beginning, as per usual.
2. Place the candle at the center of your altar, projecting energy, confidence, and good fortune. Anoint with the basil oil, bringing your way clarity of thought and associations with wealth.
3. Write down the job you want, if you are seeking a specific post, or write down aspects of your dream job: the more

specific your intentions, the better your results. Fold the paper into a triangle and place it in front of your candle.

4. Light the candle and recite your spell: *"I attract this work to me, with my will I ask let it be. Bring this job, three times three, with my power, let it be."* Let the candle burn for nine minutes, then snuff it.
5. Repeat the spell at the same time each week until the candle is completely burned. After the spell is completed, put the triangle paper in the orange pouch (add a pinch of basil, if you like, to focus on the monetary aspect of the job) and carry it with you for nine days.

Making More Money: A Spell to Get a Raise

This is a similar spell to the previous one, including the writing of intentions and the anointing of the candle. The tools are varied based on the specific intention here.

WHEN TO PERFORM THE SPELL:

Any time during the waxing moon, with Thursday being perhaps the most auspicious

HOW LONG IT TAKES:

As long as it takes the candle to burn down

WHAT YOU'LL NEED:

1 green taper candle

Patchouli oil

Paper and pen

STEPS:

1. Cleanse your space: you might use rosemary or basil for this spell, as they both contain purification properties and money attraction.
2. Place the candle in the center of your altar and anoint it with patchouli oil; the oil attracts money, along with other powerful emotions.
3. Write your name and a symbol for money on the paper, fold it in half and place it next to the candle. Light the candle and

recite: *"Rewards for good work shall come to me, hard work pays off, my raise shall be."*

4. After the candle has formed some wax, use it to seal your written intention (be careful when handling hot wax). Let your candle burn down, then slip the intention into your purse or wallet, carrying it with you until your request is granted.

First Impressions: An Attraction Spell

This is an excellent way to calm your nerves before an important job interview, though it could also be modified to apply to a first date or any other meeting wherein your vibrancy and intelligence need to shine.

WHEN TO PERFORM THE SPELL:

Best during a full moon but performed when the sun is at its strongest, mid-day

HOW LONG IT TAKES:

As long as it takes the candle to burn down plus a preparatory bath

WHAT YOU'LL NEED:

An orange

Rose petals or dried rose

1 white tea candle

Vanilla essential oil (or extract)

STEPS:

1. Begin by taking a ritual bath; you want to slough off any negative energy, while also feeling clean, beautiful, and confident. Cut your orange into six pieces, and put these into the bath along with a handful of rose petals or a few pinches of dried rose. Give yourself some time to relax and clarify your intentions.

2. After your cleansing bath, prepare your altar and anoint your white candle—symbolic of the purified you—with vanilla, the scent of attraction and beauty.
3. Light the candle and recite your intention: *"All I meet will see no wrong, as my impression is as lovely as a song. All remember when first we met, because I am clearly the best you can get."*
4. Let the candle burn down, and bury the remains in your garden so they take root.

Sorcery for Success: A Spell to Do Well at Work

This spell can be cast at any time of the year, but it is particularly potent when cast at the close of one year or the beginning of the next, during what used to be called Yule season. This is akin to the making of New Year's Resolutions. Again, it can be cast at other times but its power is intended to last throughout the year, so choose what you feel to be an auspicious moment. The spell also requires an investment of time, so plan accordingly.

WHEN TO PERFORM THE SPELL:

During a full moon

HOW LONG IT TAKES:

As long as it takes the candle to burn down, as well as time to make oil (3+ days)

WHAT YOU'LL NEED:

Ingredients to make your own anointing oil: olive oil, pine needles, poinsettia leaves, fresh or dried cranberries

1 white votive candle, 1 green votive candle, and 1 yellow votive candle

STEPS:

1. Cleanse your kitchen, as you are going to work in there to make your customized essential oil. Warm the olive oil (about ½ cup) in a small saucepan, then add a few pinches of pine needles for strength and perseverance, three poinsettia

leaves for motivation and positivity, and eight fresh or dried cranberries to banish negative energy. Let this mixture cool before pouring it into a container and covering with plastic wrap.

2. Steep this for three days before straining it into a container, preferably an apothecary jar with a dropper or other easily pourable container.

3. Cleanse your altar, then arrange your candles with the white candle at the apex of a triangle pattern. Light them and clarify your intentions: *"As surely as the sun comes up by day, keep me focused and successful in my way. As surely as the day goes long, help me stay clear and strong."*

4. Let the candles burn down as you contemplate what activities you will excel in at work. Use the anointing oil to cast a quick booster spell whenever you have an important meeting or a project due.

Practicing Peace: A Spell to End Workplace Strife

One of the trickiest issues to deal with in the workplace is one that requires an equally crafty spell. Remember, though, that your intentions with candle magic are always to reinforce positive energies, never to wish ill or harm on others. Also keep the focus on yourself and how you fit into the larger picture at work; your spell will have more success if you aren't interested in controlling what's going on but rather changing the energy and direction of events.

WHEN TO PERFORM THE SPELL:

Any time during a waxing moon

HOW LONG IT TAKES:

As long as it takes the candle to burn down

WHAT YOU'LL NEED:

1 white taper candle

1 pink taper candle

1 black taper candle

Lavender or jasmine essential oil

STEPS:

1. Cleanse your space as per usual, and arrange your candles in a triangle, with the white candle at the apex.
2. The white candle represents yourself, negotiating between amity (the pink) and animosity (which the black will banish).

You can carve names into the candles, if there are specific parties who are in need of nudging toward friendship and/or away from conflict.

3. Anoint the candles with the peaceful lavender or jasmine oil, soothing the reconciliation. Light them, starting with the white candle, then recite your intentions: *"I am here to wish all involved well, to start to heal the wounds on which we dwell. Clear our space peaceful as before, so we can work together once more."*

4. Let the candles burn down and dispose of them in kind: the white and pink should be buried someplace where their energies will be fruitful, while the black banishment remnants should be sent out by water.

Practicing Procrastination: A Spell to End Bad Habits

If you find yourself slipping into bad habits at work—the most common of these being procrastination—I recommend you do this quick banishing spell. I like to cast it on the hump day of Wednesday, which symbolizes the work day of the week where my bad habits (like laziness, inattention, or procrastination) are likeliest to crop up.

WHEN TO PERFORM THE SPELL:

Any time during a waning moon

HOW LONG IT TAKES:

As long as it takes the candle to burn down plus 21 days

WHAT YOU'LL NEED:

Salt

1 black taper candle

Pen and paper

Clear quartz crystal

STEPS:

1. Smudge your space well, using the powerful sage herb, and cast a circle around your black candle using salt. This helps with the banishment part of the spell.
2. Write down your bad habit, such as procrastination. Light your candle and state your intentions: *"I wish to rid myself*

of the bad, to find a way to instead be glad. I replace this habit with the good, a reminder of all things I should."

3. Either let the candle burn down to the paper or ignite the paper in the flame (have a flameproof container handy nearby), scattering the ashes to the wind and setting the candle off by water. Close your circle and dispose of your salt.

4. The next day, preferably at the same time, write down the good habit you wish to use as a replacement for the bad (habits aren't so much broken as exchanged). Put it under the clear quartz crystal at the center of your altar. Each day, for the next 21 days, rewrite the good habit and place the slip of paper under the quartz. On the 22nd day, bury the slips of paper near the foundation of your home. Be sure to recharge the quartz before using it in another spell, as this spell requires a lot of its energy.

Warding off Downsizing: A Protection Spell

This protection spell is designed to prevent you from getting fired or laid off, though it is also good to have some practice at protection spells in general. You can use this as a basis for any number of personalized protection spells; also look to Chapter 11 for more.

WHEN TO PERFORM THE SPELL:

During the full moon

HOW LONG IT TAKES:

As long as it takes the candle to burn down

WHAT YOU'LL NEED:

1 black taper candle

Lavender essential oil

1 obsidian stone

Dried sage, thyme, and rose

Small white or black pouch

STEPS:

1. Cleanse your altar, and consider placing some objects of good fortune at the four cardinal directions: this is optional, though it enhances the flow of energy for this spell.
2. Place your candle at the center of your altar, and light it while reciting your intention: *"Protect me from all*

negativity and cloak me in purity. Keep me safe from workplace wrongs so I can remain protected and strong." Pass the obsidian stone through the flame three times, allowing the power of the intention to strengthen the stone's resolve.

3. Once the candle has burned down and the stone has cooled, place the stone, any wax remains (or at least a bit of these remains while burying the rest), and the herbs in your pouch. The cleansing sage and protective thyme, along with the rose for confidence and well-being, will empower the protective obsidian. A white pouch is perhaps more attuned against outright firing, while the black functions more specifically in a downsizing situation.
4. Carry or wear the pouch with you until the next full moon.

Magical Motivation: A Spell to Keep you Keeping on

This spell should invigorate you just as the ingredients intend. All of these scents and colors are used to wake us up, refresh us, and expand our creativity.

WHEN TO PERFORM THE SPELL:

This is a sun spell, so choose a day with maximum sunshine, preferably a Sunday or a Wednesday

HOW LONG IT TAKES:

As long as it takes the candle to burn down

WHAT YOU'LL NEED:

1 orange taper candle

Mint essential oil

Blend of rosemary, cinnamon, and ginger

STEPS:

1. Cleanse your space as per usual, and anoint your orange candle with mint oil, then roll it in your spice blend.
2. The orange candle signifies vitality and vigor, while the mint awakens your senses. Rosemary is always good for both protection and invigoration (while also being linked to wealth), while cinnamon increases your power and passion, as ginger creates an energized spirit.
3. State your intentions clearly, preferably coming up with your

own personal list of things to do: ideally, your incantation will state what needs to be done, followed by an affirmation of the rewards in getting it done.

4. Let the candle burn down and keep the remnants at your altar for a full week.

Channeling Certainty: A Spell to Make Good Decisions

This is a spell to increase your psychic energy, attracting positive energies and clarifying the mind. It's equally good to use when faced with personal decisions, in addition to those related to work and career.

WHEN TO PERFORM THE SPELL:

During a full moon

HOW LONG IT TAKES:

As long as it takes the candles to burn down

WHAT YOU'LL NEED:

4 purple tea candles

1 white tea candle

Jasmine essential oil

STEPS:

1. Cleanse your space, and consider whether to take a ritual bath in preparation. If the decision you're contemplating is a life-changing one, I'd suggest you put in the extra time.
2. Place your purple candles, signifying psychic power and awareness, at each of the four cardinal directions: you want energy from all of the elements to help you sort through all of the factors involved in your decision.

3. Place your white candle, representing yourself, in the center, and anoint all of your candles with jasmine oil for clarity.
4. Light your candles, beginning with the north, then going clockwise and ending with the white candle. Cast your intentions: *"Help me here to decide for the best, I need to choose one and discard all the rest. I request clarity of mind, so I can make the best of my time."*
5. Let the candles burn down, then bury them someplace where good things grow. This spell can be repeated at the full moon for three consecutive months, if necessary.

10

HEALTH AND WELL-BEING SPELLS

When we start to practice magic, we begin to realize the interconnectedness of many things, from the elements and the four cardinal directions to the many correspondences among colors and scents, phases and times, magical tools in general. Health itself is no different, and healing spells rarely target one area; instead, they are intended to heal and bring together the mind, the body, and the spirit—true well-being is balance and harmony among all of these areas. If we begin to view our health in an interconnected and holistic manner, then we are better able to understand how to channel various natural energies to improve our overall health and well-being: our emotional states directly impact our physical strength, as well as our spiritual sensibility.

In general, healing spells are intended for the practitioner, though they can be turned outward toward helping others, with different intentions. Be careful, though, when attempting to perform healing spells for others: you should seek permission before assuming your actions are welcome, and be respectful if they're not.

Finally, I advocate these health and well-being spells because they help me to reorient my state of mind to the positive, as well as promote feelings of security against ill feelings and bad health. They are performed with an overall intention of putting me in a happier and fitter state of mind. I do not, as you should not, use these spells in place of professional medical advice; these are used in conjunction with traditional medicine to boost positive energies and create a vibrant, supportive space for healing.

Conjuring Relief from Anxiety and Depression

This spell can be used for either anxiety, which boils down to a fear of the future, or depression, which often indicates being stuck in the regrets of the past. The ritual is the same for either, though the signifying colors of the candle are distinct.

WHEN TO PERFORM THE SPELL:

Any time during the waning moon

HOW LONG IT TAKES:

As long as it takes the candles to burn down over the course of nine days

WHAT YOU'LL NEED:

1 white pillar candle for anxiety OR

1 red pillar candle for depression

Orange essential oil

Crystal or stone (optional)

STEPS:

1. Smudge your space well: you want your energy to be clear and fresh.
2. Place your candle in the center of the altar and anoint with orange essential oil. This replaces the anxiety or depression with strength and vitality. The white candle is to purify your

mind of anxiety, while the red candle fortifies you with courage.

3. Light the candle and, if you like, choose a particular crystal or stone to pass through the flame, drawing symbolic energy to you (a moonstone for peace, perhaps, or a bloodstone for courage). As the candle burns, recite your incantation: *"My power of self is so clearly strong, that no worries or troubles can come along. I cast protection against these worries in my soul, because might is my weapon and harmony is my goal."*

4. Let the candle burn for a few minutes as you meditate on peacefulness and strength, then snuff it. Repeat this ritual each day at the same time for nine consecutive days.

The End of Envy: A Banishing Spell

One of the most destructive emotions, envy can impede not only our joy and happiness but also our magic itself. It shuts down our mind, keeping it closed to tolerance and compassion, which are crucial to the energies we release in casting spells. I find myself casting this spell at the beginning of a new season, when change is in the air (and people are often conspicuously spending money for gifts at the holidays or travel during the summer) and I'm in need of a refreshed mindset.

WHEN TO PERFORM THE SPELL:

During a full moon

HOW LONG IT TAKES:

As long as it takes the candles to burn down

WHAT YOU'LL NEED:

1 green pillar candle

1 black pillar candle

A penknife

Clove of garlic

STEPS:

1. This is another spell that is best cast outdoors: you want to send your envious feelings away with the wind. Again, always use caution when burning candles outdoors.

2. Cast a circle around your space using pebbles, sticks, or simple energy to demarcate a cleansed space.
3. Carve the word "envy" into the black candle, and rub your green candle with protective garlic. Light the black candle first, using its flame to light the green candle.
4. Clarify your intentions: *"I cast aside this envy and other feelings poor, I bid them gone from my life forevermore."* Let the candles burn all the way through the center as you meditate on the beauty of nature, reminding yourself that what you have is enough; in fact, it is abundant.
5. Bury the green candle so your new good fortune can take root, protected from envy, while disposing of the black candle far from your home.

Blocking Illness: A Protection Spell

Most people who practice magic acquire a repertoire of healing and protective tools, including amulets, sachets, potions, and spells. Herbs, in particular, are key to most healing rituals, and can be used in a variety of combinations for a myriad of results. Here is a general health spell using candles: you can amplify its power or specify its intentions with the addition of particular herbal oils or dried herbs, depending on your needs.

WHEN TO PERFORM THE SPELL:

During a full moon

HOW LONG IT TAKES:

As long as it takes the candles to burn down

WHAT YOU'LL NEED:

1 white taper candle

1 indigo taper candle

1 purple taper candle

STEPS:

1. Smudge your space with a mix of sage and rosemary for maximum protection and cleansing.
2. Arrange your candles in a triangle with the white "self" candle at the apex. The indigo represents physical health, while the purple candle symbolizes spiritual well-being.

3. Call upon each of the elements to aid in protection: *"I call upon the earth to keep me grounded. I call upon the fire to purge me of fever. I call upon the water to wash away infection. I call upon the wind to whisk away bad energies."*

4. Let the candles burn all the way down, and when the wax remnants are cool, keep them under your pillow until the next full moon, then bury them beneath a strong and sturdy tree.

Rapid Recovery: A Spell for Quick Healing

This spell is appropriate for a particular wound or illness. While the previous spell is, at its core, a protection spell, this is a more focused conjuring. It may not be powerful enough to heal chronic conditions, but I have used it to good effect when dealing with sprained ankles and head colds.

WHEN TO PERFORM THE SPELL:

Any time it's needed

HOW LONG IT TAKES:

As long as it takes the candle to burn down

WHAT YOU'LL NEED:

1 white taper candle

Eucalyptus essential oil

Black cord or string

STEPS:

1. Cleanse your space and set your candle at the center of your altar.
2. Anoint the candle with the healing and cleansing eucalyptus oil. Use the cord or string to tie around the injured or ill part of the body, as close to the area as you can.
3. Light the candle and state your intention: *"Close this wound, end the sick, make me healthy, sure and quick."*

4. Let the candle burn down, untying the cord and letting it burn—use caution. In the last moments of the dying flame, imagine the injury or illness being consumed by the flame. Be sure to get rid of remnants directly, sending them far away.

Divining Dreams: A Spell for Good Sleep

This spell should help you get a solid night's sleep. If you want to invite dreams, then add a stick of frankincense or lavender incense to burn during the spell.

WHEN TO PERFORM THE SPELL:

Anytime you need deep sleep

HOW LONG IT TAKES:

As long as it takes the candle to burn down

WHAT YOU'LL NEED:

1 blue tea candle

Amethyst or smoke quartz crystal

STEPS:

1. Perform this spell directly in your bedroom, and prepare yourself and the room for good sleep. Obviously, you want to cleanse the space thoroughly, as usual, but you also want to invest in some more practical aids for good sleep. Put fresh, clean sheets on your bed, have a comfy blanket and your favorite pillow handy, turn off screens and keep lighting dim, consider playing some sleep-inducing music.
2. When you are ready for bed, light your candle first and recite your incantation, with your crystal in your hand. The crystal is representative of the moon itself, inviting nighttime

serenity. State your intentions clearly: *"Here in my hand, I hold the moon, so its calming light will soothe me soon."*

3. Let your tea candle burn down safely, as you tuck the crystal under your pillow and yourself into bed.

Negating Nightmares: Another Spell for Good Sleep

This spell can also be aided with herbal potions that help you sleep soundly (or just some unfussy chamomile tea), as nightmares are often caused by an agitated mind. If your nightmares come from a psychic interference, or some deep well of anxiety or trauma, you may need to perform this spell fairly regularly for it to produce results. Casting it in conjunction with anxiety spells or other banishing spells can also increase its efficacy.

WHEN TO PERFORM THE SPELL:

When necessary for peaceful sleep

HOW LONG IT TAKES:

About 10-15 minutes before bedtime

WHAT YOU'LL NEED:

1 black taper candle

1 silver ribbon

1 silver coin

STEPS:

1. As with the previous spell, prepare your bedroom not only with cleansing or smudging but also with practical considerations (clean sheets, comfy blanket and pillow, soothing music, and so on).
2. Tie your silver ribbon around your black candle: the silver

symbolizes spiritual awakening and higher thinking, as it binds the banishing candle.

3. Hold your coin in your left hand as you light your candle and cast your spell: *"These dreams that come before the dawn, make not me a frightened pawn. I ask the moon, so calm and sure to bring me peace just like a cure."*

4. Let the candle burn for a few minutes, as you visualize a peaceful scene or a previous happy dream. Put the coin on your windowsill, snuff the black candle, and tie the ribbon around your wrist before bed. You can reuse these magical tools for three nights in a row, if necessary.

Conjuring Creativity

If you feel that your magic is blocked, this spell can also help you revitalize your energy and connection with the natural elements.

WHEN TO PERFORM THE SPELL:

Any time during a waxing moon

HOW LONG IT TAKES:

15-20 minutes

WHAT YOU'LL NEED:

Small glass jar with lid

Orange candle of whatever size

Herb-spice blend including dried basil, mistletoe, bay leaf, cinnamon, rosemary, and sage (two teaspoons each)

STEPS:

1. Cleanse your space, as per usual. You can do this spell at your altar or in your kitchen, where it might be more convenient.
2. Make sure your jar is sterilized and magically purified (soap and water first, then some lemon and/or salt). Light your candle so it provides enlightening guidance as you layer your spices: start with a teaspoon each of basil and mistletoe for creative thought, bay leaf for success, cinnamon for energy, rosemary for clarity, and sage for wisdom.
3. You can place a symbol of your creativity in the jar, if you

like, be that a sigil or a slip of paper with a word or phrase on it, or an object that symbolizes your creative pursuits.
4. Finish the layering with another teaspoon of each of the above herbs.
5. State your intention clearly: *"Sleep no more, inspiration. Awakened be. Rouse up muses, come to me."* Then use the melted candle wax to seal the bottle (with caution, of course).
6. Keep your creativity jar on your altar for up to three months.

Hearty and Hale: A Spell to Improve Health

This spell uses candle magic in a slightly different way: you are focusing your magic on your homemade incense blend, using the candle to release the scents and energies into the atmosphere. This incense blend can also be brewed into a tea, assuming that you've used kitchen-grade products safe for consumption.

WHEN TO PERFORM THE SPELL:

During a full moon

HOW LONG IT TAKES:

A couple of hours (mostly inactive)

WHAT YOU'LL NEED:

Incense ingredients: dried orange peel, caraway seeds, black peppercorns, dried sage, rosemary, cinnamon, and natural sugar (such as demerara)

1 orange or red tea candle

Flameproof incense burner or other vessel

STEPS:

1. This is best prepared in the kitchen, so smudge the kitchen with a strong sage bundle.
2. Prepare your incense mixture by combining one tablespoon each of dried orange peel for vitality, caraway seeds for antiseptic properties, black peppercorns for endurance, sage

for mental strength, rosemary for memory, cinnamon for physical strength, and sugar for sweetness (of life).

3. Put your ingredients in an incense burner or other flameproof container and light your tea candle underneath the incense, releasing its scents and intentions into the room.

4. Let it burn until it's spent, then bury the remnants in a place where healthy plants grow.

Casting Out Fear

This is a very basic banishment spell that uses clear symbolism to rid you of unwanted fears. I find that this simple spell will put you in the right mindset for dispelling a fear, but it takes a lot of time and energy to get over a true phobia. For example, I have an intense fear of flying, so I always cast this spell before I get on a plane. The fear doesn't go away, but my mind is soothed and my energies can be spent on more positive things.

WHEN TO PERFORM THE SPELL:

When needed

HOW LONG IT TAKES:

As long as it takes to burn and scatter intention

WHAT YOU'LL NEED:

1 black taper candle

Pen and paper

Flameproof dish or cauldron

STEPS:

1. Cleanse your altar space, taking the time to both purify your space with lemon and/or salt and smudging with sage: fear is a negative energy that clings to much in our lives.
2. Write down your fear on a slip of paper and read it aloud: confronting the fear head on bolsters our courage.

3. Light your candle and cast your spell: *"Keep close to me those things so dear, crowding out implacable fear. Now I request you disappear, be gone from my life, irrational fear."*
4. Ignite your piece of paper with the candle flame, then let it burn to ash in your flameproof bowl or dish. Scatter the ashes away from your home, and send the waxy remnants of the candle to a watery grave.

11

PROTECTION SPELLS

Another incredibly useful category in the armament of candle magic is the protection spell. Not only is this kind of magic incredibly practical, but it bestows upon you a peace of mind that is invaluable for continuing your magical studies—and for daily life, in general. The spells you will find in this chapter are, again, confined to candle magic, simple and straightforward, but they should give you a sense of the wide world of protective magic that exists for interested parties. Amulets and talismans are frequently employed in these spells and can be repurposed for all sorts of protective purposes. Protection spells are also very important because, in order for you to be able to practice any kind of magic, you must be able to connect to the flow of energies that come from nature and the fundamental elements. If negative energies (or people or spells) are blocking your ability to call upon these forces, then your ability to do magic is hampered. So, keep your space cleansed, positively charge your magical tools, and learn to deflect any negative energy that is directed your way.

This is not to suggest that protection spells are retribution against any other person (or that they can somehow completely control external forces); rather, they function to build up a surplus of positive energy that surrounds and protects you and your home, your sacred space, and your loved ones, and keep negative influences at bay.

Protecting Home and Hearth

This spell is ideal for when you first move into a new living space: you can ensure that any negative energy put out by previous occupants is dispelled, and reassure your own sense of safety. To fortify, recast the spell each year at the anniversary of your initial move-in.

WHEN TO PERFORM THE SPELL:

When needed

HOW LONG IT TAKES:

Two days

WHAT YOU'LL NEED:

1 black taper candle

1 white taper candle

Lemon and rose essential oils

4 small glass jars

Dried lavender, basil, salt and rice

STEPS:

1. The day before you intend to cast the spell, thoroughly smudge your entire house. Get up at sunrise (an auspicious time) and tidy everything before doing a sage smudging.
2. Fill each of your jars with lavender, basil, salt, and rice, respectively, and place them at the four cardinal directions in

your home—in a windowsill, if possible—or out in the garden, if you have one. The lavender brings peacefulness to the household, while the basil offers protection; the salt wards off negative energies, while the rice is thought to bring good fortune. Let the moonlight charge these containers overnight.

3. The next day, preferably at sunrise, arrange your jars at the four cardinal directions on your altar with the candles in between. Light your black candle to banish evil, your white candle to purify. Anoint the black candle with lemon essential oil for protection, your white candle with rose oil for blessings.

4. Cast your spell with clear intentions: *"Bless this house, with peace and love. Cleanse all that should be rid of. Protect all those dwelling here, to keep us close, safe, and dear."*

5. Let the candles burn down entirely, and bury the wax remnants near your foundation. You can keep the jars on your window sills for a few weeks, if you like, and/or you can use the contents to conjure up some magically enhanced potions and meals. Some practitioners don't use the herbs or other edible ingredients that have been a part of their spells, but I find it perfectly acceptable, not only because it infuses some magic into what I eat, but also because it keeps with the spirit of economy and recycling that is a part of any good spellcaster's philosophy.

Conjuring Peace: A Spell for a Happy Household

This spell attracts the positive energies needed to keep everyone in your home getting along with one another. The spell jar is intended to sit at a central place in your home, where it will draw on all the fundamental elements to keep the positive energy flowing.

WHEN TO PERFORM THE SPELL:

Any time during a waxing moon, though a Friday is thought to be best

HOW LONG IT TAKES:

As long as it takes for the candles to burn

WHAT YOU'LL NEED:

2 blue tea candles

2 yellow tea candles

Vanilla essential oil

Small glass jar

Dried basil, lavender, thyme, catnip, and lemon peel

Lapis lazuli stone

Rose quartz stone

A couple drops of sun-charged water

STEPS:

1. Cleanse your altar space, as per usual, and prepare your spell jar. Add a tablespoon each of basil for protection and luck, lavender for peace, thyme for joy, catnip for attraction, and lemon peel for happiness.
2. Anoint the stones with a couple of drops of sun-charged water (water that has been exposed to full sunlight for three hours), then place them in the jar: the lapis lazuli soothes and invites intuition, while the rose quartz promotes friendship and romantic love.
3. Place your candles at the four cardinal directions—the blue at north/earth and west/water, the yellow at south/fire and east/air—and anoint them with soothing vanilla essential oil.
4. As you light the candles, cast your spell: *"Here I ask for this home to have peace, for all negative energy and strife to cease. I invite much happiness and joy to all who dwell here, girl and boy."*
5. Let the candles burn down, and bury their remains at the foundation of your home.

Vanquishing Visitors: A Spell to Get Rid of Unwanted Guests

We all know what it's like to have the obtuse guest who doesn't realize it's time to leave, whether that be an annoying uncle at the holidays or an old friend who's crashing on your couch. Here's a simple, but gentle, banishment spell to restore your privacy.

WHEN TO PERFORM THE SPELL:

When needed

HOW LONG IT TAKES:

As long as it takes for the candle to burn

WHAT YOU'LL NEED:

1 black taper candle

Lemon or mint essential oil

Black pepper, cayenne, and cinnamon

STEPS:

1. Cleanse your altar or space. You might consider smudging the area in which the unwanted guest has been sleeping (if you can do so while they aren't around).
2. Anoint your black banishment candle with lemon or mint oil; both provide purification and protection for your space. Mix together your spices, about a tablespoon of each, and roll your candle in them: black pepper provides stamina and

courage; cayenne sends away negative energy; and cinnamon brings protection.

3. Light your candle and recite your incantation: *"Hear me now as I ask my guest to go, give me peace and end this woe."* Repeat this seven times as you watch the candle burn.

4. Be sure to get rid of the remnants as soon as possible: this might be an occasion for a handy toilet flush!

Under Your Thumb No More: A Spell to Free Yourself from Influence

If you've ever been involved in an unhealthy relationship, whether a romantic relationship or friendship gone sour, or even a domineering family member, this spell can help you free yourself from that negative influence. You might also try casting a decision-making spell, as well, or a confidence spell to get you back to your own clarity of thinking.

WHEN TO PERFORM THE SPELL:

Any time during a waning moon

HOW LONG IT TAKES:

As long as it takes to burn and scatter ashes

WHAT YOU'LL NEED:

2 white taper candles

1 red or purple taper candle

Pen and paper

Flameproof bowl or dish

STEPS:

1. Cleanse your altar space, as per usual, and line up your candles with the red or purple candle in between your white candles. Choose red if the person of influence has controlled

you with passion or anger; choose purple if that influence has been more psychological or spiritual. The white candles will pull that energy from the central candle, purifying your intentions.

2. Write the person's name on the piece of paper and set it alight while you cast your spell: *"I ask that you step away from my life, freeing me from this constant strife. I reclaim my mind and soul, rejecting your influence and becoming whole."*

3. When your candles and paper have burned, scatter the ashes to the winds, bury the remnants of the white candles somewhere that brings you joy, and send the red or purple candle away in water.

Safe Voyages: A Protection Spell for Travel

This is a quick and easy spell that you can perform whenever you're going on a trip. I also carry a protection pouch with me, complete with a wooden orange-colored *maneki neko* cat for luck (I did previously mention that I have a fear of flying, so I cover all my bases).

WHEN TO PERFORM THE SPELL:

When needed: best on the Wednesday before you embark on your journey

HOW LONG IT TAKES:

As long as it takes the candle to burn down

WHAT YOU'LL NEED:

1 white taper candle

Rosemary essential oil

Rose quartz crystal

STEPS:

1. Consider smudging your entire house, rather than just your altar for this spell. This will also banish negative energies in your home, keeping everything positive for your return.
2. Anoint your candle and the crystal with the protective rosemary oil, light the candle, and cast your spell: *"I call upon the spirit of the moon, to help me reach my destination soon. I want my trip happy and safe to be, for*

all involved, including me." Pass the crystal through the flame three times while you repeat your incantation.

3. Carry the crystal with you on your journey. Store the remnants of the candle somewhere safe until you return, then bury them close to your home.

Avoiding Accidents: A Prevention Spell

Essentially, this spell teaches you how to make a talisman that you can carry with you for general safety. I keep this pouch of ingredients in my car and thus far it's worked like a literal charm!

WHEN TO PERFORM THE SPELL:

During a full moon

HOW LONG IT TAKES:

As long as it takes for the candle to burn

WHAT YOU'LL NEED:

1 black taper candle

Small pouch

Dried sage, rosemary, and salt

Amethyst crystal

Personal item (see steps below)

STEPS:

1. Cleanse your altar before you begin, and if you have the time, charge the crystal in moonlight before you cast your spell.
2. Place your candle in the center of your space, and light it while reciting your incantation: *"Here I ask that safe I'll be, no matter how wild and free. Use these things to protect*

me from harm, infuse them with power to work like a charm."

3. As you let your candle burn, fill the pouch with your ingredients: a teaspoon or two of each of your protection herbs, along with the salt; add the amethyst crystal for soothing fear; and put in a personal item that you feel has magical properties to you. For example, I use whiskers from my cats (not pulled out, of course. I collect them as they are shed). But you can use anything you feel is a personal good luck charm.

4. Keep the talismanic pouch in your car or in your purse or briefcase so that it watches over you at all times.

Legal Relief: A Spell to Win a Court Case

As anyone knows who has ever faced any kind of legal snafu, this can take a toll on your peace of mind (not to mention your time and energy). This spell can help you "sweeten the deal," as it were, and bring positive results to any kind of court case you find yourself negotiating.

WHEN TO PERFORM THE SPELL:

Seven days before the court date

HOW LONG IT TAKES:

As long as it takes for the candle to burn

WHAT YOU'LL NEED:

1 brown tea candle

Small jar

Honey

Black mustard seeds, cayenne pepper, and galangal root

Pen and paper (optional)

STEPS:

1. Cleanse your space before you begin. You can put this together in your kitchen, if you like, after a good sage smudging.
2. Pour the honey into the jar, and add a tablespoon of black mustard seeds to confuse your opponents, a couple of

pinches of cayenne pepper to ward off negative energy, and three slices of fresh galangal root (or a couple of teaspoons powdered) for good luck and protection.

3. Light your brown tea candle and recite your incantation: *"Keep me grounded and help me win, vanquish my enemies and save my skin!"* Let the candle burn all the way down, then place the remnants in your spell jar and keep it in an auspicious place until the results are in.

Karmic Returns: A Spell to Reverse Evil Sent to You

One of the most fundamental tenets of working magic is that you never wish harm on others. If you do, that karmic energy will return to you threefold. If you suspect someone has been engaging in this kind of magic against you, then you can return it to them—and let them rue the day they expelled that negative nonsense!

WHEN TO PERFORM THE SPELL:

Start or end at the full moon

HOW LONG IT TAKES:

About 10 minutes a day for nine days

WHAT YOU'LL NEED:

1 black pillar candle

1 white pillar candle

1 red pillar candle

Cinnamon essential oil

Penknife

STEPS:

1. Cleanse your space well; this spell requires a lot of power behind it.
2. Prepare your candles: pick out some runes to carve into each candle. A pentacle is a banishing rune, which can work, or

the algiz for protection in general (when rendered upside down, this rune also constitutes a warning), or the eihwaz for defense. Depictions of all of these can be found online. Alternately, you can carve your own symbology onto the candles, according to what works best for you. This can be as simple as carving your name into the white candle, your opponent's name into the black candle, and the offending deed into the red candle.

3. Arrange your candles in a triangle, with the white candle at the apex and anoint with cinnamon oil, which brings both energy and protection to your spell.
4. Cast your spell: *"I send back evil your way, three times three. Your bad intentions won't stay with me, as I return them to you, three times three."* Recite the incantation three times, then snuff the candles.
5. Repeat the spell each day (ideally at the same time) for nine days.

Magicking Away Misfortune

This is a very basic banishment spell to clear your space and life of negative energies that cause misfortune. If you feel that recent events haven't been going your way—the little irritations keep piling up—then this spell can reset your aura.

WHEN TO PERFORM THE SPELL:

When needed

HOW LONG IT TAKES:

As long as it takes for candles to burn

WHAT YOU'LL NEED:

1 white taper candle

1 black taper candle

2 purple taper candles

Incense (optional)

STEPS:

1. Cleanse your space well before beginning, and consider burning some incense for an added boost of energy (sandalwood, with its powers to bless and to heal, is a good choice here).
2. Arrange your candles according to the four cardinal directions, with the white candle (representing the purification of the self) and the black banishing candle at

opposite energies (either north and south, or west and east). The two purple candles, which are to bring about psychic healing, should be at the other two opposing points.

3. Light your candles starting at the north and moving clockwise, as you recite your spell: *"Increase my power and let it grow, so I am free from the misfortune that has been sown."* Continue to repeat your spell until all candles are lit.

4. As the candles burn, imagine all of your misfortune wafting away on the smoke, dissipating into the air. Breathe deeply and envision peacefulness and happiness in your life.

5. Be sure to dispose of the waxy remnants according to what they represent to you, either burying them close by or releasing them in water to send them far away.

FINAL WORDS

At this point, you have likely cast many a crafty spell to improve the quality of your life. From love relationships to friendships, prosperity and career goals, overall health and well-being to protection from any number of misfortunes, your candle magic has certainly illuminated the many pathways to success and happiness that is within your power to direct. I hope that you have seen and felt your powers grow alongside your confidence and knowledge of how to practice this simple magic with great success.

My greatest hope is that you use these explanations, interpretations, and magical templates to cultivate your own special brand of candle magic. There is nothing so potent as discovering your own particular talents and personal correspondences that will enable you to take control of your own destiny. Just about any branch of magic, including candle magic, lends itself to personalization and improvisation—that's why we practitioners are often called crafty! As you begin to trust your own intuitions and get better at identifying your particular intentions, return to the correspondences listed in Chapter 2 to structure your own successful spells. While I have found success with a handful of magical objects and other tools, you may find that some other items mentioned in that chapter work better for you. Once you get the hang of what intention corresponds with what item—be it candle or color, herb or stone, moon phase or day of the week—you will grow more and more adept at customizing your own special spells, to be brandished for your own precise purposes.

Inevitably, as you develop your magical skills further and discover the many potent energies that are available for your own empowerment, you will move beyond the basic candle magic that you find in this book. But never forget that the candle, even if it is not central to the casting of a spell, is a magically, spiritually, historically, and culturally significant object that contains layers of meaning and symbolic import, reminding us of the wondrous world in which we reside. A candle represents the all-consuming powers of the fire element—destructive and regenerative at the same time. The fire element, and its attendant tool, the candle, can evoke the warming comforts of hearth and home, affirming our connection to loved ones and larger communities; this is why the candle is central to so many love and friendship spells. It can also remind us of the purifying forces of the flame, as we are reborn from the ashes, which is why candles are often used in both protection and healing spells. The spells in this book are all about the ways in which the flickering flame of the candle can enhance your life, attracting good fortune, great love or grand passion, prosperity and well-being, while also warding off negative energies and events.

In that mesmerizing spark, you can focus your energies and bring about positive change that will reverberate throughout your life. Channel your intentions through that flame, its wisp of smoke telegraphing your message to the fundamental elements, the natural world, and the ethereal plane. The candle itself represents a convergence of all of these magical realms, allowing you the opportunity to enhance the power of your intention, of your needs and desires, gently nudging those dreams into fruition. Use the light of the candle as your beacon of purpose, signaling your intention to build your best and most beautiful life!

THE CRYSTAL MAGIC SPELL BOOK

A BEGINNER'S GUIDE FOR HEALING, LOVE, AND PROSPERITY

INTRODUCTION

For centuries, the practice of magic and witchcraft has had a bad rap. Stereotyping and stigma, linking witchcraft to devil worshiping and other unflattering depictions, are finally falling by the wayside. Nowadays, practicing magic has developed into an appealing and modern belief system. One such type of specialized magic is used for attracting that special person. While love spells do seem contemporary, they date back to ancient times. Between the 1400s and the 1700s in the United Kingdom, witchcraft was continuously honored by some villagers who would frequently visit those who were believed to practice witchcraft with their problems related to love, marriage, and attraction. At that time, and still today, love spells are cast in the form of rituals, potions, written text, or by utilizing items such as candles or dolls.

More than ten years ago, after a bad break-up with my partner and losing my job, I felt as if my life was spiraling out of control. I wanted to get back on a spiritually positive path and regain my self-worth. I was introduced to magic by a close friend. Just some basic magical spells and rituals; a way to distract myself from my woes. I never imagined that I would not only regain control over my emotions, but also the power to be the captain of my own ship and the master of my destiny. Like Humpty Dumpty, I was put back together again. I was first attracted to crystals as a young child, when my mom took me with her to a small shop. I felt "pulled" towards a particular crystal and begged my mother to buy it. I then collected several more as I grew up, long before I knew anything about magic. Today, I believe crystals were my "gateway drug" into magic and have come to realize that crystals are like that for many people. Most who believe in the healing powers of crystals have come to realize they are practicing magic. The spells set forth in this book will help you to learn how to harness your magical powers and amplify the potential power of crystals.

Mineral stones and crystals are extremely versatile and surprisingly powerful tools of magic. Practitioners of modern magic use crystals for more than just divination; they are used for attracting love, gaining wealth, improving health, and much more. If you have ever picked up a crystal and held it up to the light, looking closely as you turn it over and inspect its wonder from all different angles, you can't help but notice the mysterious sense of awe evoked by these special stones. The word "crystal" means any substance formed naturally by geological processes under the Earth's ground. Each one has its own unique chemical composition, along with its own magical energy signature. The most familiar crystal stone is probably clear quartz. This is what real or true "crystal balls" are made from. Next comes amethyst and rose quartz. Other stones commonly used for magic include jade, bloodstone, and lapis lazuli, which are made from a combination of more than a single mineral and therefore are not considered to be "true" crystals. Other stones referred to as crystals, such as jet and amber, are actually organic substances that over time have become fossilized, rather than stones. For the sake of simplicity, most people who practice crystal magic use the term stones and crystals interchangeably.

While crystals are classified as inorganic, many who practice magic think of them as "alive" because they provide healing energy to all living things. Scientists call the effects of tourmaline and quartz piezoelectric because, when tapped by a hammer, they radiate an electric charge observable to the human eye. This is clear evidence of their innate energy and power. Magical practitioners understand that the crystal's power is the same as the power naturally occurring in the wind or flowing waters. All of energy, both seen and unseen, is interconnected. Since our intentions and thoughts are also forms of energy, we can use crystals as conduits to send positive energy and healing powers out into the universe. These energies come back to us in the spiritual realm and bring with them healing and positive vibes, manifesting as real change in our lives.

I

UNDERSTANDING CRYSTAL MAGIC

Crystals are natural elements that vibrate with their own magical resonance, and that resonance can be used in your magic. Their vibrations can heal, bring balance, and help you to reorganize the universe according to your will. But before you can jump into casting spells, you'll need to understand and take to heart some basic crystal magic knowledge.

1

THE MAGIC OF CRYSTALS

Once upon a time, crystals were considered "hippy" nonsense, and were dismissed as such. Nowadays, it seems that mysticism has gone mainstream. Crystals are embellishing everything from handbags to fine jewelry. The wellness industry has a huge global presence and includes crystals that have found their place in the everyday routine of alternative and complementary healthcare and fitness. Their physical attributes make crystals stand out, as they have the unique qualities that refract light and give it a dark, yet transparent appearance. This is part of the reason people from many different societies and cultures ascribe magical powers to them. There are many differing types of crystals, each with their own unique abilities to heal you physically, emotionally, and spiritually. They are known to enhance the flow of positive energy and help clear the mind and body of negative energy for emotional and physical benefits.

Acceptance, reflection, and mindfulness are the key ingredients to indulging in this experience of wellness and self-care.

Historically, crystals are referenced all the way back to the Ancient Sumerians, who used them in their magic formulas. Turquoise, emeralds, quartz, and carnelian adorned the Ancient Egyptians and their amulets, while they also used peridot and topaz to rid the body of evil spirits and for other forms of protection and good health. Emeralds have been utilized throughout history, including in ancient Mexico, as a symbol of the heart of the dead, and were included in burials. The origin word 'crystal' is from Greek, meaning ice. It was thought at the time that clear quartz was water so frozen that it would never thaw. Likewise rooted in Greek origin is the amethyst, meaning "sober," which was often worn to prevent hangovers and drunkenness! You would think the world would be sold out of amethysts! Stemming from the Greek word for blood, "hematite" was worn by soldiers and sailors while preparing for and during battle, and to keep them safe at sea because of its reddish color. In ancient China, jade was of great value due to its healing properties, especially for kidney stones. It is still revered today. Jade is also considered to be very lucky in New Zealand and in other parts of the world where the tradition of the lucky stone has been passed down through generations. Knowing how different cultures perceived crystals throughout history tells us why we are so fascinated with them to this day.

Consider how I perceive my own collection, in layman's terms: when I hold my citrine crystal, it reminds me to check in with my intentions and to hit head-on any obstacles that may be in my way. Even if you are new to crystal vibrational energies, just remember that it is about gaining the highest self-awareness and finding balance in your life. It is not about simply buying a few beautiful crystals and speaking some magical words over them. It is about building a personal relationship and a connectedness with them if you want them to successfully work with you.

Why Crystals are a Great Place to Start with Magic

Crystals are powerful healing agents because they permit fruitful and positive vibrations to flow into the body and take the negativity and toxic energy away. They work by channeling your vibrational energy levels to focus on healing your body from its core. Each crystal has its own unique frequency and vibration, arising from their composition on a molecular level. The way the crystal's molecules interact and create energies and vibrations is behind the beneficial aspects they provide. Crystals are magnets that absorb negative energies and enhance positive vibes. Because they are created naturally, they harness the energies of the oceans, the moon, and the sun and use those energies for healing, lifting our moods, and improving our overall state of being. When you hold a crystal in your hand it interacts with the chakras in your body and enhances emotional and physical wellness. Crystals vibrate at the same frequencies as you and I and help the healing abilities already within us to reach their full potential. This comfort provided by the stones, when placed on your body, helps you to feel protected and at ease.

Crystals' Vibrational Energy

Making a personal connection with your crystals and gems is one of the essential elements of working with them. Learning how to feel and recognize the crystal's energy is how you establish and strengthen your connection. If you are just starting out, here are a few tips: work with a crystal that has been freshly charged and cleansed to feel the strongest energies. You can cleanse and charge your crystal with sage, sunlight, Palo Santo, dirt, and water. There is no "wrong" or "right" way to sense or feel the energy of your crystal. It has to feel right to you. You are the best avenue for discovering your deep connection to crystal energy over time. Depending on your connection and familiarity with the crystal, the energy can be very powerful or very subtle. Try not to feel disappointed or frustrated if you do not feel anything right away. When it is subtle, crystal energy can be difficult to discern or recognize during the first few times you try. Like everything worthwhile in life, it takes practice. The more you practice and focus on making a connection, the easier it will become to sense the crystal.

Here are some quick tips for your "vibes to rise" and for you to feel energy:

1. Set aside preconceived notions.
2. Take off any other crystal jewelry (including your engagement or wedding rings). It is much easier to feel the crystal's vibration if you are only focusing on one stone.
3. Remove or turn off all distractions, such as your cell phone, tv, radio, etc.
4. Start with one that attracts you.
5. The crystal will resonate with your own natural frequencies!
6. Close your eyes. Meditate before holding the crystal.
7. Take several deep breaths through your nose and exhale

slowly out of your mouth while visualizing the energy of the crystal with each breath.

8. First start by rubbing your hands together to prepare the energy centers in your palms.
9. Place the crystal in your non-dominant hand or the one you feel is most receptive.
10. Spend a minute or two tuning into the crystal energy. Focus on your crystal and note any sensations you feel in your hands or anywhere in your body as you hold the crystal (starting with your hands). Notice any physical or emotional sensations.
11. Notice if the crystal feels cold or hot to your hand. Do you feel any shaking, vibration, or buzzing from the crystal? Is your skin tingling? Concentrate on any feelings while focusing on your crystal. If you get goosebumps or chills, it is an indication that you are picking up the crystal's energy and vibrations.
12. Allow the energy to begin to take shape with each inhale and exhale, let it grow while you inhale its healing energy into every cell in your body, and exhale it back out to share its healing energy with the Earth.
13. Without any expectations for an outcome, let the crystal take you on a peaceful journey while filling you with its healing light.
14. While holding your crystal, focus on your mental state. Notice your experience; do you have clarity? Can you notice stress dissipating and anxiety decreasing? Let any negativity

release itself from your body as you become more grounded. Be mindful of the moment.

15. Do you feel waves of relaxation or calmness, joy, love, protection? Perhaps you feel excited, positive, or motivated. If you feel sadness, know you are being healed. Just notice your feelings as you hold the crystal. Each crystal has its own unique properties and each one will have a different effect.
16. Remind yourself the crystal came from the Earth's heart and feel the connection.
17. Slowly, begin to open your eyes as you ease yourself back into the material world (aka reality), becoming mindful of your surroundings.
18. Take a few slow breaths during this transition.
19. Look at and then thank your crystal.

Familiarizing yourself with each of your crystal's energies will tell you how that specific stone will help you in your life. When you find the crystal that helped you to relax, that will be the perfect stone to help you sleep or calm your nerves. If you notice feeling energized or motivated, this will be the crystal for enhancing your productivity. If you are having a rough day, choose the crystal that makes you feel comforted and loved. Trust what comes to your mind and continue to strengthen and grow in your connection to your crystals.

There is a growing body of evidence suggesting a strong connection between our bodies and our minds, so holding your crystal may first affect you physically; then as you focus on your stone, your emotions will start to change. With the ability to effect change in the vibrations in your body comes the power to better your physical health, change your mood (hopefully for the better), elevate your intentions, achieve your aspirations, and find peace through contentment. The experts in the field of vibrational energy know that certain emotions create specific vibrations. Joy, acceptance, and peace construct vibrations with high frequencies, while fear, hate, anger, and despair give off lower rate vibrations.

Hermetic principle #3:

"Nothing rests; Everything moves; Everything vibrates."

— THE KYBALION

Crystals vibrate at different frequencies depending on their matter, size, thickness, and their color (light frequency). The next step is to learn what stones resonate at the correct frequency for what you are trying to achieve. Thankfully, much experimentation has already been done for thousands of years by the ancients with the art of 'laying on of stones' and they've already figured out what stones help with what needs... for most. There are four scientific characteristics to crystal vibration: matter, color, size, and thickness. These attributes describe how the atoms and particles that make up all matter move in a back-and-forth motion. As previously mentioned, some thoughts and emotions have the highest vibrations, such as unconditional love and peace. To quote Tesla "If you want to understand the universe think in terms of energy, frequency, and vibration." The Hermetic principle #3 holds vibration as the driving force in understanding all creations in the universe. You may be wondering, "How do I sense my crystal's vibration?" The answer to this question is based on your degree of self-awareness. Are you experiencing grief, anger, or jealousy? If so, you may be in a low vibration emotional state. So, practicing how to shift your thoughts and emotions into a grateful high vibration is a good place to start. Different crystals react differently to different people - it depends on the person's own vibrational frequency and how it matches up with the crystal's vibrational frequency.

Daily Crystal Practice

1. Crystal magic is a part of daily self-care and will bring good feelings and balance into your life. Crystals will teach you to look inward for answers, how to go with the flow, and how to align your actions and thoughts with feelings associated with what you desire to attract. While you have hundreds of feelings at any given moment, it is your intuition that shows you which crystals, at that very moment, you need in your life. Carrying amethyst, selenite, and clear quartz with you on a daily basis will provide you with peace, stability, and receptiveness. All three have their own unique energies they radiate, and when together, they overlap in some places, which gives them heightened magical powers.
2. Smudge your crystal. Wave some burning juniper or sage, cedar, or mugwort over your crystal and in all of the corners of your space, leaving all of the doors, windows, cabinets, and drawers open so that any lingering negativity finds a way out.
3. While holding your crystal, practice radical honesty about where you can recognize negative emotions. Take a look at any resentment you have and make the decision that it is time to let them go. They are dead weight anyway. You might be carrying around resentment as if it delivers some sort of punishment to the person who wronged you. That person, however, may never think about it and may be off

traveling the world, having fun, or even winning the lottery. Isn't resentment a waste of time? Meanwhile, here you are with a dark spot in your heart and low frequency energy. Practice banishing these feelings with your crystal.

4. Finding clarity is important if you want to have a clear vision of what your heart desires and with what your intent is with your crystal ritual. With an open mind, imagine your desire as if you already have it. That way you can get rid of any thoughts blocking your way to success.

5. Practice a daily morning ritual. Spending a few moments aligning your energy right after you wake up in the morning sets the tone for the rest of your day. Choose your favorite ritual, such as a bit of yoga, positive affirmations, mindful meditation, etc. (something empowering). Next, prepare yourself for your crystal ritual; set your intention and submerge yourself in that positive energy for what you want to happen for you during the day.

6. Make a habit of letting your creative juices flow when working with your crystal. Try to remember how it felt when you were a child and found awe in the smallest of things. Dance like nobody's watching, finger paint, color yourself creative in the kitchen. These are all good things. Consider this your energy-generated permission slip to dive into the world of positivity.

7. Your crystal practice is a way of treating yourself with kindness and love. Self-dialogue has a direct impact on how you feel. Get rid of negative self-dialogue, and even if you

have to pretend at first, talk to yourself with compassion and understanding and your crystal will welcome the good vibes.

8. Along with getting to know your crystals, it is also important to lay off the toxins. Ridding your body of toxins will lift your vibrational energy. The more toxic an environment is, the harder it is to clean. The same goes for your mind and body. But when it comes to positive energy, put some thought into it. It will make a world of difference in your energy frequency communicated to your crystal.

9. Spiritual exercises are powerful ways of elevating your vibration. Connect with your crystal's energy and your special spirit or "higher power" because it will help you know you are not alone and that you are loved and protected.

10. Avoid adopting someone else's low frequency vibrations. Taking on someone else's emotions is not the same as caring. You have the power within you to set boundaries and say to yourself, "Those are not my feelings."

11. Pause throughout your day and admire your crystals. Most of us have to-do lists that are a mile long. Practice some breathing techniques and don't forget to "stop and smell the roses." Einstein said, "He who does not pause to stand rapt in awe, is dead." Taking a short walk several times a day is a fantastic way to increase your frequency; it's like stopping to refuel your gas tank.

2

CRYSTAL BASICS

With a bit of gentle guidance, you can discover the wondrous powers of crystals. Learn how to cope with anxiety and stress and how to profile, select, and organize your own collection of crystals. Ever since that day my mother took me to the store and I begged her to buy me that stone, I have loved how just being around crystals makes me feel. Now, this passion is realized in every corner of my home and office. Some people like to use them for mental health or physical healing, some to find love, and others for prosperity. Some people just love to look at their beauty. Crystals are known to emit and store vibrations (or energy), as well as to amp up your own personal intentions and vibes. The best thing about doing magic with crystals is that there are no directions "set in stone" (pun intended). Just do what feels right to you.

Crystal Formation Experiment

Most crystals and other gems form because of forces that have been generating for billions of years. That is how many years it takes for hot magma to bubble from the center of the Earth and push its way to the top crust to form a mineral. Minerals then interlock, forming crystals. The rarest and finest crystals are polished after being cut and turned into gemstones. Some form as water evaporates and some grow inside of gaseous bubbles after the magma has pushed its way to the Earth's crust. Energy has always been here in some form or another; it cannot be created nor can it be destroyed but it can be transformed into another form of energy and here lies the magic of the crystal.

If you want to actually see crystals being formed, here is a little at-home experiment that is amazing.

1. Pour a ½ cup of water into a large cup or bowl.
2. Add ½ cup of Epsom salts to the water. (You can use table salt but it takes longer.)
3. Wait 24 hours.
4. As the water evaporates, the sodium atoms get closer together and form a cluster. They will keep coming together into a formation. This is the crystal you made yourself!

How Crystals Are Different from Gems, Minerals, and Rocks

Crystal is made from highly ordered and microscopic atoms that are naturally arranged to form a three-dimensional pattern also known by the term "crystal lattice." Billions of atoms form and shape the structure of the crystal in a process referred to as crystallization. Each mineral's crystal structure is fixed; should it change, it would not be the same mineral. The structure of the crystal defines the mineral variety. For instance, the structure of a quartz crystal will always be the same. Over time, some crystals grow quickly, while others can take millions of years, depending on how slow the magma cooling process is. The slower the cooling process, the bigger the crystal. Snowflakes can be made of a single crystal or they can be made of a collection of many crystals. When impurities infiltrate a crystal, it can affect the process of crystallization, and thereby create a change in color because its molecular makeup has been altered. Heat also alters the chemical process of crystallization and can also change its color.

Crystals have been heated by man for millennia, working to change or enhance their color. They can also be affected by a natural heating source such as the sun during their formation. Most of the finest gems in the world have been through some type of heating process. Gemstones are formed when a mineral or a piece of a rock is cut and often polished to be used in a piece of jewelry. That is how it becomes a gemstone. To be considered a gemstone, it must possess certain characteristics, such as rarity, durability, color, and beauty. Obviously, you can't just cut and polish any old rock and make it a gem. The four characteristics play an important role in their classification, with beauty being of the most importance. Many gemstones are cut from crystals.

Rocks are made from at least two different types of minerals bonded together. Granite and marble are two examples of rock. Rocks differ from crystals because they lack a crystalline structure.

The Meaning of the Shapes of Crystals

Crystals come in different colors (rose, amethyst, aquamarine) and are used for varying purposes, such as protection, attraction, health and wellness, sleep improvement, etc. But they are also formed into many differing shapes. The crystalline structure doesn't affect the type of energy it puts out; however, the shape of the crystal does affect the way you receive its energy. The shape of your crystal can help to ramp up your experience and your purpose. So, choosing the shape of a crystal should complement your intention and magnify and enhance your transformation.

Here are some of the crystal shapes and their influences:

1. Cubes

A cube-shaped crystal is the one you need if you're looking for some grounding energy. Placing a cubic crystal in your hands connects you to the vibrational energies of the Earth. You can also place them in each corner of your office or home for protection.

2. Pyramids

Pyramid-shaped crystals have very strong powers when it comes to manifesting your desires. This is because their strong base support works as an anchor for your intention. Its apex shape puts your intention out into the universe, whether it is for money or love. Pyramid crystals take it up a notch to fulfill your desire.

3. Spheres

Sphere-shaped crystals serve as a reminder that you are interconnected to all of the energies in your environment; part of a greater good; like imagining that you have the world in the palm of your hand. Sphere-shaped crystals give off a Zen vibe, making them perfect for meditation. Collecting a few small spheres to add to your crystal collection will assure your relaxation time will be special.

4. Tumbled Crystals

These are small and smooth crystals, considered to be the stepping stones into the magical world of vibrational energy. Don't let their small size fool you! The good news is they are travel-friendly and powerful indeed. You can take them with you anywhere you go; keep them close so you can reach out and grab them wherever you are and reconnect to their energy to be reminded of your intention all day long. They are like carrying around your best friend. I love them.

5. Crystal points

Points are powerful crystals that will keep you sharp-minded. A point crystal is the one to use when you need to stay super-focused on something. Pen your intention, desire, or affirmation on a sheet of paper. Fold up the paper and place it under your crystal point in a pyramid fashion. It will send all of the intention written on the paper upward and outward into the universe and into the atmosphere surrounding you.

6. Crystal hearts

Crystals that are heart-shaped have been cut and polished this way. They do not naturally occur but they still promote powerful love energy. Meditate on your intention and focus on a gentle loving light, filling your heart and clearing it of any old trauma, scars, or wounds; bring healing love and peace into your body.

7. Crystal Clusters

So beautiful are crystal points clustered together! They hold mystical vibrations and sparkle in their natural form. Put a crystal cluster on the coffee table, entranceway table, or dining room table, or on a conference table at work, to promote community and open-mindedness. I have one on my family dining table and it never goes unnoticed or without discussion, even though it has been there for years.

What is a Crystal Grid?

A crystal grid is a wonderfully powerful energy instrument to use when manifesting your intentions, goals, and desires. It is the way you arrange your crystals in a specific layout created for your exact intention. If you set your crystals up after much consideration and with intent, they are considered a grid. Just placing crystals near each other without a specific purpose is not considered a grid. If you are wondering why you should create a crystal grid instead of just using individual crystals, know that the grid power is derived from the union of energetic vibrations created between healing crystals. Using your intention to design a type of sacred geometrical pattern of crystals is an effective way to amplify their power. Using a crystal grid combines the power in the pattern you created, multiplying the crystals' energies. Working together, they will greatly strengthen their powers and your intention and bring about much faster results than you would be able to achieve using only single stones.

How to use a crystal grid depends on what your goal or intention is, as each grid can be designed for a different purpose or goal. Whatever your goal may be, you can create a powerful crystal grid to hold your intention and manifest it.

Step by Step Guide on Choosing the Shape of a Crystal:

1. Do a bit of homework about the vibrational and energetic characteristics of your crystal from a trusted source.
2. Consider your intent when selecting a shape that offers the benefits you are interested in.
3. Consider the way you are going to work with the crystal and where it will be stationed, such as on your altar, for chakra healing, or in a crystal grid.

The Colors of Crystals

The color of each crystal holds within it a vibrational energy, a specific intention, and an emotional response. The colors of the crystals are connected to the chakra system in our bodies, which refers to the energy centers corresponding to nerve bundles in our spine. It is inevitable that the stress of everyday life can throw your chakras out of balance. When this happens, it negatively affects you both physically and emotionally. Each chakra is associated with a color, beginning with purple at the top of your head down to red (the root chakra) at the base of your spine. These beautiful colors connected to the chakras have a deeper meaning; they are related directly to how each of the nerve bundles within that chakra functions.

By practicing with crystals in your meditations and rituals, you can enhance the magic of your present intentions and reap the effects you desire in your life. There are a multitude of crystals associated with every color known to man. My favorite way to bond with a new magical crystal is to let myself gaze through an assortment and notice where my eyes land first. You always know deep down inside what you need and your intuition leads you there. For starters, here are some of the colors I know well:

Red is an intense and powerful color that invokes our determination, passions, and inner strength. Red celebrates with us that we are alive! Red is connected to our root chakra and increases our self-confidence and courage, while releasing any lingering feelings of guilt and shame. When you need to pull out your warrior-self, use red to awaken your distinctive power and sensuality. When I am feeling the "go getter" in me, I wear my garnet earrings. Other red crystals include red calcite, cinnabar, sardonyx, rose quartz, and more.

Orange is a bit milder than red. It is a fun and flirty way to boost your creativity and motivate you toward success. It doesn't hurt to have it around in the bedroom too! If you really want to get your creative juices flowing, try a carnelian crystal. It is sure to do the trick. Orange crystals are associated with our sacral chakra and are the color of creation.

Yellow is obviously bright and happy. Yellow crystals provide new perspectives and a batch of clarity for when or if you are feeling confusion. Holding a yellow calcite will boost your confidence while clearing you of any self-doubt. Reach for a yellow crystal if your memory needs a quick boost or if you are attempting to learn a new skill.

Green is a color most of us could do with a bit more in our lives. It is connected to the heart chakra, as it facilitates abundance, healing, and nurturing. I love working with this vibrant shade along with others for a double dose of healing results. My favorite is malachite when my intention is focused on balance, money, manifestation, and transformation.

Blue is a favorite of many, as it represents total calmness. When holding a blue crystal, meditate on the vastness of the oceans and skies. It is associated with our throat chakra, and therefore, it works to enhance our communication skills and to clear up miscommunications from our lives. I love working with lapis lazuli when I am looking deep within myself for my inner truths and need clarification on how to appropriately communicate them to others.

Purple is associated with the crown chakra, and has a highly spiritual function, which serves to offer tranquility, enlightenment, protection, a good night's sleep, and enhanced intuition. Amethyst (Earth's natural tranquilizer) is the best-known purple crystal and possibly one of the most spiritually energetic stones to have in your collection. Other purple crystals include spirit quartz, lepidolite, charoite, and sugilite. Purple crystals relieve strain and stress while soothing irritability, alleviating grief, and diffusing negativity.

Clear and white clear away the mind's clutter and purify your thoughts and behaviors. White symbolizes cleanliness and purity. These crystals are perfect for new beginnings and for those just starting out with crystal magic, as white and clear crystals seem to be the easiest with which to work and connect. Whenever you have a need to promote peace and serenity or get a good night's sleep, use these crystals, ruled by the moon; its warm white rays of light will bring you tranquility.

Pink gives you a fuzzy warm feeling just by looking at it. Pink crystals carry a much more subtle power than red crystals. Their energy is loving, gentle, and warm, yet still provides you with the commitment, determination, and energy of the red crystals. Pink crystals carry with them energies of compassion, kindness, understanding, and love that everyone needs. Pink crystals will help you with the attributes of self-forgiveness or forgiveness for others, letting go of the mistakes of your past. They provide you with soothing emotional healing.

Aquamarine's properties include serenity, calm, and healing. It is fantastic for healing your stomach, liver, throat, and allergies. Also, it helps with pituitary and thyroid problems. To use aquamarine crystals, just place them over your throat for healing and for thyroid issues. Place over the brow to provide you with clarity, and over your heart to alleviate anxiety.

Agate's properties include vitality and strength. The color calms the stomach and helps with digestion. It also promotes psychological stability and balanced emotions. To use, simply keep it in your pocket, tucked in your bra, or in your purse where you can touch it often for strength.

Aventurine's properties include protection, anxiety reduction, and hopefulness. It comes in more than one color and works to relieve itchy skin and nausea and provide heart health and vision. Green aventurine quartz is used for economical abundance. To use, stick a green aventurine quartz in your pocket on your way to the casino or carry it in your purse for abundance and self-confidence. Hold it over your heart for blood pressure stability and heart health.

Rose quartz's properties include healing circulation, heart health and heartbreak, and fatigue. It also works to attract a new love interest or enhance the relationship you are in. It is also helpful for self-acceptance and self-care. To use it, keep it under your pillow in the bedroom. For heart health, place it on your chest while in a resting position. You can also hold it in your hand, rub your hands gently together and drop it in a glass of filtered water. Let it sit for one minute and then drink it.

Moonstone's properties include help with hormonal/menopausal problems, weight gain, joint pain, edema, migraines, and insomnia. To use moonstone, wear it as jewelry to stay safe during travel. You can also put it in the console on your car or under your pillow for a good night's rest.

Tourmaline comes in pink, black, brown, red, blue, yellow, colorless, or a combination of two or more of the above-mentioned colors. Tourmaline's vibrational energies depend on its color or combination of colors. Tourmaline crystals provide protection, grounding energy, and promote balance and stability. They are also useful for nerve damage, hearing problems, pain relief, flatulence, constipation, anxiety, and stress. Use it to absorb negative energy (make sure you clean it after use).

Clear quartz's properties include energizing, reducing anxiety and sensory nervous complaints, pain relief, calming respiratory issues, skin irritations, and congestion and swelling of mucous membranes. To use, carry in your pocket or purse, place under a pillow, meditate with it, decorate your home or office, give it as a gift, wear it as jewelry, or place it in your planters or in a sunny area just to relish in its beauty.

Shopping Tips for Crystals

As I mentioned, when I was 9 or 10 years old, my mother took me to a very cluttered antique shop, well hidden somewhere between my house and Timbuktu. I say Timbuktu because at the age of 9, anything more than 15 minutes in the car seemed like days. I didn't mind going to antique shops, because there were always interesting items, but none that I ever deeply felt a need to take home with me. However, this specific trip was anything but ordinary. I saw the glass case by the cash register and felt the most amazing pull towards this crystal. In the corner of the case were "the round ones." They were small spheres of crystal quartz, and believe it or not, I felt compelled to grab one. I immediately called my mother over to show her. All of a sudden, I felt drawn to a beautiful pink crystal. I told the lady behind the counter that I couldn't make up my mind which one I wanted. She said, "I'll make it much less complicated for you." She told me to "stick out my hands" and placed the clear crystal in one hand and the pink crystal in the other. She asked me to take a gander around the shop without thinking about holding the stones. Then she said, "Trust me, you will know today which crystal is meant for you to take home."

With that, I began looking around the shop. I remember admiring some Russian nesting dolls, all sorts of candles, long strings of beads, petrified pieces of wood, and wishing I could have them all. I continued to gaze around the shop while my mother was deciding which piece of artwork she wanted. Suddenly, I felt a strong electric shock run through my hand. I gasped. I figured it was somehow static electricity coming from the carpet I was walking on. All of the customers in the shop turned and looked at me like I had hurt myself. I asked the lady behind the counter if the crystals had batteries in them. She smiled at me and said, "Of course not; it looks like the pink crystal chose you."

It helps to learn a bit about the traditions of crystal healing vibrations and uses when it comes to shopping for a crystal. I have learned from my childhood experience to walk around the store and wait for the crystal to call out to me. If you feel a sensation from any of the crystals you are admiring, such as a tingle, pulse, peaceful feeling, or heat or cool sensations, this is a good indication that a crystal matches your needs. Make sure you don't overthink it. If you don't quite feel anything yet, pick out a few you love because of their beauty or uniqueness. Don't pick crystals based on the little information cards neatly stacked in front of them; just keep track of your collection. Once you get home you can do a bit of research on the ones you chose and you will find that they just so happened to be exactly what you needed.

3

CRYSTALS AND CHAKRAS

Some scholars in the Western world believe that the chakra system started around 1500 BC in India, when the earliest texts on yoga, the Vedas, were penned. Most of the scholars from India think the chakra system is very much older than that. In the chakra philosophy, the entire universe is acknowledged as being created, transfixed, and sustained by two perfect forces in a permanently indestructible union known as "Shiva" and "Shak" which are represented biologically as the feminine and masculine poles. The word chakra translates from Sanskrit to mean "wheel" and refers to the different energy points in the human body. They are thought of as spinning disks of energy that should stay aligned or "open" because they are associated with major organs, nerve bundles, and specific energetic areas of our bodies that affect our physical and psychological or emotional well-being. According to some, there are 114 different chakras in the human body, but seven of them are considered to be the main chakras which run along our spine. These seven chakras are the ones usually referred to in this manuscript.

Healing with Chakra Crystals

Each one of the seven main chakras is associated with a name, number, color, health focus, and a specific spinal area starting at the sacrum (just above the tailbone) and going to the top of your head, known as the crown. The sacrum energy is also known as the "root" chakra. Chakra crystals can be used in varying ways. Wearing jewelry adorned with them is an easy way to use them. Wearing a pendant of crystal can enhance your vibrational energy throughout the day. Carrying a crystal in a pocket or purse, somewhere where it is easy to touch, caress, or hold with a quick affirmation, works as well. Chakra crystals are also beneficial during healing practices. As you are meditating, rest one of your healing crystals just under your navel and it will bring increased focus and healing to your routine. If you are sitting and meditating, cup a crystal in your hands as you rest them in your lap for the same great outcome. Let's first take a look at the corresponding numbers and colors of the chakras before we go into the details of each one.

Chakras

#1 Root Chakra

#1 Root Chakra (Muladhara) is the first of the chakras, found at the base of the tailbone. It is important because, when balanced, it forms the base foundation for opening all of the chakras above it. Having a safe home means having a solid foundation upon which it can sit. If you want to live there for a while, you will need a firm foundation to

provide the stability necessary to create a happy home for years to come. The root chakra is made up of whatever provides your stability in life; your grounding force. The root chakra comprises the basic human necessities, such as water, food, safety, and shelter. It is also responsible for your emotional well-being, including your ability to conquer fear. When aligned, you feel safe, grounded, and less worried throughout your day. Your root chakra has much to do with early childhood experiences because that is when it develops. If an individual has a traumatic childhood, they may find themselves in a root chakra blockage. If there is an imbalance in the root chakra, anxiety disorders, along with phobias and night terrors, as well as eating disorders, may develop. Physical imbalances can manifest as bladder and colon problems, lower extremity issues, and for men, prostate problems. When chakras are "out of whack," blocked, or misaligned, certain physical and emotional issues arise. If the root chakra is blocked, manifestations such as constipation, arthritis, urinary issues, and anxieties about basic needs and money insecurities occur. When your root chakras open, you will feel secure and grounded, both emotionally and physically.

How to Balance #1 Root Chakra

Meditation and staying connected to your higher spiritual plane will help keep you grounded. You cannot always trust the outer world to provide you with safety or survival but you can trust in your spiritual self and in a power greater than yourself to provide you with emotional safety. It doesn't matter what name you give to that higher spirit; it can be Nature, God, or the Universe. If you think about it, animals are not positive when they will find food, but they do trust that Nature will provide. Smell is the sense organ associated with your root chakra.

> **Balancing Tip:** Focus on the very tip of your nose while meditating and it will help in aligning your root chakra. The root chakra colors are red, black, and deep pink. Its crystals include hematite, garnet, ruby, black tourmaline, and black onyx.

#2 Sacral Chakra

#2 Sacral Chakra (Svadhisthana) is the second chakra and it is located in the lower abdominal area. It carries a few nicknames, including "the social chakra," "the creation chakra," and "the sex chakra." This chakra commands the reproductive organs and processes, sexuality, emotions, relationships, and your sense of adventure seeking. This chakra is concerned with much more than just sex. The reality is that it oversees pleasure and passion, not only by reproduction, but by creating other things, like beautiful artwork, music, or even your work, as well as just enjoying life. It does, however, govern sensuality, in the manner of embracing your own natural sexuality. Its crystal is the tiger's eye, its element is water, and its color is orange. When the sacral chakra is blocked or misaligned, urinary problems can pop up, as well as a loss of libido. Other reproductive issues can also arise, such as menstrual cramps accompanied by lower back pain. Emotionally, if your sacral chakra is blocked, you may feel closed off, ashamed of your sexuality, or plain old uncomfortable in your own skin. You may also feel a lack of creativity and find it difficult to pursue spontaneous endeavors. Fortunately, there

are ways to conquer this and bring your sacral chakra back into alignment.

How to Balance #2 Sacral Chakra

First, exercises involving your hips can be beneficial in bringing balance back to your sacral chakra. Getting a hula hoop is a good idea, as it will help redirect your circulation and energy to the chakra, raising its vibrational energy. Of course, for all of the chakras, yoga and meditation are highly recommended. For realigning my sacral chakra, I perform the low lunge, goddess pose, and pigeon pose yoga asanas. Try your own yoga routine, such as yin yoga and creative yoga combined with affirmations to help keep your sacral chakra balanced and enhance your sensuality. Sound meditation works, too. Slowly let out the sound "vam" (or "lam" for your root chakra). This is pronounced like "lawn." Slowly, let the vocal vibrations seep through this area of your sacral chakra. This is a restorative and quick method for aligning your sacral chakra. Don't forget to practice affirmations as a powerful tool for balancing all of your chakras. For instance, for your sacral chakra, say "I am grateful for my body," "I accept myself," and "I am happy to be me." Another method for balancing and realigning your sacral chakra is aromatherapy.

The sacral chakra color is orange and it is associated with the moon, so orange and yellow crystals such as citrine (also good for cleansing) and orange carnelian are good for unblocking your sacral chakra or for opening it. Orange calcite also has cleansing characteristics which can open a blockage in your sacral chakra. Also, eating foods bright orange in color, such as sweet potatoes, carrots, and tangerines can help to restore balance to your sacral chakra. Moonstone crystals carry unique properties and they can soothe and open your sacral chakra. They are connected to the moon, which also governs the sacral region of the body! Since the moon controls the tides, if you want to become spiritually connected to your sacral chakra, spend some time at the beach, by a pond, river, or lake. These are relaxing locations that pair well with the feelings of adventure and pleasure with which the sacral chakra is associated.

#3 Navel or Solar Plexus Chakra

#3 Navel or Solar Plexus Chakra (Manipura) is set just behind your navel and governs your sense of purpose, confidence, self-worth, personal identity, and self-esteem. The Manipura is also associated with your metabolism and digestive system. When it is balanced and you have removed the negative aspects of your sacral chakra (Svadhishthana), you are aligned. As the foundation of digestive fire, the naval chakra oversees your pancreas and digestive tract; therefore, when it is blocked, a plethora of medical issues can arise. Ulcers, circulatory problems, diabetes, and hypertension are among them. However, when it is aligned, balanced, and strong it will help you to avoid these types of illnesses, as well as overcome them. The Manipura chakra balances your energy and keeps you healthy. When your Manipura is in good shape, you will feel confident, know who you are and what you want in life. The quality of your life will mean more to you than material gains; you will feel a sense of purpose. The emotional signs of a blocked #3 chakra can lead you into feeling powerless, removed, easily angered, controlling, and sometimes aggressive; it can also make you feel the opposite, feeling like a victim with low self-worth and neediness.

The colors of the third energy or naval chakra are golden or yellow, so any yellow or goldish crystals will open the Manipura. Tiger's eye, topaz, amber, yellow jasper, or yellow calcite are all good choices. Also, citrine is associated with abundance and good decision-making, and golden calcite helps with personal growth. Yellow is connected to a renewal of your nervous system and balance. Furthermore, it is the color of intellect. Manipura crystals draw their energies from the sun, and their frequencies connect to your conscious mind's frequency. If your self-confidence needs a boost, sport some amber earrings or yellow walking shoes. Aragonite crystals also come in yellow and are helpful for prosperity, concentration, and focus. Aragonite is a great grounding gem.

How to Balance # 3 Navel or Solar Plexus Chakra

The third chakra will help you find your truth - your authentic self. So, stepping outside of your comfort zone and trying something new is a great way to bring balance and open your solar plexus chakra. The word Manipura in Sanskrit means "city of jewels," so it is no surprise that it resonates with the element of fire and yellow crystals. It is the first relationship chakra, so placing a yellow crystal just below your navel while lying down will restore balance. Citrine crystals harness the energy of the sun, so using citrine as a healing stone will balance the energy of your solar plexus. Citrine broadens your perspectives about life; using it will raise your emotional vibration and give you the physical boost you need to remove any fears that may be holding you back in life. *Yellow jasper* is a naval chakra crystal that will encourage self-esteem and motivate you going forward. It is a crystal of protection that soaks up positive energy, providing you with more joy. Yellow jasper brings a sense of inner calmness and raises your stamina, giving you an uncanny ability to clear any misunderstandings that you may encounter.

#4 Heart Chakra

#4 Heart Chakra (Anahata) governs love, empathy, change, compassion, forgiveness, trust, peace, generosity, and gratitude. It is situated at heart level at the center of the spine. Anahata in Sanskrit means "unhurt." The fourth chakra is associated with the air element and is considered special because it is the exact middle point of the chakra system, so it acts as the spiritual and physical chakras' unifier. By connecting the lower three chakras (root, sacral, and navel) with the upper three chakras (throat, third eye, and crown) the heart chakra provides the connectedness between spirit and earth. Of course, its mantra is "I love." If your heart chakra is blocked or misaligned, you may feel a sense of unhappiness, insecurity, or as if your heart is broken and you are unlovable. You will be likely to distance yourself from your friends and put up emotional barriers, or become resentful, bitter, or even worse, totally shut down emotionally.

This is not a good chakra to have blocked; not that any of them are good to have blocked, but if you think about it, a blocked heart chakra is the worst because it makes you feel unloved and unlovable. However, if you're feeling a bit co-dependent, your heart chakra may be overactive. When your heart chakra is putting out too much vibration, it's in overdrive and causing an imbalance, which affects you in every way. It can leave you feeling emotionally bankrupt or lead you to toxic relationships. A heart chakra in overdrive can have you feeling ruled by your emotions. Believe me, everything is not okay when you are giving so much of yourself that you are neglecting yourself. Fortunately, there are methods for shaping up your heart chakra balance.

How to Unblock #4 Heart Chakra

The heart chakra has a unique frequency and its corresponding colors are pink and green. One might think that because it is the heart, the associated color would be red, but it is not. The fourth chakra symbolizes the ability to give and receive empathy, love, kindness, compassion, and healing, among other positive abilities. If you have an unbalanced Anahata, you might experience loss, pain, low self-esteem, or regret. Rose quartz crystals, jade, any of the pink or green crystals, green tourmaline, and green calcite attract love and open the heart chakra. You can wear jewelry, such as a rose quartz pendant, and experience its joy throughout your day. Display it in the corner of the tub when you bathe or conduct a healing session with it placed directly over your heart. As with all of the crystals, cupping a rose quartz in your hand while meditating will balance your heart chakra and remove any blockage. You can also create a grid with any of the heart chakra crystals if you want to attract a special someone.

#5 Throat Chakra

#5 Throat Chakra (Vishudha) is associated with self-expression (talking), truth, and communication (how you speak while expressing your emotions). The Vishudha is situated within the throat and neck area above the heart chakra in the body. This is your essential communication center where you store your vibrational energy for conscious dialogue and knowing how to strike a balance between

speaking and listening. Having your throat chakra open is very important because communication is not only a necessary survival mechanism but it is also the key component of human interaction. You will know if your throat chakra is open when you express yourself with ease. A noticeable eloquence happens with an open and balanced throat chakra. You will have the ability to share your unique experiences, your perspectives on life and your valuable feedback with total confidence. The color associated with Vishudha is blue, due to its calming, honest, and empathetic properties.

How to Unblock #5 Throat Chakra

There are various ways to use crystals for opening, balancing, and aligning your throat chakra. Choose one of your blue crystals, such as amazonite, aquamarine, lapis lazuli, or the one you are most drawn to and lay them over your throat chakra (at the base of the throat) while meditating. You can also make your own jewelry. While focusing on your intention and holding two pieces of wire, twist them together in at least four twists, creating a V-shape at the bottom. Wrap wire around your blue crystal and make a loop at the top. It is that easy. Keep a crystal in your pocket for all-day energy. Amazonite will balance you emotionally and relieve your anxiety.

#6 Third Eye Chakra

#6 Third Eye Chakra (Ajna) is associated with your intuition, wisdom, and creativity. It is a vehicle for connecting you with different perspectives by opening your mind beyond the realm of the physical senses. It is difficult to put into words what it means to have a different way of seeing things because the visions are often subtle

and involve the third eye. It takes some practice to sustain awareness of your Ajna chakra energy. Visions may be ghost-like or dreamy, cloudy, or blurry; however, at times they will be as clear as can be. The third eye chakra is situated on your forehead, between your eyes. The third eye chakra is connected to quintessential dimensions of the spirit world, those of wisdom, imagination, and truth.

How to Unblock #6 Third Eye Chakra

The third eye chakra is associated with the color of wisdom, purple. There are various crystals utilized during healing sessions for the Ajna. Sodalite is very helpful for procuring balance, focus, and mental clarity. It will keep you in a creative and calm head space when kept close by, such as on your desk or on the conference table. It is a violet-bluish color decorated with beautiful earth tones. For great penmanship, wear a sodalite ring. Don't be surprised to know I am wearing one right now to facilitate my creative writing skills. I just love it. When I started writing this book, there were so many wonderful aspects of crystal healing techniques running through my mind and so many directions in which the writing could flow. I found a royal blue sodalite crystal that had white calcium marbling. I had it set in silver and as soon as I slid it on my right ring finger, I felt a tingle throughout my whole body. My creative juices began to rush through me, and any writer's block I was experiencing seemed to fade away, as a sense of calmness and direction took over my fingers on the keyboard. This crystal has honestly made a difference in the way I express myself in writing.

#7 Crown Chakra

#7 Crown Chakra (Sahasrara) is situated at the very top of the head. It provides access to a higher state of being and opens you to things beyond your normal state of consciousness. What sets it apart from the other chakras is that it is actually just above the top of your head in what is considered to be your spiritual entity. It is not associated with a physical organ in the body, but with your consciousness. There are really no words to describe its unconditional love. Its color is white or indigo (light purple). However, when your Sahasrara is imbalanced, it can manifest itself in cynicism. When overactive, the opposite occurs and a feeling of closed-mindedness and disconnect from your body (living in your head) takes over.

How to Heal #7 Crown Chakra

The best way to heal your crown chakra is with your crystals. With access to the Sahasrara, your connection to the universe is made stronger. You acquire prana (pure life energy), which broadens your perspectives. You will also feel more motivated and highly spiritual. Here are some tips for using crystals to heal and/or balance your crown chakra. One of the best methods for healing your Sahasrara is through meditation.

Lay down and place a flat crystal on your crown (the top of your head). Amethyst is known for being a highly spiritual crystal and connects deeply with the crown chakra. It can calm the chaos in your mind and enlighten your soul to the spirit world. It takes you to the next level of spiritual development.

Lepidolite holds a gentle energy that connects on a deep level with the crown chakra. It does not open the chakra, but it will help you to stay calm during stressful times.

Clear quartz crystals are also known as master healers. They hold a high vibration with positive forces to bring about good health and wellness in all areas of your life. They awaken all of the chakras and can unblock your crown chakra and its beneficial energies. They will provide you with mental and spiritual clarity and improve your mental focus. Set your intention and time the first five minutes, while you hone your focus. Do this twice a day until you feel the healing process. Use this method to keep your crown chakra open and well-balanced.

Try using each of the above-mentioned crystals. I use clear quartz as a "winner take all" crystal because it makes me feel like all of my chakras open up as soon as I put it in my hands. Place a Sugilite crystal under your pillow. With its beautiful violet color, it has been used for thousands of years by healers and shamans.

Wear a moonstone in your hair. It will gently heal your crown chakra as it draws its energy from the moon.

4

ESSENTIAL CRYSTALS

Choosing the right crystal for spell work can be a bit confusing. Maybe you are just not sure about where to start. There can be so many reasons you want to take advantage of the healing powers of crystals in your life, and there is a plethora of crystals from which to choose. I use crystals every day of my life for healing and for my magical ventures. From amethyst to zebra jasper, choosing the right crystal is an amazing experience. Vibrational energies flow through and emerge differently according to the class of crystal you choose.

Your body will react accordingly to the unique properties and energies that crystals hold. Keep in mind that when picking the right crystal for your magic, one of the purposes of the crystal is to remind you of your deep connection to the earth's healing vibrations. Believing and focusing your intention on a particular crystal transmits that energy to the crystal you choose. This is the magic set in motion for your desired spiritual or physical healing. Think of crystals as your anchor to the Earth, always revealing themselves with universal healing characteristics and the elements of the world. They serve as wondrous aides and guides, inspiring and reinforcing our healing journey. Varying ailments require varying healing characteristics; therefore, some crystals are for protection while others are for balance, harmony, or love. Still others are for prosperity and clarity, and some are specific crystals with properties associated with alleviating health problems.

Now let's talk about balance. First off, balance is represented and deeply connected to the earth element. With how fast all of our emotions, thoughts, texting and typing, computing and overall emotional anxieties move nowadays, we have to somehow find balance by taking it easy and being mindful of our bodies. The concept of balance is dynamically ever-changing but needs a center point. So, if you are feeling out of balance, you need to check in with yourself over and over again, to find your center. We really can't discuss "balance" without talking about feminine and masculine energy. The whole world would be off kilter if it wasn't for the balanced yin yang or The Hermetic Principle of Polarity. Work your magic by balancing your chakras with your crystals and getting in touch with both your masculine and feminine energies. The same can be said about focusing on one type of magic. If you find yourself focusing on sun-powered magic, switch it up and spend some time with the Moon. The same goes for focusing on a single deity. If you have an element or god that you regularly work with, try learning how to work with a goddess too. You just need to experience balance; it doesn't mean you are holding the new goddess/god or element above the other.

The following are just thirty of the crystals I have the most experience using. I include the color, chakra, element, and magical uses of each of them:

1. AGATE

Colors: Brown, white, red, gray, pink, black, and yellow

Chakra: There is an agate for each of the chakras.

- Blue lace agate: throat chakra and the third eye chakra.
- Crazy lace agate: third eye chakra.
- Fire agate (red and brown): root chakra. Gold or orange fire agate: sacral chakra and solar plexus chakra. Green fire agates: heart chakra.
- Laguna agate: root chakra.
- Moss agate: heart chakra.

Element: Earth

Magical Uses: Speaking the truth, balancing between throat and heart chakras, loving unconditionally, living in peace and understanding.

2. AMBER

Color: Golden

Chakra: #2 Sacral Chakra (Svadisthana)

Element: Fire

Magical Uses: Naturally purifies the spirit and the mind. Amazing ability to draw disease and pain away from the body, physically, mentally, and spiritually through the absorption of stagnant or negative energies and transform them into positive and clear energy. Unblocks the sacral and navel chakras. I use it as part of my cleansing rituals or when I cast healing spells. I put it on top of the photo of the person for whom I desire healing magic.

3. AMETHYST

Colors: Purple, violet, dark purple

Chakra: #6 Third Eye Chakra (Ajna)

Element: Air

Magical Uses: Boosts the immune system, improves endocrine function, enhances the skin's appearance, promotes a healthy digestive system, alleviates headaches, balances hormones, reduces stress and anxiety, promotes cleansing, cures insomnia.

4. AQUAMARINE

Colors: Blue, greenish blue, dark blue

Chakra: #5 Throat Chakra (Vishudha)

Element: Water

Magical Uses: Releases creativity and wisdom. Provides increased fortitude due to its calming effect. Promotes harmony in relationships as it inspires tolerance and compromise. Strengthens fidelity and commitment like the waters that flow upon the Earth. Protection crystal while at sea or with any water-related activity. Promotes allergy healing and a healthy immune system, pituitary gland, and liver.

5. AZURITE

Color: Deep blue

Chakra: #6 Third Eye Chakra (Ajna)

Element: Water

Magical Uses: Emotionally healing vibrational energy. Strengthens and cleans the emotional body, letting go of worry and stress. Provides an acceptance and understanding of irrational fears and where they came from. Used for spinal alignments and vertebral disorders, pain related to malformed rib-cage development and small bones, and healing properties for arthritis and joint problems.

6. BLACK KYANITE

Colors: Black, orange, green, indigo, yellow, rare white, pink, gray

Chakra: #1 Root Chakra (Muladhara)

Element: Water

Magical Uses: Manifesting intentions, promotes psychic abilities, healing energy, effective communication, strengthens relationships, balances root chakra. Place it between your feet on the floor for grounding energy. It is my favorite grounding crystal. Carries very high vibrations while offering protection and opens the earth star chakra.

The earth star chakra is a more recently discovered chakra situated under your feet (not part of the physical body) and is directly connected to the Earth's core. It grounds the entire chakra system.

7. BLACK OBSIDIAN

Color: Black

Chakra: #1 Root Chakra (Muladhara)

Element: Water

Magical Uses: Extremely powerful crystal for protection. Helps you examine and recognize your dark side (we all have a dark side) and clears it from your psyche. It does not hide from dark energies; instead, it shines a light on the darkness and negativity and strips it from your path, leading you toward love and light. While often utilized for protection, the black obsidian crystal has amazing healing properties for grief and loss, as well as broken heartedness and other emotional struggles.

8. BLUE CALCITE

Colors: Blue, clear, whitish, pale (*blue* is special)

Chakra: #5 Throat Chakra (Vishudha)

Element: Water

Magical Uses: Is there a speaker in the house? Blue calcite takes away any shyness and helps you to articulate your words, even when you are communicating electronically, even when you're texting. Communication is still energy and energy doesn't discriminate. It is soothing to the nervous system and helps alleviate anxiety. It connects the intellectual mind to the emotional mind and balances them, giving way to better health and wellness. Physically it keeps your bones and teeth strong due to its relationship with calcium.

9. BLOODSTONE

Colors: Red, green

Chakra: #1 Root Chakra (Muladhara) and #4 Heart Chakra (Anahata)

Element: Fire

Magical Uses: Grounding, decision making, protection, courage, friendships, idealism, unselfishness, spiritual harmony, intense healing. Boosts the immune system, purifies blood, kidneys, liver, spleen, bladder, eliminates toxins, aids in circulation, in blood disorders such as anemia, and heals infections. This is a very important crystal to use on a regular basis. There are numerous scholarly articles on the benefits and healing properties of bloodstone crystals. Women have been using them for centuries to prevent miscarriages and to give themselves strength during labor and childbirth. The bloodstone has an amazing ability to alleviate problems associated with PMS and menopause.

10. CELESTITE

Colors: Gray, green, orange, yellow, brown, blue

Chakra: #6 Third Eye Chakra (Ajna)

Element: Spirit

Magical Uses: Healing eyes, nasal, ears, digestion, mental illness. Removes toxins from the bloodstream, alleviates pain, brings good luck, balance, peace, truth, and enlightenment. Restores chakra balance, provides purification of the chakra, inner wisdom, helps you to remember your dreams. The thing I love most about this crystal is that it really helps me spiritually. When I place it on the third eye chakra, I get a sense of levitation and divine love! It balances my yin and yang energies.

11. CLEAR QUARTZ

Color: Translucent

Chakra: #7 Crown Chakra (Sahasrara)

Element: Spirit

Magical Uses: Master of all healers, boosts the immune system, amps up physical, emotional, and spiritual energies, powers up your intention, acts as pain relief, and promotes positivity. The clear quartz crystal enhances people's auras. I have seen it with my own eyes! I use it to keep my whole body in check. It opens, cleanses, unblocks, and activates all chakras. Keep it close by if you are studying, as it strongly influences concentration.

12. CITRINE

Color: Yellowish

Chakra: #3 Navel Chakra (Solar Plexus Chakra) (Manipura), all of the chakras

Element: Fire

Magical Uses: Self-discipline, prosperity, chakra cleanser, harmony within the family, healing agent for digestive, bowel, and spine problems. It is also an energy enhancer, weight loss help, optimism promoter, and CFS (chronic fatigue syndrome) healer. Cupping the crystal each day and stating your goals aloud to the universe will ramp up its energy tenfold. Citrine works with your root chakra and helps you to realize your dreams. It is an energy provider. That is why it helps those who are suffering from fatigue. But, if you think about it, with increased energy comes professional growth. I use it the same way I take my vitamin C.

13. FLUORITE

Colors: Purple, clear, green, blue, rare yellow, rainbow

Chakra: Purple- #6 Third Eye Chakra (Ajna); Blue- #7 Crown Chakra (Sahasrara); Green- #4 Heart Chakra (Anahata); Yellow- #3 Navel Chakra (Manipura); Rainbow- all chakras.

Element: Air and Water

Magical Uses: Detoxes the mind! Blue fluorite: the crystal of singers. Calm, spirituality, clarity, and logical thinking. Green fluorite:

helps with addictions, cleansing, and creativity. Purple fluorite increases self-confidence, improves coordination and balance, and concentration. Rainbow fluorite helps with nervous system irregularities, promotes accurate fortune telling (runes, tarot, etc.), and has anti-viral properties. Yellow fluorite is a liver healing crystal that also lowers cholesterol and removes toxins.

14. GARNET

Colors: Dark red, green or olive, dark yellow, black

Chakra: #4 Heart Chakra (Anahata)

Element: Fire

Magical Uses: Honesty, sincerity, libido, self-confidence. It also keeps you steady on your feet during crisis intervention and improves your courage. Garnet aids in blood disorders and improves circulation. Something about Garnet makes me feel very safe. Passions are ignited with garnet!

15. GREEN AVENTURINE

Color: Green

Chakra: #4 Heart Chakra (Anahata)

Element: Earth

Magical Uses: Money and wealth. Transforms negative energy into positive energy. Protects your home and garden from electromagnetic pollution. Promotes compassion and self-confidence. This crystal protects you from heartbreak, and in later years, if you desire, will attract a love interest of great potential. Gives you the power to embrace change and fills you with an understanding of true acceptance.

16. GREEN JADE

Color: Green

Chakra: #4 Heart Chakra (Anahata)

Element: Earth

Magical Uses: Money. Inspires devotion, loyalty, love, protects against misfortune and accidents. Helps with disorders of the kidney and heart and helps with anxiety. Whenever I am involved with green jade, I always seem to be able to vividly remember my dreams. It enhances clarity, wisdom, emotional balance, and inner peace.

17. HEMATITE

Colors: Black, gray, red, brown; all have a distinguishing characteristic of a reddish-brown streak.

Chakra: #1 Root Chakra (Muladhara)

Element: Fire

Magical Uses: Stress reduction. Grounding and protection. Pulls in positive vibrational energy. Brings harmony to the mind, body, and spirit. Helps with legalities. Brings money, aids in decision-making, works for manifestation, focus, clarity, stability, protection, balance, divination, problem-solving, emotions, doubt, anxiety, communication, and strength.

18. LAPIS LAZULI

Color: Deep blue

Chakra: #5 Throat Chakra (Vishudha) and #6 Third Eye Chakra (Ajna)

Element: Water

Magical Uses: Wards off evil. Improves eyesight. Alleviates headaches, skin problems, anxiety, and stress. Protection, self-expression, truthfulness, and moral compass. Stimulates clarity, objectivity, and creativity. Reveals your inner-most truths. It really helps new relationships to bond and allows for freedom of expression.

19. LEPIDOLITE

Colors: Lilac and rose-violet

Chakra: #4 Heart Chakra (Anahata), #6 Third Eye Chakra (Ajna) and #7 Crown Chakra (Sahasrara)

Element: Water

Magical Uses: Meditation, transition, awareness, and emotional balance. It rids the mind and body of negativity, opens the heart, throat, and third eye chakras, aids in overcoming addiction and provides a much-needed boost to the immune system for everyone, but most importantly for addicts. I have an ol' friend who swears by Lepidolite for treating his sciatica and diabetic neuropathy! It is a stress reliever and helps anxiety. A number of articles on the Internet discussed the use of Lepidolite for treating bipolar disorder.

20. ORANGE AVENTURINE

Color: Orange

Chakra: #2 Sacral Chakra (Svadisthana)

Element: Water

Magical Uses: Promotes normal sexual functioning. Enhances creativity and spiritual growth. Helps with problem-solving and decision-making. Helps you to be mindful of the present moment and how you are feeling right now. Enhances feelings of contentment, joy, happiness, and positivity. This crystal does an amazing job at relaxing me and allowing me to notice the simple pleasures in life. It also helps individuals suffering from PTSD.

21. ROSE QUARTZ

Color: Pink

Chakra: #4 Heart Chakra (Anahata) and #5 Throat Chakra (Vishudha)

Element: Water

Magical Uses: Heals the heart and soul. Prevents heart attacks and thrombosis. Improves circulation and keeps your heart muscles strong and running smoothly. Protection during pregnancy for both unborn child and mother. Promotes the flow of unconditional love and unbreakable bonds. It is the heart stone. Because of its relationship with the heart, rose quartz crystals also attract romantic love interests. It heals the pain of deep emotional trauma and improves self-worth.

Carries the warmth of motherhood and teaches you how to soothe the self; to heal yourself with your own hands.

22. MOONSTONE

Colors: Opalescent, milky whites with variants of blue, gray, pink or green

Chakra: #3 Navel Chakra (Solar Plexus Chakra) (Manipura)

Element: Water

Magical Uses: Helps with reproduction, childbirth, and hormonal issues and breastfeeding. Balance, self-care, stress relief, insight, healing, and work productivity. Eliminates excess body fluids and toxins, aids in digestion, and nourishes fleshy organs such as your pancreas and liver. Helps men and women to be more open to their emotional selves. I read a lot of articles that referred to moonstone helping men open up to their emotions. However, my experience is that it makes me more receptive to my emotions, too.

23. OPAL

Colors: Nearly all colors (rainbow hues). It is a magnificent play of color energies used to vitalize chakras that correspond with each other and then link them to the crown chakra.

Chakra: #7 Crown Chakra (Sahasrara)

Element: Air and Water

Magical Uses: Brings alive your mystical and psychic characteristics, while advancing your cosmic intuition and consciousness. It raises your insight, allowing you to journey deep into self-healing or regress into past lives. It is a protector and can be used as a shamanic guide. It is my primary grounding crystal because of its magnificent way of helping me to invoke visions. It is physically beneficial for the health of hair, nails, eyes, and skin.

24. RUBY

Color: Pure red

Chakra: #1 Root Chakra (Muladhara)

Element: Fire

Magical Uses: The queen of crystals and an aphrodisiac! Helps with fatigue and lethargy, Stimulates energy and circulation of the entire body. It can be overly stimulating for some, yet also calming to those who are hyperactive. If you are planning on entering a debate, make sure to sport a ruby somewhere on your person. It fights exhaustion and lethargy.

25. SAPPHIRE

Colors: Blue, yellow, black, pink, white, indigo, green

Chakra: Black- #1 Root Chakra (Muladhara); Blue- #5 Throat Chakra (Vishudha); Green- #4 Heart Chakra (Anahata); Indigo- #6 Third Eye Chakra (Ajna); Pink- #4 Heart Chakra (Anahata); White- #7 Crown Chakra (Sahasrara); Yellow- #3 Navel/Solar Plexus Chakra (Manipura)

Element: Water

Magical Uses: All sapphires have the following qualities, but some are stronger with specific colors: grounding, memory, good luck and wisdom, intuition, attraction, generosity, spirituality, increased self-worth, loyalty, and independence. Works to combat blood and circulatory disorders, throat problems, and nerve disorders.

26. SUGILITE

Color: Violet

Chakra: #7 Crown Chakra (Sahasrara)

Element: Spirit

Magical Uses: Awakens the crown chakra and permeates light throughout your body. Encourages acceptance, forgiveness, and hope. Stress reduction; it also instills confidence and increases self-esteem. Provides a greater awareness of the mind-body connection. Brings light to the darkness and combats fears and anxieties. Opens the third eye chakra and helps you to recover your dreams and makes them rich in meaning and significance. Relieves headaches. Also, a grounding force. Removes negative karma. Inspires awe!

27. SUN STONE

Colors: Gold, orange, red and brown

Chakra: #2 Sacral Chakra (Svadisthana)

Element: Fire

Magical Uses: The abundance crystal encourages originality and independence. This one can make you rich and famous. It is a good luck charm when participating in any competition. It will inspire you to reveal your talents and do so without fear! Brings about great enthusiasm and will make a fitness program seem appealing. If your job requires labor or long hours, you can count on a sun stone in your pocket to give you the energy you need to succeed. In the workplace, it is nice to keep one on your desk, as it will enhance your profile and bring you new opportunities for advancement and leadership. Keep one next to your computer, especially if you have an online business. It will also protect you from any beings that are emotionally draining as it is a stress reducer by nature. It shines light on dark places with its brilliance, so it helps those with phobias or fear of the dark.

28. TIGER'S EYE

Color: Golden to red brown

Chakra: #1 Root Chakra (Muladhara), #2 Sacral Chakra (Svadhisthana), and Navel Chakra (Manipura)

Element: Fire and Earth

Magical Uses: Brings good luck, promotes clarity, problem-solving, improves focus, balances yin and yang, and is a mood stabilizer. Enhances purpose, courage, willpower, self-worth; reduces stress and tension. Heightened awareness, optimism, sheds light on situations, helping you to see things more clearly. Inspiration, grounding, empowerment, helps you to look at things logically. Enhances libido. Aids in reducing fatigue by providing positive energy.

29. TURQUOISE

Color: Blue

Chakra: #5 Throat Chakra (Vishudha)

Element: Air

Magical Uses: Helps to heal any areas associated with the throat, ears, nose, and lungs. Alleviates allergies, headaches, asthma, and any other bronchial problems due to its cool and soothing properties. Calms panic attacks and is great for grounding. It is one of the oldest crystals known to man. It strengthens your immune system and rebalances the mind, soul, and body. I love it because it really helps to clear up my thinking when I feel overwhelmed.

30. ZEBRA JASPER

Colors: White with black stripes, green, red, and brown with white

Chakra: #1 Root Chakra (Muladhara)

Element: Fire

Magical Uses: Balances and unites feminine and masculine energies and your chakras. Encourages optimism, even when under stressful conditions. Inspires you to turn your dreams into reality. Helps with muscle pain, kidney and bladder issues, skin conditions, and strengthens your teeth and bones. Grounding properties. I always feel very connected to Mother Earth when I use this crystal. When I do that successfully, I am filled with joy!

5

PREPARATION

When it comes to preparing for spell casting, there is much to do in order for your manifestations to be successful. You can think about casting a spell in the same manner as you would follow a recipe for your favorite dish. You know you want it to come out right! Knowing how to prepare to cast your spells is every bit as important as how you cast your spell. As you know by now, the clarity of your INTENTION is the most important thing. You don't have to build an altar to do a spell, but it will make your magic more organized and will provide you with a sacred space for you to focus your energy and intention. It can also be a beautiful place for you to turn to when you want to feel good about yourself and the universe.

Start out by finding a beautiful and meaningful piece of material. Your altar cloth can be green if your intention is abundance, for example. You can build your altar wherever you choose. I have mine on a table in the corner of my bedroom facing east to catch the rising sun. Years ago, I started out with one on my dresser and then on my coffee table. Finally, I wanted a place that could be devoted to my altar, so I bought a handcrafted wooden spell table with the tree of life etched on it. It's beautiful. There are many to choose from online starting at around $35. Every item selected for your altar should be something to which you feel spiritually and personally connected. Every witch's journey is unique, so make use of items from which you feel a positive emotional vibration or energy.

Preparing Your Altar

Choosing the color of your cloth (make sure you use cloth you are drawn to and that feels good on your skin) depends on what you want to achieve:

- *Red (fire element):* Love, courage, passion, power, professional goals, and creativity.
- *Orange (fire element):* Attraction, success, property, and justice.
- *Yellow (air element):* Happiness, learning, memory, and intelligence.
- *Green (earth element):* Abundance, money, fertility, nature, health, and personal growth.
- *Blue (water element):* Serenity, spirituality, patience, wisdom, psychic abilities, and protection.
- *Purple (water element):* Power, psychic abilities, ambition, acceptance, and royalty.
- *Pink (fire element):* Friendship, romance, health and well-being, love, and nurturing.

- *White (air element):* Cleansing, peace, and purity, confidence, clarity, and inspiration.
- *Silver (water element):* Dreams, astral projections, intuition, telepathy, communication, and positivity.
- *Gold (fire element):* Success, happiness, prosperity, luck, wealth, attention, enlightenment, and popularity.
- *Brown (earth element):* Animals, favors, family, health, friendships, grounding, strength, and balance.

If you give glory to a deity, include symbols referencing them and their magic. Trust your intuition when placing items on your altar. Usually, at least four candles are placed on the altar to connect it to north, south, east, and west. Items representing each of the elements are also used. I have a gorgeous crystal bowl filled with blessed water and small floating candles in it, and at the bottom I have a tiny moonstone crystal. I am honoring water on the western side of my altar. You can use any symbols you want, but here are some suggestions:

- *East (air)* — feather, wand, knife, magnifying glass, wing
- *West (water)* — goblet, river stones, bowl of water, seashells, salt
- *South (fire)* — yellow flowers, orange or red crystals, matches
- *North (earth)* — bones, plant, rocks, bonsai

How to Cleanse Your Altar

It is essential to cleanse your altar on a regular basis because it rids the room of unwanted or negative energies and allows space for beneficial and positive energies. Just like cleaning our homes, we should clean our altars. Negative energies can come to the altar by way of items or people coming into and leaving the room. Cleansing your altar imbues it with respect. To charge your altar means to fill the area with your energy and intentions or with an element's or deity's intentions. Charging your altar is also important to your magical process. Here is how I charge and cleanse my altar. You can tailor or change it to fit your preferences or needs.

Necessary items:

- Sage or other smudge item or incense (and something to light it with).
- Fireproof plate or abalone shell (to hold under your smudge bundle); you can use an incense holder.
- Witch hazel, holy water, or lemon juice and a clean cloth.

Steps for cleansing:

1. Remove everything from the altar and put to the side.
2. Wipe down the entire altar in a counterclockwise motion. The whole time you are cleansing, speak aloud "begone negative energies from my altar." Clean it thoroughly so that it is acceptable to you for communicating with divine energy.
3. Continuing with your intentions, clean all of the items, tools, or any other magical supplies before placing them on the altar.
4. Light your smudge bundle and wave its smoke in a counterclockwise direction all around your altar. While

waving the smoke, imagine it evaporating all negative vibrations. Then do the same for all of your items.

Charging Your Crystals

In order to successfully improve and change your life for the better using crystals, you have to be dedicated to their cleansing and charging on a regular basis. The positive vibrational energies given by crystals require upkeep and attention. With charging comes added energy, enhancing your crystal's vibrancy and magical longevity before it has to be cleansed again. Also, charging your crystal can raise its intensity and the intensity of any spell placed into it.

Moonlight Charging

Moonlight charges your crystals with a gentle and soft feminine energy and works well as a facilitator for change, like switching jobs, moving to a new home, or a relationship breakup. It also works well in providing you clarity and introspection.

For sunlight and moonlight charging, lay your crystals out either in a grid or pattern, according to your intuition, so that they receive direct moonlight or sunlight. If you can, expose your crystals for 24 hours so they can get the most energy from both. Full moons symbolize new beginnings. Energies differ according to the phases of the moon, which offers feminine energies:

- Full moon: waning energy.
- The new moon: growth energy.

Sunlight Charging

1. The following is a list of crystals that will not fade in the sun and work best with the sun-powered energy:
2. Obsidian: it is commonly found in its original state outdoors; it is volcanic and will not fade.
3. Clear quartz: because there is no pigmentation in this crystal, it does well in direct sunlight for charging, but be careful it does not ignite sparks and starts a fire.
4. Tourmaline: this is a fantastic grounding crystal that is safe to charge in sunlight.
5. Moonstone: this crystal is perfect for charging under the moon and the sun, so its feminine and masculine energies become balanced.
6. Charging your crystals in indirect sunlight is good for those prone to fading or becoming brittle if exposed to direct sunlight. Pick a nice shady spot in your yard, garden or windowsill that faces a sun-filled area but is not quite reachable to the sun. You can also cup your crystal and meditate outside for 15 minutes or so. If all else fails, place your crystals under a representative of the sun such as a glowing candle. Do it in a room that is dark so the candle can shine brightly.

Earth Charging

You can either place your crystal directly into the earth and bury it or you can put it in a box or a jar to retrieve later. Charge your crystals this way for at least seven hours. Call the earth and soil back to your stones for charging. This is a natural charging method that allows your crystals to reprogram their connection to the Earth so they can renew their powerful healing energies. Crystals that work best with this method are:

- Agate
- Boji stone
- Calcite
- Carnelian
- Jasper
- Mahogany
- Obsidian

Setting the Intention of the Crystal

It is imperative that you communicate exactly what support you want and where you want it from your crystals. Your intentions may change over time. Intention setting is a powerful and helpful exercise in crystal magic and can bring you more joy, positivity, happiness, balance, abundance, and all-around good vibrations. Whatever your intended goals may be, they all start with an intention, and your crystals are the tools to use to set you on your journey of manifesting your personal dreams and objectives. Crystals have tremendous power to bring your intentions to fruition. They serve as a visual aid to remind you of your objectives in life and can be a useful physical tool for setting your intentions routinely. If setting your intention to your crystals is a new practice, here is an easy step-by-step technique.

Note that you can always change your ritual to compliment your gut feelings; the more you make it yours the more powerful your magic:

1. Cleanse and connect: You will be drawn to varying crystals for different reasons. Maybe one day, a certain color makes you resonate with a specific crystal. Or maybe you looked up the properties of a certain crystal to meet a certain need or power you want to harness. Trusting your intuition is the most important part of connecting and then going with the crystal(s) you are drawn to.
2. Once you have chosen the crystal(s) you want to set your intentions to, use the previous methods to clean and charge them.
3. Clear your mind of all negativity and take several deep breaths or meditate for a few moments with your crystal.
4. Choose your intention that fits your objectives, something you need rather than want.
5. Keeping a still mind, focus on your intention and your crystal.
6. Write your intention on a piece of paper while maintaining your focus on your connection to your crystal.
7. Speak aloud your intention to your crystal while holding it over your third eye.
8. Continue the process until your mind and body feel that your intention is set.
9. After setting your intention, keep your crystal close to keep your objectives at the forefront of your brain. You can place it under your pillow and sleep on it. It is best if you can see it,

though, such as on your desk. I keep my clear quartz and green tourmaline on a small glass plate. This was the glass top to one of my candles and now it is a perfect little vessel for my crystals to sit on while I am writing or networking on my computer.
10. Say thank you! Whenever doing magic, it is important to express your appreciation to the spirits for your blessings. It is also a beautiful way to end your rituals. You can do this with a quick gratitude list where you write down three things you are grateful for or make an offering to a deity of your choice; whichever fits your personal beliefs.
11. Reset and revisit your intentions to help you as you continue on your unique spiritual journey. You may choose to set your rituals for each full or new moon, thereby making it a monthly ritual.

How to Store Your Crystals

You can keep from chipping your crystals if you store them in individual containers or pouches. Many spiritual advisors recommend only using natural materials, so they stay free from negative or outside energy. But I found that natural materials actually work as conductors of energy, so I keep my small crystals in small plastic boxes to steer clear of outside influences. I keep them in a daily medicine container because they have divided compartments. I also put a piece of tissue underneath so that the crystal is resting on a soft bed. Do your best not to store hard crystals with very soft ones, so as to avoid scratching or nicking the soft crystals. Calcite and fluorite crystals break easily, so use caution when storing hard stones. If you want them to be displayed while stored, keep them away from direct sunlight and any extreme changes in temperature.

Take the time to look up crystals in your collection for helpful hints on what can potentially damage them. For example, lodestone and hematite oxidize or they can rust if left out in the open air. Some crystals, such as selenite, dissolve in hot water. Moldavite fractures in hot water. For these reasons, I emphasize the importance of doing your homework. Check out the Mohs scale of mineral hardness. It tells you how easily crystals scratch, with 1 being very soft and 10 being the hardest (which is a diamond). It is a good guide to use to tell you if you can carry your crystal safely in your pocket or if it should be in a velvet pouch. In general, if your crystal has a rating of 6 or higher on the Mohs scale, you can safely clean it in water.

6

CRYSTAL GRIDS

When our most precious crystals are combined with a bit of geometry for the specific intention of manifesting our deepest desires, goals, dreams, and objectives, we have a crystal grid. If you think about it, geometry is sacred and it is everywhere, it is in our architecture, the branches and leaves of the trees, the galaxies and their spirals, and the cells in our bodies. By studying geometry we can better understand the world around us and unlock the mysteries of creation. When placed under a microscope, crystals reveal that they are made up of a perfect crystalline foundation that show patterns that repeat themselves in perfect geometrical form. So, by making crystal grids, you are aligning your intentions with the right crystals and their geometric form necessary to manifest your objectives.

Select at least four crystals to start your grid, keeping your intention in mind. You can use all of the same type or combine types, again depending on your intention. It's best to place the biggest one in the middle. Once you have decided on your crystals, gather them together and cleanse and charge them using any of the techniques previously discussed. Once you have performed your cleansing and charging ritual, consider your combinations. Here are some suggestions for enhancing your grid:

- For banishing: onyx, obsidian, hematite, and jade.
- For healing: agate, amethyst, jasper, tourmaline, rose quartz, or stones representing your chakras.
- For personal growth: sunstone, clear quartz, and carnelian.

Forming your Crystal Grid Pattern

Decide on a geometric pattern. This can be a pentacle, circle, spiral or any of a thousand others out there. Pick one that you feel connected to. You can even use a deity as a template. Some geometric patterns lend themselves to healing, abundance, protection, and well-being. One of my favorite patterns for my most recent crystal grid is a part of the flower of life (the basic spatial pattern of our universe), namely, the seed of life, because it symbolizes all possible beginnings and all possible journeys, a path to infinite possibilities.

Here are instructions on how to draw the seed of life pattern.

1. Start by using a compass to draw a circle.
2. Draw another circle anywhere along the circle you just drew.

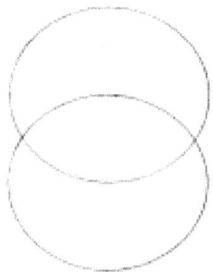

3. Place the tip of the compass at the intersecting points of the circles and draw two more circles. Repeat the process until you have six circles.

4. Put the tip of the compass where the black dot is below and draw the 7th circle.

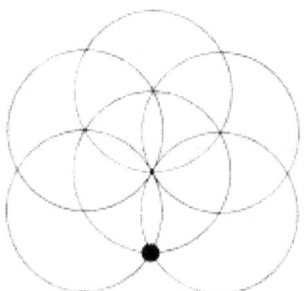

5. These 7 circles comprise what is known as the Seed of Life.

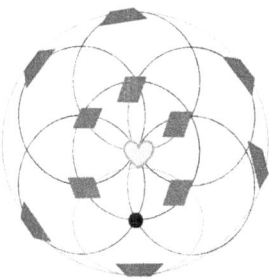

There aren't any fast rules or rules set in stone when it comes to constructing your crystal grids; it always goes back to working with how you feel the crystals are guiding you; your intuition. There are many tutorials on how to best make them. For me personally, I think the most powerful manifesting comes from your own intuition. Some like to use their crystal grid as part of a more complex ritual. You may also want to keep it very simple. Other shapes include:

- The egg of life is the addition of six more circles to your seed of life, symbolizing fertility, life, and rebirth.
- The flower of life is composed of 19 circles and is thought to be the basic structure of the universe; every atom, every molecule, and every life form.
- The tree of life is our connection to everything unseen. It is a reminder that you are not alone but part of an interconnected universe. It shows a hierarchical formation for all of the universe's forces and is made up of 10 spheres (Sephiroth). Beginning at the top, the first sphere symbolizes cosmic consciousness, and the sphere at the bottom symbolizes the material world. The spheres in between symbolize different aspects of the soul.

- The fruit of life is the holiest of the sacred geometry because it is hidden within the pattern of the flower of life. It has 13 spheres, representing the transition and unity between dimensions/worlds. Think about the keys on a piano; the thirteenth note is actually a higher frequency of the first note.
- Metatron's cube is the culmination of the centers of the 13 spheres connecting into 78 lines. This sacred geometrical structure has all of the above-mentioned patterns and every possible law of geometry, making up what we experience as physical reality.

Where to Place your Crystal Grid

You can place it on a cloth or paper with sacred geometry drawn on it, or you can put leaves or flowers within your grid. What you place underneath your grid is unique to your liking; you can use living energy such as bamboo or other types of wood, or you can use a mirror or glass to spread your crystal's energy. You can put your grid right on the ground and feel connected to Mother Earth's field of energy. Since crystal grids serve as a reminder of your intentions, every time you see it, your mind can focus. For this reason, it is nice to have it on display. I don't think there is a specific room in which to place your crystal grid, but it could be that your space is limited. If you meditate on it, some ideas may come to mind. For instance, if your intention is prosperity, you may have it in your office. If your intention is protection, you may want your crystal grid by the front or back door. Of course, if you have created it for better sleep, well, I guess you know where it goes! However, I highly suggest putting some space between your crystal grid and your bed or where you sleep (don't put it under your bed) because their strong energy fields can cause a sleep disturbance. You can always test it out yourself, but if you are limited in space, and have the crystal grid near your sleeping area, only put it there when you don't have to get up early.

Setting up your Grid

As I said earlier, when designing your crystal grid, using your intuition is the best method to follow. However, usually crystal grids have crystals (called Way Stones) surrounding a center stone. Crystals that amplify the other crystals are also important. Crystals have "auras" just like all living things. People have their chakra line to center them. When you design a crystal grid, the center crystal is the grid's anchor, which behaves as an antenna to let the universe and spiritual realm know your intentions. The central crystal is commonly the largest stone with the highest vibrational energy. The crystals surrounding the center stone are the ones geometrically arranged. The number of surrounding crystals depends on how complex or simple you want to make your grid, and the shape you have decided upon. These surrounding crystals are the great grid communicators, broadcasting and receiving your intention out into the universe like satellites. If you have formatted your crystals in a square or wheel pattern, create a spoke-type energy pattern by moving your finger from the surrounding crystals to the center crystal.

If you want to make a more complex grid, tumbles or quartz points typically function as *amplification stones*. They are optional, but they do amp up the grid even more. The amplification stones are placed geometrically between the surrounding crystals. You can also place an item, referred to as an object of importance, on your grid. Some examples include a photo of a special person in our life, flowers, a letter, jewelry, leaves, or any other important object aligned with your intention. If you use the keyword 'crystal grid' and click on images in your search engine of choice, you will see hundreds, if not thousands of examples. Choose carefully where this grid will be set up and take into consideration how much time will be needed for the grid to manifest its purpose.

Activating your Grid

At this point, either with your hands, a favorite crystal, or a metal wand, extend your field of energy to transmit and magnify your intention into the grid. Prior to activation, conjure up a concise announcement of what you plan to manifest. While waving your wand, pendulum, crystal, or hands, speak aloud your intention to the center crystal. Imagine it beginning to glow with your intention and the heightened energy being produced. Then, with your hand or wand hovering above each crystal and moving in a counterclockwise motion, connecting the crystals, visualize the aura surrounding the grid. When you think the time is right, end with an expression of gratitude for the support and encouragement of your crystals. To increase or stimulate your crystal grid's energy, imagine connecting lines that link each individual crystal's energy, making one cohesive unit. If you bump crystals out of place, you will need to reactivate the grid. With your intention set to linking all of the crystals' energy, starting at the center, use your wand or smudge bundle and make a line connecting to a crystal on the outside of the grid. Then in a clockwise fashion make a line to the next crystal and then back to the center crystal again. Go back over the same line and move clockwise to the next surrounding crystal and then back to the center crystal again. Once you have outlined the surrounding crystals, if you have amplifying crystals in the grid, make a line with your wand, finger, or smudge bundle to include them. Make sure to end up with your point toward the center crystal to charge it with universal energy so that it may manifest your objective. Keep in mind that crystals are magical on their own, but when combined with your intention and intuition, their power is unstoppable.

7

CRYSTAL ELIXIRS

Essential oils are soothing to the mind, the soul, and the body. Essential oils combined with the healing and magical powers of crystals will promote your health and wellness, as well as clearing, unblocking, and balancing your chakras. Crystals and essential oils work synergistically to enhance your intention, and the energy you want to manifest. In case you are wondering what the two have in common, well, both are made from natural resources in the earth and both are used for magic and healing purposes. Crystals naturally occur as minerals in the earth and are discovered all over the globe. Essential oils are directly distilled from trees, plants, and flowers. I have been experimenting with essential oil and crystal pairings for quite some time now, and I have come to realize that when the crystal and oil have a similar vibrational energy, they enhance each other's ways of guiding you toward the state of being that you want to achieve. To do this, get a small crystal that will fit into a small essential oil glass container. Place the crystal in the bottle and fill the container ¾ of the way with the essential oil.

The following is a list of pairings between crystals and essential oils and their magical uses:

AMETHYST: Pairs with cypress, sandalwood, and frankincense.
Magical use: Provides balance, protection, and self-confidence.

AMAZONITE: Pairs with orange, bergamot, clove, juniper, geranium, and spruce.
Magical use: Provides truth and courage, dispels worry, negative energy, and fear.

APATITE: Pairs with orange, nutmeg, peppermint, and grapefruit.
Magical use: Stimulates growth, motivation, goal setting, energy.

AQUAMARINE: Pairs with ginger, lavender, helichrysum, clove, and chamomile.
Magical use: Enhances self-expression, helpful for closure, relaxes the mind.

BLUE CALCITE: Pairs with geranium, basil, frankincense, vetiver, and lavender.
Magical use: Facilitates communication and is considered the crystal of trust.

CITRINE: Pairs with ginger, orange, patchouli, sandalwood and clove.
Magical use: Creativity, success, power, and abundance.

CHRYSOCOLLA: Pairs with ylang ylang, helichrysum, tangerine, sandalwood, basil, and lavender.
Magical use: Teaching crystal, encourages peace, compassion, and forgiveness.

CLEAR QUARTZ: Pairs with all essential oils.
Magical use: Amps up any intent or energy that is invested into it.

EMERALD: Pairs with cedarwood, jasmine, rose, patchouli, and lavender.
Magical use: Promotes unity and friendship, relaxing effect, encourages positivity.

EMERALD CALCITE: Pairs with ylang ylang, clue tansy, tangerine, and patchouli.
Magical use: Crystal of peace, supportive during any transitions in life.

GARNET: Pairs with jasmine, lemon, ylang ylang, frankincense, and orange.
Magical use: Positive crystal, inspires devotion and love, antidepressant.

HERKIMER DIAMOND: Pairs with sage, tea tree, clove, lemon, and frankincense.
Magical use: Promotes self-appreciation and works as a healing agent; emotional, spiritual, and physical.

LABRADORITE: Pairs with peppermint, neroli, basil, and lemon.
Magical use: Inspiration, clarity, lets you envision many possibilities all at the same time.

LAPIS LAZULI: Pairs with spruce, lime, basil, jasmine, and frankincense.
Magical use: Inspires knowledge and good judgment, creates a desire for the truth and wisdom; considered a stone of truth.

ORANGE KYANITE: Pairs with grapefruit, jasmine, orange, lavender, and geranium.
Magical use: Encourages optimism, playfulness, enhances self-esteem.

PERIDOT: Pairs with cypress, jasmine, cinnamon, patchouli, and bergamot.
Magical use: Helps to overcome resentment and fear, assisting you to move forward with your life, manifests prosperity and abundance.

PINK LEMURIAN (quartz): Pairs with sage, ylang ylang, lavender, and bergamot.
Magical use: Feminine energy, love, heightened spirituality, meditation, unconditional love; attracts angels into your life.

PINK OPAL: Pairs with orange, sandalwood, juniper and frankincense.
Magical use: Crystal of renewal, balances your emotions, calming effect.

PYRITE: Pairs with grapefruit, clove, peppermint, and frankincense.
Magical use: Promotes leadership, energizes creativity, and acts as a protective agent.

RAINBOW MOONSTONE: Pairs with bergamot, cypress, rose, vetiver, and lavender.
Magical use: Calming crystal, helps during change by providing insight.

RHODOLITE (a variety of Garnet): Pairs with cedarwood, coriander, rosemary, spruce, and tangerine.
Magical use: A warming crystal that inspires your intuition and promotes contemplation.

ROSE QUARTZ: Pairs with bergamot, lavender, ylang ylang, rose, and jasmine.
Magical use: The crystal of love and relationships.

RUBY: Pairs with cinnamon, rose, ginger, peppermint, and ylang ylang.
Magical uses: Makes you motivated and able to concentrate. Gives you energy; associated with love.

SAPPHIRE: Pairs with orange, vetiver, lavender, bergamot, and ylang ylang.
Magical use: Brings joy, commitment and love, balances chakras.

SUNSTONE: Pairs with myrrh, frankincense, clove, and orange.
Magical use: Inspires self-nurturing and is considered the crystal of joy.

TANGERINE QUARTZ: Pairs with fir, chamomile, tangerine, patchouli, and frankincense.
Magical use: Grounding crystal that allows you to leave the past behind, boosts creativity, and is soothing.

TANZANITE: Pairs with rose, sandalwood, chamomile, frankincense, and geranium.
Magical use: Meditation crystal, connects your heart and mind, enhances communication.

TOPAZ: Pairs with bergamot, orange, jasmine, rosemary, and sandalwood.
Magical use: Crystal of good fortune, enhances confidence, prompts joyfulness and goal attainment.

TOURMALINE: Pairs with myrrh, geranium, orange, bergamot, hyssop, and fir.
Magical use: Enhances self-awareness; an inspirational crystal that promotes compassion and understanding.

TURQUOISE: Pairs with fennel, rosemary, clove, Palo Santo, cypress, and frankincense.
Magical use: Calming crystal, protection, and creativity.

II

THE SPELLS

Crystals, obviously, are beautiful to look at and full of positive energy. They are the fastest way to make your space magic. But the most powerful way to use your crystals is by using them in your magic. Whether it is for love or healing, abundance or success, you can harness their natural energy for many of your mystical endeavors. Part Two will fill your enquiring mind with spells from A to Z.

HEALING SPELLS

Crystals, inherently, vary in their energies and professed healing properties. To harness their energy, you must program your crystals with a specific intention. As you continue to practice with one stone, you will have an even deeper connection with your intention. The crystal's magic amplifies your intentions, and the two together make a powerful healing tool. By using your clear and specific intention, you can program your crystals and manifest your desire in healing.

Grief and Loss Spell Jar

Dealing with loss is far from easy but grief can feel all-consuming. There are many painful types of loss, such as losing a loved one, losing a job, or even our years as they pass by. There is no straight path through grief, but there are techniques to help you ease or shift the overwhelming energy that is the product of loss. Your crystals can't wipe away your pain, but they can give you a gentle source of healing and comfort vibrations to help usher through such difficult times. Some crystals can bring you inner strength, while others can bring an ease of acceptance, and still others will bring you gentle compassion. While their powers vary, they all have the same goal of working towards helping you cope with the loss and find some peace of mind.

> HOW LONG IT TAKES:
> 15 minutes
> WHAT YOU'LL NEED:
> Hawaiian black salt
> Myrrh
> Lapis lazuli
> Amethyst
> Aloe vera
> Globe amaranth

Amethyst is a universal and powerful healing crystal, and it can greatly benefit someone experiencing grief. During the period of grieving, it is normal to feel anxiety, stress, and nervousness, making your day-to-day activities very difficult. Amethyst is created with immense heat and pressure, ever reminding you that something can be beautiful when stressed.

STEPS:

1. Cleanse and smudge a medium size jar with a cork. Charge the jar with your intentions; speak aloud three times:

> *My friend is the wind, my friend is the rain.*
> *Ease my heart from grief and pain.*
> *So it is and should be.*

2. Place black sea salt in the bottom of the jar.

3. Continue layering materials according to their number from the bottom.

4. Place the cork in the jar.

5. Anoint the jar with chamomile oil or the essential oil that comforts you the most.

Grief Behind is Peace of Mind Spell

There is not one specific factor that drives individuals forward after a period of grief, or that holds them back. Most people who think of grieving rituals think of social displays of bereavement, such as "sitting shiva," funerals, wearing black for a certain number of days, etc. However, inner healing is necessary, so that a person can continue with their life and gain back their peace of mind. That is why I created the "Grief Behind Peace of Mind" spell.

> HOW LONG IT TAKES:
> 15 minutes
> WHAT YOU'LL NEED:
> Neroli oil
> 1 quartz stone
> 1 bowl of water
> 3 tablespoons of salt

STEPS:

1. Cup the crystal in your strong hand. Visualize your grief and pain in your mind's eye. Imagine the pain and grief spilling from within you and through your body to your hand and into the crystal.

As you do this, speak aloud:

> *Grief is a passage,*
> *Not a place to stay.*
> *Calm my heart,*

So I can greet the day.
So it is.

2. In a counterclockwise motion, stir the salt into the bowl of water.

3. Add the quartz crystal to the bowl.

4. In a counterclockwise motion, swish the crystal and salt water around three times.

5. Leave the crystal in the water for ten minutes.

6. Remove the crystal and throw it as far away from you as possible.

Life is a Balancing Act Spell

Chapter Four contains a list of crystals and their associated chakras. The word chakra, in Sanskrit, means "wheel," in reference to your body's energy centers. The spinning wheels of energy correspond to specific nerve bundles and the major organs in your body. If you or someone you care about needs a spell for balance, make sure to review Chapter Four if you sense a blockage, imbalance, or physical or emotional issues associated with a specific chakra. This is the best spell for balance. Since there are over 100 chakras in your body, it's no wonder that we fall off kilter every now and then.

> HOW LONG IT TAKES:
> 5 minutes for 7 days
> WHAT YOU'LL NEED:
> Crystals chosen depend on imbalance

STEPS:

1. Wear crystals as jewelry over your chakra locations.

2. Meditate with the crystals.

3. Keep a crystal somewhere on you (pocket, brassiere, belt).

4. Place in the corners of your bath.

5. Keep a crystal under your pillow or on your nightstand when sleeping.

Now I Lay Me Down to Sleep Spell

Spells manifest the best when cast with a clear head and intense focus on the objective you desire. The magic is within you, it doesn't happen on its own. So, when it comes to a good night's sleep, I highly recommend you combine your spell with some deep breathing, a spiritual bathing ritual, and some relaxation techniques. When you are ready, prepare your sleeping space, making it as comfortable for yourself as possible before you do your spell. Have your lights down low or light a candle. Change the bed clothes. I am always amazed at the difference in the quality of my sleep when it is on freshly cleaned sheets. If you have a lavender candle or lavender essential oil, let it dance around your room until you achieve a beautiful, calming effect. Finish everything you have to do, like going to the bathroom, and get ready for bed.

HOW LONG IT TAKES:
30-45 minutes, as needed
WHAT YOU'LL NEED:
1 smoky quartz crystal
1 snow quartz crystal
10 dried lavender stamps
1 sheet of paper (untreated if possible)

STEPS:

1. Sit in your bed in a comfortable position. Place your spell materials next to you.

2. Hold a crystal in each hand. Focus your intent on each crystal's energy and how it feels in your hands.

3. With your eyes closed, gently move the crystals around in your hands; notice every ridge and bump. Slowly feel them starting to warm up with your touch. Let their energy pass through your hands and throughout your whole body.

4. Turn your attention to the smoky quartz and feel its calming-grounding energy transforming all of your negativity into positive and peaceful sensations.

5. Send this energy down to your toes.

6. Turn your attention to your snow quartz and feel its hope radiating in your palms. Feel the snow quartz flowing through you.

7. Let yourself fall into the powers of the crystals and their protective energy.

8. Allow your mind to quiet.

9. After a moment, quietly chant:

> *Peaceful sleep come to me.*
> *My spirit, my mind will now roam free.*
> *Grant calm serenity tonight.*
> *Tomorrow is a beautiful sight.*
> *As it is and should be.*

10. When ready, gently and slowly open your eyes. If you can still feel the energies coursing through your body, close your eyes again for as long as you need.

11. When you're ready, take the lavender sprigs and the crystals and put them on the piece of paper.

Wrap them up carefully and place the package on your nightstand.

12. Ease yourself down into your bed and warm yourself in the comfort enveloping you. Thank your materials and fall gently into a deep slumber.

Color Me Creative Spell

Being creative can be a bit tricky, as it seems to come and go. In my experience, creativity has a tendency to arrive at the most inconvenient time. It usually happens when I am trying to fall asleep or while I'm driving in heavy traffic; it then vanishes at the exact time I need it. Creativity is governed by the sacral chakra, which just so happens to govern our passion and pleasure. So, it should come as no surprise that creativity is derived from our pleasure and passion center. Using the mega strong carnelian crystal will open your creative powers, allowing you to feel more original and inspired in every area of your life. Carnelian works together with your sacral chakra, creating a highly creative and powerful energy. It wakes up your creative side, so that you can imagine and inspire all that is good in your life. The power of words with intent is amazing, so speaking your creativity into existence and amplifying it with your crystal will give you a quick and powerful spell.

HOW LONG IT TAKES:
30 seconds
WHAT YOU'LL NEED:
1 carnelian crystal

STEPS:

1. Cup your carnelian crystal in both hands and speak aloud three times:

I am creative, talented, and smart.
As it is and should be.

Over the Moon Water Recipe for Spells

Soak the amethyst and clear quartz crystals in the moon water. The really neat part about this dynamic duo is that the amethyst powerfully charges the moon brew and works especially well with any creativity spells. The clear quartz amplifies the whole spell. The crystals charge the water and the water charges the crystals. This enhances your psychic attributes and works wonders with dream magic.

HOW LONG IT TAKES:

30 minutes prep and 13 hours moon brewing

WHAT YOU'LL NEED:

1 clear quartz or moonstone crystal

1 amethyst crystal

The full moon

1 floating white candle

1 cinnamon stick

1 lavender-colored flower

A corked glass bottle

A pot for boiling (preferably cast iron or use your cauldron)

A glass bowl

Cheesecloth, coffee filter, or strainer

Funnel

STEPS:

1. Wait for a full moon. It helps to know in advance when this will occur so you can get excited about what you are about to do.

2. On the evening of the full moon, put your cinnamon and flower in water and gently bring to a boil.

3. Strain the liquid in a tied off coffee filter or wrap the components in a cheesecloth before boiling.

4. Let the brew simmer on low heat for 30 minutes.

5. When it has cooled down, pour into a glass bowl. Strain the herbs if you didn't use a filter or cheesecloth.

6. At the stroke of midnight, take your brew outside and place it under the moonlight (so you can see the reflection of the moon in the water).

7. Place your amethyst and clear quartz or moonstone crystal in the center of the bowl of water.

8. Send your lit candle adrift in your brew. If you feel it's okay, meditate for a few minutes and leave it overnight.

9. The next morning, pluck out the cold wax.

10. Funnel the water into your bottle and cork it.

11. Thank the moon and your materials.

12. Enjoy!

I Think It's Time for a Change Spell

In every person's life, there comes a moment where they want to make some type of vital change. It may be losing weight, starting a new job, or improving your financial state. Casting this spell can bring on that change. Your timing for this spell is crucial. It has to be during a new moon because fresh beginnings are aligned with the new moon. The new moon's energy will help you to let go of your past. Moldavite is the stone of transformation, maybe because moldavite itself was created through an intensely changing process. It is the crystal to choose if you want to make a vital change in your life, or if you wish to have good luck while you navigate change.

> HOW LONG IT TAKES:
> Bath time + 30 minutes or until candle burns down
> WHAT YOU'LL NEED:
> 1 moldavite crystal
> 3 white candles
> Sea salts
> Candles (red for love; green for money; orange for creativity)
> Paper
> Candle snuffer
> Ribbon (same color as the candle).

STEPS:

1. Cleansing bath ritual. Fill the tub with warm water and sea salts. Light three white candles around the tub. The purpose of this bath is

for calming yourself while preparing for your spell work, not to imagine the future.

2. Place your colored candle in front of you or on your altar. Write down your intention, describing your life post change. Do this in the present tense.

3. Cup your moldavite crystal in your hand and visualize and feel the positive emotions this change has in your life.

4. Fold the paper in a direction toward yourself, so the energy is directed back at you and place it under the moldavite crystal.

5. Scribe your intention on your candle. Either a symbol such as $$ or in words.

6. Light the candle.

7. Place the parcel and the Moldavite crystal so it is hit by the glow of the candle.

8. As you gaze into the flame, speak aloud:

> *I make this claim,*
> *as I ignite this flame.*
> *I embrace this change,*
> *but self-love remains.*
> *As it is and should be.*

9. Either snuff out the candle or stay with it until it burns all the way down. You want to receive all of the energy from the charging Moldavite.

10. When the spell is complete, take back the parcel and unfold it. Roll the parcel that has your intention writing on it into the shape of a cylinder.

11. Take the cylinder and the Moldavite and put them together where they cannot be disturbed or ever found.

12. Your future is yours!

I'm Not Angry Spell

On any given day we can experience turbulence in our emotional landscape. Some days, I feel pushed and pulled in all the wrong places, anxious, overwhelmed, and every once in a while, downright angry. If this ever happens to you, and you don't want those feelings to hang around, cast this "I'm Not Angry Spell" as part of your handy self-care spell rituals. Anger stems from an unbalanced or blocked flow of your natural energy in the throat and root chakras.

HOW LONG IT TAKES:
Bath time + 30 minutes or until candle burns down
WHAT YOU'LL NEED:
Howlite
Peridot
Smoky quartz
Amethyst
Bloodstone

STEPS:

1. Meditate with any of the crystals above for anger releasing and to channel positivity into your life.

2. Hold sessions with your family, friends, or group and communicate while holding the crystal and it will help you get to the root of the problem.

3. Keep the crystal in your pocket. It is best if it is touching you at all times. So, wearing it in aring, or other type of jewelry is a great idea. Keep touching it so it can suck the anger right out of your mind.

4. Have a crystal where you feel the angriest. If you lose your temper at work, at home, or in any other stressful environment, let the crystal slowly rid your environment of all toxicity.

5. Place them around where you notice the maximum concentration of negative energy and conflict.

Begone Negativity Spell

Some think an illness or a disease is the reason for having fatigue or prolonged aches and pains, but have you ever considered that negativity might be either part of the problem or the cause of the problem? Negative thinking affects more than just your state of mind; in fact, I believe it festers into everything from headaches to heart problems and prolongs the recovery time if you are sick. Practice the "Begone Negativity Spell" to help you transform your negative energy into positive energy.

HOW LONG IT TAKES:
21 days
WHAT YOU'LL NEED:
Lepidolite crystal
Amethyst crystal
Blue lace agate
Moonstone crystals
Sage
Lavender
Juniper

STEPS:

1. Make sure your crystals for this spell are cleansed and charged.

2. Use the same method for cleaning your crystals that you use for your aura and your soul. Sage, lavender, and juniper, combined with amethyst, blue lace agate, or a moonstone grid can be used. Smudge

your crystal and then your body from head to toe. Visualize all of the negative energy disappearing.

Cleansing Negative Energy Spell

The color of clouds under a midnight full moon seems to transport me to the mystical world. A smoky quartz crystal is for the soul as a multivitamin is for the body. It stands ready to neutralize any negativity headed your way. It is your anchor in the storm of doubt. The smoky quartz will detox and purge the "stuff" that is deep down and glued to your aura. You don't want negative energy to fester and become denser in your physical body. Smoky quartz is a type of naturally irradiated crystal formed when the molecules are exposed to gamma-rays. The process is slow and completely natural. The crystal knows bad juju because gamma-rays are released into the earth from elements that are naturally decaying, such as uranium. So, this crystal soaks up any decaying energy in you!

HOW LONG IT TAKES:
21 days
WHAT YOU'LL NEED:
Smoky quartz crystal
Sweetgrass
Frankincense

STEPS:

1. Place the crystal on your altar with some sweetgrass and frankincense. If you need an instant cleaning and you are busy, simply hold the crystal and plants in your hands while you are working or tending to clients throughout the day.

Energy Boosting Spell

Most of us know the feeling of all our energy being drained; that overly-tired time of the day or night when no matter how alluring something seems, we cannot seem to get ourselves psyched-up enough for it. It's even more difficult to notice low-frequency energy drains, where you don't always experience the normal signs of fatigue. All you know is that you just don't feel that get-up-and-go energy for things you normally love. I lose my focus when I am experiencing periods of low energy, so I created this spell for me and you for those times when we need a bit more than a cup of java to feel good.

> HOW LONG IT TAKES:
> 15 minutes
> WHAT YOU'LL NEED:
> Your favorite music
> Rose quartz crystal
> Vervain herb
> Abalone shell

STEPS:

1. This spell is best done when you are by yourself, so you can turn up the music.
2. Select a song that makes you want to get up and dance, one that is uplifting and makes you want to swing your hips.
3. Put your vervain herb in the abalone shell and light it.
4. Place your rose quartz next to the smoking vervain.

5. Turn up the music.
6. Feel the energy flowing into your body from the charging rose quartz and vervain.
7. Off you go!

You've Got a Friend Spell

Friendships require mutual respect and continuous effort to keep them healthy. As time goes by and people mature, sometimes friendships can grow apart. If you are looking for a new friendship or you have a friend who is upset with you, this spell helps witches bond with new friends and improve the relationships with the ones they already have. I recommend doing this spell whenever you crave closeness.

HOW LONG IT TAKES:
12-24 hours
WHAT YOU'LL NEED:
1 bowl or dish of water (can be your moon water)
1 rose quartz crystal
1 blue candle
Rose oil
A waterproof item from your friend or a waterproof item you would gift a new friend

STEPS:

1. If this spell is to enhance a current friendship, get your friend's permission first. Trust is the foundation of any friendship, so you do not want your friend to ever think you were trying to manipulate them without their knowledge.

2. Put two drops of essential rose oil on the rose quartz crystal.

3. Put two drops of essential rose oil into the center of the blue candle.

4. Put the crystal into the center of the bowl.

5. Light the candle and place it next to the bowl.

6. Speak aloud:

> *I call on the power of the element of water to bind together candle, oil, and stone, as it will bind together my everlasting (new) friendship or friendship with (friend's name) in harmony.*
> *And it is done.*

7. Snuff out the candle.

8. Place the bowl with the crystal under a waning moon overnight or leave it in overnight if you used your own moon water.

9. Take the crystal out of the water. You can save this water in a bottle and label it as a new *"The Moon is my Friend Blessed Water"* for rituals.

10. Give your item to your new friend or close friend whenever you feel distance. Hold it in your hand and tell your friend to do the same. Keep it in a place where you sit on a regular basis.

LOVE SPELLS

This chapter is going to cover issues surrounding unrequited love, finding new love, how to win over someone's heart and how to use the power of crystals to fill their mind with images of you! Let's say there is already a bit of chemistry happening between you and your love interest; manifesting a love spell will influence your love interest in a way that will make you the center of their thoughts and dreams. Love spells are crafted for differing circumstances and situations. That's why I have crafted the following spell to suit your specific needs. Therefore, you must take into consideration the primary purpose of the spell and why you use it.

Looking for Love in All the Wrong Places Spell for Wholeness

I am sure you've heard the song "Looking for Love in all the Wrong Places." Well, this is true if you are not looking within to find love. We want other people to deeply love us, when much of the time we are not practicing self-love! How can you possibly receive from someone else what you do not believe deep inside that you deserve from yourself? It is like being in a plane crash and putting the oxygen mask on another person first. For me, I feel quite disturbed by the thought of having to depend on love from outside of myself. Wouldn't it be nice if all the love you receive comes on top of your own self-love? That is why I have created this spell for wholeness ritual; it is to help you find yourself when you feel lost and to get to know yourself on a deeper level than you have ever experienced before.

HOW LONG IT TAKES:
15 Minutes
WHAT YOU'LL NEED:
Moonstone crystal
Black onyx crystal
Celestite crystal

STEPS:

1. Identify where you feel empty inside and choose a crystal. Maybe you're battling eczema or Crohn's disease, or maybe you feel lost and depressed and can't find the origin of your pain.

2. Focus on filling the void. Be specific and call it by name. Here are the crystals I usually use when I am not feeling whole:

3. Moonstone is the crystal of new beginnings and works for me when my stomach is tied in knots. Charge and anoint it and wear it around your neck.

4. Celestite is for a good night's sleep and lifting your mood. Keep it next to your bed, on a nightstand to feel calm and healed.

5. Black onyx will ground you. One of my best friends gave me a black onyx when I was leaving for college, and I gave one to my new roommate to eliminate negativity and bring peace.

6. Cleanse, anoint, and charge the three crystals. Since you are performing healing rituals, it is very important to rid your crystals of any negative energy. You can smudge them, clean them with salt, or rinse them with spring water. For healing and wholeness, you need fresh energy, not stale energy. Just the thought of a crystal being weighed down with stale energy is repugnant to me.

7. Set an intention to will yourself to be whole. If you are feeling down, hold the celestite crystal to the back of your neck or to any part of your body that needs healing. Hold the black onyx to your forehead if you need to feel one with the earth. Know that you will be healed.

8. Whether you are new to energy healing or you are a fourth-generation witch, you can practice your intentions to manifest positive changes and improve your health.

My Eyes are Drawn to You and Yours to Mine Spell

It is important to cast this spell on a Friday, the day of Venus. Also, you want to cast this spell on a full moon or a new moon when love spells are most effective.

> HOW LONG IT TAKES:
> 30 minutes
> WHAT YOU WILL NEED:
> 1 pink candle
> 1 rhodochrosite
> 1 rose quartz
> Palo Santo smudging bundle
> Rose petals

STEPS:

1. The most important part of this spell is setting your intention. Imagine a clear picture in your mind of who, what, where, and when you want this love spell to work. This spell is for new love and works best when you have seen someone you are attracted to and you want them to notice you back. Meditate on whether you are in a good place in life to enter into a relationship with your love interest. I know a few witches who cast a love spell only to wish that they had done it at a better time. For example, if you have children, you may want to wait until after summer break. Same, if you are a college student, you may want to wait until after final exams. Make sure to steer clear of any intentions involving manipulation, control, or domination.

2. Make sure to charge your crystals.

3. Place the crystals on each side of the candle.

4. Light the candle and move one crystal one inch clockwise and the other crystal one inch counterclockwise.

5. Do this once a day until the crystals touch each other.

6. Once they are touching, place them atop the rose petals and chant:

> *My heart and soul so filled with fire,*
> *Bring to me my heart's desire.*
> *Crystal of love shimmers so bright,*
> *I'm looking for true love tonight.*
> *So it is done.*

7. Blow out the candle and be patient. Carry the crystals together in the same pouch or pocket until the love you have been waiting for arrives.

Let's Talk Communication Spell

Do you wish you knew how to communicate better with your significant other(s); that you knew how to say what you mean before you say something that can cause a disconnect or conflict between you? Do you suddenly find yourself in the middle of an argument without knowing how you got there? Are you having difficulty explaining yourself or expressing your feelings? Good communication requires mutual respect and effective listening. I created this spell to help ease communication efforts, but you have to be willing to listen to your loved one without preparing a rebuttal while they are talking. If you are thinking about what you are going to say when the other person is talking, it is impossible to hear them. Stay calm, cast this spell, and then listen.

HOW LONG IT TAKES:
20 minutes

WHAT YOU'LL NEED:
1 blue candle
Lilac incense
Lapis lazuli crystal
Lavender buds
1 small dish
Amber oil
Abalone shell

STEPS:

1. This spell is best cast on your altar.

2. Light your lilac incense and wave over your lapis lazuli crystal to charge it.

3. Put your incense in your abalone shell.

4. Light your blue candle.

5. Put your lavender buds into the small dish and place the crystal in the center.

6. Rub the amber oil on your throat in a clockwise motion and speak three times:

> **Communication breeds trust.**
> *Trust is a must.*
> *I'll talk to you.*
> *You'll talk to me.*
> *Together with trust, we'll be.*
> *And so it is done.*

7. Let your candle burn down or snuff it out. Repeat this spell every day for three days.

Light My Fire Rekindling Passion Spell

We all want passion in our relationships; to feel a sense of adventure with our connections and intimacy. But sometimes the passion starts to fade and the relationship begins to suffer. Before you practice your magic, ask yourself what you believe has caused the stagnation. Maybe time has just gone by and the two of you now have more of a companionship than an intimate relationship. Is it one-sided? Or maybe you have both stopped putting the same effort into it that you once did because of kids, work, or age? Whatever the reason your excitement has waned, you now want to rekindle the passion, excitement, and lust you and your partner once had. This is a tried-and-true spell, so get ready!

HOW LONG IT TAKES:
90 minutes
WHAT YOU'LL NEED:
A sunny day
1 orange carnelian crystal
1 rose quartz
2 red candles
Red cellophane
1 elastic band
1 glass of water
Rose essence
1 red rose

STEPS:

1. Put your rose on your altar in some water.

2. Put a few drops of rose oil on both crystals.

3. Put the crystals at the bottom of a bowl.

4. Place the bowl on your windowsill, letting it get sunlight for one hour.

5. After dark, put the candles in the middle of a table and light them.

6. Gaze into the candles and think of you and your partner becoming one in unity.

7. Put one drop of rose oil on two rose petals and float them in the bowl with the crystals.

8. While gazing at the candles for three minutes and thinking about passionate closeness, chant the following aloud three times:

> *Crystals and candles together ignite.*
> *Bring alive our passion tonight.*
> *Desire between us will be true.*
> *Some passion for me and some passion for you.*
> *Let it be done.*

9. Burn the candles for one hour and then snuff them out.

10. Sleep with the crystals under your pillow until the passion reignites.

11. Once it does, put them together on your altar for keeps.

It's Over: Letting Go of Lost Love Spell

Oh, the pain of letting go! It is just an awful feeling. Even when you know it is the best for both of you, tending to a broken heart is never any fun. However, it can be a very exciting time to set your intentions on self-care, self-awareness, and creativity. Here is a spell you can cast to bring in new beginnings and let go of your old ties when you find yourself nursing a broken heart.

HOW LONG IT TAKES:
One day
WHAT YOU'LL NEED:
A full moon
1 abalone shell
1 piece of paper
1 red ink pen
1 citrine crystal
1 aquamarine crystal
Scissors
1 red candle

STEPS:

1. Give back or give away all of your ex-partner's belongings. Items hold energy, so it is imperative that you clear that energy. If you have to, get a close friend to return the items to your ex, and whatever that person doesn't want back, get rid of. You can always donate items.

2. A full moon is the best time to set your letting go intention.

3. In red ink, write down the person's full name.

4. Fold up the paper.

5. Go into your backyard or somewhere you can place the crystals under the full moonlight.

6. Take the scissors and cut the parcel in two.

7. Place ½ under the citrine crystal and ½ under the aquamarine crystal.

8. Leave them there overnight.

9. Bring the pieces of paper and the crystals to your altar.

10. Light your red candle.

11. Burn both pieces of paper with the ashes in your abalone shell.

12. Collect the ashes in your shell and snuff out your candle.

13. Bury your crystals in the ground either on the side of a crossroad or in a field away from you.

14. Let the ashes blow away and say:

> *I believe it's best for you and me.*
> *I release you now so I'll be free.*
> *The relationship is gone,*
> *I am moving on.*
> *As it is and should be.*

Desirable Me Spell

The simple truth here is that you ARE desirable with or without magic. But a bit of spell work can add to your fun. You are not like anybody else. If you haven't looked in the mirror lately, that might be part of the problem. No one can rival your desirability as long as you know it to be true. Of course, everyone has their own "taste" in what they consider desirable, but that is irrelevant. Everyone wants to feel desirable. There are days when I just can't even imagine anyone finding me desirable, and I am not talking about a bad hair day. I mean when my stress level is high and it shows. It happens to the best of us. That is when this spell really comes in handy. This spell is just to boost your feelings of being desirable because you already have everything you need. So, a bit of crystal charm will help you feel it!

HOW LONG IT TAKES:
11 minutes
WHAT YOU'LL NEED:
1 sunstone crystal

STEPS:

1. Sunstone is the crystal for desirability. It keeps our sensuality from hiding within and motivates us to bloom outward instead. This crystal holds within it the sun's revitalizing energy and has the power to forge brightness back into your life and affirm your truth that you are desirable and desired!

2. Hold the sunstone over your third eye, and say aloud:

I allow my inner glitter and radiance to shine through.
I am desirable, I am anew!
As it is and should be.

3. Imagine yourself with a white glow radiating out of your pores, sparkling brilliant, and expanding with the light.

4. Put your sunstone by your dressing mirror for three days.

Faithfully Yours Spell

Trust and faithfulness are inherent and complex needs. We look to trust other people, and we want others to think of us as trustworthy. Most human interactions depend on mutual trust. However, some relationships often lack mutual trust. Much of the time we fear or lack trust in our relationships due to our own insecurities. I have noticed in my life, the more confident I am in myself, the less I worry about faithfulness in others. In this spell, you will be using blue crystals because they are tremendously helpful in overcoming insecurities. In almost every case I have ever known, unfaithfulness has torn apart relationships, making them seem nearly impossible to repair. The best way to avoid this heart-wrenching pain is to avoid infidelity yourself. If you are the one trying to stay faithful or keep your loved one faithful, use blue crystals. Sodalite and lapis lazuli work best for this spell.

HOW LONG IT TAKES:
5 minutes
WHAT YOU'LL NEED:
Licorice herb
Rosemary
Cumin
Sodalite
Lapis lazuli
1 dark colored pouch with drawstring

STEPS:

1. Scatter ½ of the licorice herb over your partner's footprints.

2. Put the other ½ of the licorice herb in the pouch.

3. Add some cumin to a meal you both eat at the same time.

4. Hold a crystal in each hand, chant the following, and then put the crystals in the pouch.

> *I trust myself and know the truth.*
> *I have the faith to trust in you.*
> *Our love is one that can't be beat.*
> *You nor I will ever cheat.*
> *And so it is and should be.*

5. Place all of the materials/ingredients in the pouch and put it under the side of the bed on which your lover sleeps and s/he will always be faithful.

Peaceful Endings Spell

For any witch wanting to replace the pain, confusion, stress, and hurt that comes along with the ending of a relationship (even if they are the one who wanted it over) with peace of mind, clarity, and tranquility for all involved, taking this cleansing bath ritual is the way to go. A witch friend of mine was headed to the dreaded divorce court after 11 years of marriage. They had one child who was eight years old. It was an awful time for everyone involved, but it was better than staying in an unhappy situation. She said this spell changed her, to the point that the whole family practiced it once a week during the difficult time and the couple peacefully and amicably separated.

HOW LONG IT TAKES:
30-45 minutes
WHAT YOU'LL NEED:
1 rose quartz crystal
5 drops of lavender essential oil
4 drops of rose essential oil
3 drops of rosemary essential oil
1 cup Epsom salts
½ cup coarse Himalayan pink salt

STEPS:

1. Place all of your ingredients into a potion jar, including the rose quartz crystal.

2. Infuse the potion with your positive intention by holding your hands or wand over the potion. Imagine peaceful love flowing from a

never-ending source within your heart, down your arms, into your hands, through your fingers, into your wand, and into the potion of salts.

Interloper Be Gone Spell

Sometimes it is very necessary to remove negative people who just don't seem to get the message. It is not always that they are negative in their own right. Sometimes, their involvement in your affairs is what creates negativity in your life. I had a friend who was a bit down on his luck, going through a tough breakup. He had lost his job and was having a great deal of anxiety. Of course, I wanted to help and invited him to stay with me, for what in my mind was going to be a week or so. I did everything I could to ease his suffering. I don't think I ever put my wand down and my crystals were starting to grow heavy. I just couldn't seem to tell him he had to leave.

After a month, he was still on my couch. It was driving me nuts. I had finally had it. I very gently and kindly said to him, "I think it is time for you to move on and find a new place where you can be happy." He said he agreed, but then another week went by and it was as if the conversation had never happened. In this case, I could not ask his permission to do magic to get him to leave. But I did tell him I would cast a spell wishing him better times. And so I did. Two days later, another friend of his invited him to Florida. Happy days were here again and I didn't have to worry about any karmic backlash. Here is the spell, just in case you find yourself in a similar predicament.

HOW LONG IT TAKES:
15 minutes
WHAT YOU'LL NEED:
Black obsidian tumblers
1 black candle

1 piece of paper
Pen
1 bowl

STEPS:

1. Write the full name of the person on the piece of paper.

2. Place the black candle in the center of the bowl.

3. Create a sacred barrier around the candle with the black obsidian tumblers.

4. Light the candle and chant while burning the piece of paper:

> *Crystal of black; this candle burns slow.*
> *From my life (name) must go.*
> *As it is and should be.*

5. Snuff out the candle and bury the crystals away from your home.

6. Throw away the candle.

10

PROSPERITY SPELLS

Financial prosperity is an important aspect of our lives but is far from easy to achieve. Many people fall into debt, dislike or hate their jobs, or can't even hold down a job. Sometimes it seems like there is no end in sight, only endless days of labor just to make ends meet. There is absolutely nothing wrong with the desire for money. If you are struggling, it is only because you have to learn how to attract money; rituals will help you to do just that. Every person is concerned with becoming financially independent and enriching their lives and the lives of those they love. You would be surprised how many wealthy people in this world consult witches, fortune tellers, and psychics before they conduct their financial transactions. The most common wish when it come to money is "to make it." That, right there, often calls for magic.

Debt Relief Spell

If you are down on your luck and your debt is piling up, use this debt relief spell and watch your debt disappear. Practical steps must also be taken, obviously. This spell works in two ways; one is magic and the other is to help you to be mindful when it comes to your finances.

> HOW LONG IT TAKES:
> 25 minutes
> WHAT YOU'LL NEED:
> Photocopies of your bills
> 1 peridot crystal
> 1 malachite crystal
> 1 green aventurine crystal
> 1 black candle
> 1 cauldron

STEPS:

1. Place the black candle in the center of your cauldron.

2. Surround the candle with the crystals.

3. Tear up the photocopies of your bills into tiny pieces.

4. Light your candle and imagine all of your debt burning down to ashes. Chant 13 times:

This spell is to make me free of debt,
No more over money will tears be wept.
As it is and should be.

5. Place the crystals and ashes into a paper bag and bury the bag away from home.

Monetary Magic Spell (Draw Money)

Monetary spells are a part of white magic. Like all white magic, money spells are cast to decrease the weight of negative aspects associated with finances, and increase the positive aspects. This spell will attract financial gains into your life. Believe me, money will come. However, don't expect to win the lottery the day after you do this spell. You will come into abundance, though, such as a hike in pay, a new, high-paying job, or an unexpected monetary gift. It is hard to tell how the spell will be manifested, but it will be manifested in the form of money.

> HOW LONG IT TAKES:
> 10 minutes
> WHAT YOU'LL NEED:
> Full moon
> 1 green aventurine
> Green or silver cloth
> Tea Tree essential oil
> 1 silver coin (a silver dollar would work great)

STEPS:

1. Sit under the moonlight with your silver or green cloth on the ground.

2. Place your silver coin on your cloth.

3. Place your green aventurine crystal on top of the silver coin.

4. Gently wave your wand or your hands over your crystal and coin, while visualizing yourself picking up all of the silver the moon has spilled.

5. While you see yourself picking up all of the money, chant aloud:

> *Thank you spirit of the moon,*
> *For bringing abundance to me so soon.*
> *You filled my pockets over with silver*
> *And now the gold will flow like a river.*
> *As it is and should be.*

I Have Confidence in Me Spell

How many times in your life have you passed up an opportunity because you were so sure you either didn't deserve it or there was no chance you would be able to achieve it? Have you passed up chances to invest in your own small business or travel on a whim? Are there times you wish you had spoken up, but were too afraid of other people's reactions? After today, you can leave your insecurities and doubts behind and radically change your attitude. Going forward, you will be confident enough to be the captain of your own ship of life, thanks to a bit of magic, a few powerful crystals, and willingness with intent.

HOW LONG IT TAKES:
5 minutes at night and 15 minutes the next morning
WHAT YOU WILL NEED:
1 hematite
Plain or stationery paper
Cinnamon
1 brown candle
1 rose quartz
Ginger
Thyme
1 pink pen, marker, or pencil

STEPS:

1. Write down eight (the lucky feng shui number) positive affirmations with your pink pencil, such as, "I am confident," "I am wonderful," and "I am strong."

2. Place all the other ingredients inside the paper and fold it up, so that the crystals, ginger, and thyme are on the inside.

3. Keep it next to your mirror or wherever you get dressed in the morning.

4. In the morning, light the brown candle.

5. Sprinkle cinnamon over the top of the candle and light it while chanting:

> *Burning candle, lovely wind,*
> *Bring me confidence from within.*
> *I'm calling for courage from above.*
> *I cast this spell for strength and love.*
> *So it is as it should be.*

6. Keep the parcel with the crystals inside until you don't need it anymore.

Get a Job Spell

These days, getting a job isn't easy, especially one that you will look forward to going to every day. Thanks to spells that work by the law of attraction, coupled with your commitment and energy, all the intention you will be putting into this spell will give you what you need to get that job offer you have been waiting for. Luck, work, prosperity, and good fortune will find you, and you'll be blessed.

> HOW LONG IT TAKES:
> 1 week
> WHAT YOU'LL NEED:
> Waxing crescent moon
> 1 green aventurine crystal
> Clove essential oil
> Rice
> Bay leaf
> Sea salt
> 1 dish

STEPS:

1. Wait for a waxing crescent moon. Set your altar or cast your spell on the ground.

2. Make a circle of protection. Using sea salt, make a circle on your altar or on the ground around you for protection.

3. Set your intentions for a job into your rose quartz or tiger's eye crystal.

4. Put two drops of clove essential oil onto your crystal.

5. Place the crystal on your dish.

6. Add about a handful of rice and put the bay leaf on top of the rice.

7. Wave your hands or your wand over the dish and chant:

> *Bring to me this job I need*
> *I'll do the work--I'll do the deed*
> *The doors will open wide for me*
> *As things will be as they should be*

8. After one week, remove the crystals and keep them near you until you get the job.

You're Promoted Spell

This spell will help get you the promotion for which you have been working so long and hard. Sometimes, a bit of a crystal magic boost is just what the higher-ups need to put pen to paper, landing you that well-earned promotion. Casting this spell can bring words of praise your way, along with a raise in pay. Sometimes, the result of this spell may even be a new job offer. Take all things into consideration when projecting your intention into your spell.

> HOW LONG IT TAKES:
> 45 minutes
> WHAT YOU'LL NEED:
> 1 citrine crystal (charisma)
> 1 amethyst (wisdom)
> 1 sunstone (career success)
> 1 handheld bell

STEPS:

1. Cast a sacred circle or circle of protection.

2. Arrange your three crystals on the circle's edge with the sunstone crystal at the northernmost point.

3. Place the other two crystals according to your intuition in the southeastern and southwestern points.

4. You should be able to visualize a triangle with equal sides, with each crystal at each point of the shape.

5. Stand in front of the sunstone (northern) crystal with your bell.

6. Ring the bell three times loudly and chant:

> *May the powers of wisdom, charisma, and job success*
> *Grant me a promotion and my career be blessed.*
> *As it is and should be.*

7. Imagine your boss or higher-ups congratulating you on your promotion as if it already has happened, raise your arms over your head and chant:

> *I cast my intention for a promotion into the universe.*
> *May the spirits of luck, good fortune, and perseverance*
> *look upon me with favor. As it is and should be.*

8. Walk around your circle three times, again, but in a counterclockwise fashion; open your circle. Chant:

> *The spell is done and the circle is open.*
> *May the universe bless my intention for a promotion.*
> *As it is and should be.*

9. Pick up your crystals and put them near you at your workplace, touching them frequently until you receive your promotion.

Spell to Help You Focus

Sometimes there just aren't enough hours in the day. It's all hustle and bustle. But the ability to focus is critical to your success if you want to move ahead, learn new skills, be a better partner, and to anything else you need to do. When you lose focus, mistakes can be made and the quality of your work suffers. It is harder to solve problems and everything seems frustrating. This is when your crystals can help. For improved focus, unblocking your upper chakras does the job.

HOW LONG IT TAKES:
20 minutes
WHAT YOU'LL NEED:
1 hematite
Rosemary
Peppermint essential oil
1 cup or saucer
1 yellow candle

STEPS:

1. Smudge the hematite crystal with sage.

2. Lay the rosemary in the cup and put the crystal on top.

3. Put two drops of peppermint oil on the crystal and the candle.

4. Light the candle.

5. Hold the hematite in your hand and chant:

> *This crystal will help me with focus and memory as I work/study (name your endeavor for the following week).*

6. Snuff out the candle and pass the hematite through the smoke and say:

> *As it is and should be.*

7. Carry the hematite crystal and anoint your wrists with peppermint because it stimulates the same area of the brain as caffeine.

Business Success Spell

There is a lot going on in the world and businesses are struggling more than ever. But with the right energy, focus, and a bit of crystal magic, you can embrace your success in business whether you're new or you are already established yourself. Business is business, and you want to be successful. I am going to share with you a spell that will improve your business endeavors and raise your vibrational frequency at the same time. This will help you to cope with the stressors of being in business.

HOW LONG IT TAKES:

25 minutes

WHAT YOU'LL NEED:

1 citrine

1 green or gold sachet bag

1 piece of paper

1 green ink pen

Basil

Bay leaf

Orange zest

Gold or green thread

1 sewing needle

1 green or white candle

3 silver coins

Red rose petals

STEPS:

1. Start your spell in a peaceful room and meditate in a sitting position for a few minutes.

2. Put the bay leaf, basil, orange zest, coins, and citrine crystal into the perfume bag.

3. Write your intention on your paper in green ink. Be very specific: "I will have success in my business ventures."

4. Draw your business logo (if you have one) or any symbols of prosperity and success on the paper.

5. Fold up the paper into a parcel, put it in the bag and close the bag.

6. Hold your sewing needle over the candle flame while chanting your intention three times.

7. Sew your spell bag shut.

8. Do not blow out your candle, snuff it out.

9. Keep your charm bag with you or put it in your workspace.

10. When important business transactions or transitions take place, light your candle for a few minutes and then snuff it out, repeating your intention again.

Victory, Victory, Victory Spell

One of my favorite things about magic is that it is proactive! I just love this aspect of spell casting. Being proactive is the way to do the happy dance of victory. Getting the right crystals, keeping them cleansed and charged, keeping a sacred space, and knowing how to create a protective circle are all essential. These are all crystal-guided pathways to victory. I also love this spell. There is something very powerful about a clockwise spiral. Not sure why, but it resonates with me on a deep level and I think it will do the same for you.

HOW LONG IT TAKES:

15 minutes

WHAT YOU'LL NEED:

1 aventurine

1 hematite

1 pen

1 piece of gray or silver paper

Allspice

Cumin

Garlic

Basil

Ginger

Onion

1 abalone shell

STEPS:

1. Write the word "victory" on the piece of paper.

2. Draw the counter-clockwise spiral or the Irish victory symbol seen below.

3. Fold up the paper and put it in the abalone shell.

4. Place both crystals on top.

5. Add the herbs on top.

6. Chant the following words eight times:

> **Crystal of power, crystal of might,**
> **Grant me victory here tonight.**

Crystal of power, crystal today,
Victory, victory, I am here to say.
As it is and should be.

7. After three hours, grab the crystals and keep them on your altar or near your bed.

Legal Eagle Mojo Bag Spell

When it comes to legal issues, we either want to avoid them at all costs, or beat them at all costs. You want the results to be in your favor and any accusations taken away from you. This is where magic comes in. With the right spell, you can move things closer or farther away. This mojo bag is great to have around, just in case.

HOW LONG IT TAKES:

45 minutes

WHAT YOU'LL NEED:

1 drawstring bag

1 pen

1 piece of paper

3 hematite crystals

1 very small hematite

3 nails

Red string or thread

Sage clippings

1 drop of mugwort oil

1 vial court case oil

My Court Case Oil Recipe:

1/8 cup of almond oil

4 drops lavender oil

3 drops patchouli oil

Infuse with very small hematite crystals placed in the small sacred oil container

Store in a cool and dark place

STEPS:

1. Prepare my court case oil ahead of time.

2. Write your intention on a piece of paper.

3. Anoint three hematite crystals with the oil.

4. Tie red thread or string around the nails.

5. Put all ingredients into the pouch.

6. Carry with you until court date or when dealing with any legal issues. It is important that you **don't** take the mojo bag into any government buildings as the nails will set off metal detectors!

7. Anoint your wrists with the oil before any legal situation and state to yourself, "as it should be."

Lucky Numbers Spell

Wouldn't it be nice if we had a spell for the lottery? I often wonder if any lottery winners practice magic. Simply given the law of odds, you would think some do. However, there is much to think about when it comes to numbers and magic. People tend to choose numbers they believe are lucky. That is the same thing as believing in magic. I often ask naysayers of magic if they have a lucky number. They almost always do. Oddly enough, they don't see the irony. Let's learn this spell.

HOW LONG IT TAKES:
30 minutes
WHAT YOU'LL NEED:
6 green aventurine crystals
1 green candle
Chamomile powder
Extra virgin olive oil
2 dice
1 green ink pen
1 piece of paper
1 penny

STEPS:

1. Mix one drop of olive oil with chamomile powder and rub into your hands. Repeat this before gambling.

2. Draw a four-leaf clover on a piece of paper and put four 7's in a circle around it.

3. Place in the center of the table.

4. Put the penny on top of the paper.

5. Put the candle on top of the penny.

6. Place the green aventurine crystals around the candle.

7. Put the dice on your favorite numbers and put them inside the circle.

8. Light the candle and say:

> ***I cast this spell before the dice, powers that be, make my win nice.***
> ***As it is and should be.***

9. Snuff out the candle, put your betting shoes on and good luck!

11

PROTECTION SPELLS

The fact of the matter is, when it comes to protection spells, every home and item in the home contains energies that you or someone has brought in. It may be a purchased item or a gifted item. However, it always has its own energy. Usually, energies are neutral or good, however, they can also be negative. Sometimes, bad things happen while items are in our possession. We don't want to throw away certain things that are either expensive, have been in the family a long time, or have some other important meaning. I have come across random items that just seem to cover me with an ominous feeling, and I am not sure why, but I am sure it is a case of negative energy! This chapter will cover how to protect yourself, your home and office, your car, and any other possession you have.

Sacred Boundary Protection Spell for Your Home

In my years of practicing magic, I have counselled many on spells that can be cast to ensure protection for people, property, and homes. In reality, protecting the home is one of the more popular uses for magical work. Home protection spells have been cast since the ancient Egyptian, Greek, and Roman times, and they are cast all around the world. This spell is the one I feel is the safest, so I am happy to share it with you. This spell should forever protect your home.

HOW LONG IT TAKES:
3 days
WHAT YOU'LL NEED:
1 black tourmaline
1 citrine
1 rose quartz
1 fluorite
1 clear quartz
3 large nails
1 black candle
1 bulb of garlic
Water
Wine
1 bowl

STEPS:

1. Smudge, cleanse, and fill your crystals with your intention to protect your home.

2. Peel some of the garlic skin and lay under the iron nails.

3. Place the three nails in a bowl in the shape of a triangle on top of the garlic skin.

4. In the center of the triangle, place the clear quartz.

5. Place the other three crystals at the points of the triangle.

6. Sprinkle it with the water and wine.

7. Do this for three days.

8. On the fourth day, throw the crystals out into your yard and drive the nails into the ground.

9. Chant:

As it is and should be.

Privacy Please Spell

It can be very challenging to have to put up with negativity in our life, especially when it comes in the form of a neighbor. After working all day, coming home should be an opportunity to rejuvenate and to have some privacy. Nosy neighbors or even friends can really put a damper on relaxing in your home. After all, no one wants neighbors who project negative energy into their homes.

HOW LONG IT TAKES:
25 minutes

WHAT YOU'LL NEED:
1 bowl
1 selenite
1 smoky quartz
1 black tourmaline
Olive oil
Chamomile leaves

STEPS:

1. Cleanse your crystals thoroughly.

2. Roll them in the olive oil and then the chamomile leaves and put them one at a time in your bowl.

3. Speak your intention aloud for each crystal.

4. Write your intention on a piece of paper and tuck it under the black tourmaline crystal.

5. With your palms facing the crystals, imagine sending white light toward them.

6. Ask the universe for privacy, safety, friendliness, and positive relationships with all of your neighbors and the rest of your community.

7. Speak this chant:

> *This spell I cast is for privacy today*
> *To make nosy people go away.*
> *No harm intended to see this through.*
> *It's only solitude I pursue.*
> *As it is and should be.*

Have a Safe Trip Spell

Right up there with protecting yourself and your home, spells for safe traveling are some of the more popular spells to cast. If you think about it, many people have some form of protection charm hanging from their rearview mirror or in the glove compartment of their vehicle, in a pocket, or in a suitcase. We have all types of spells for personal space and home protection, but we need spells like this one for when we are away from our home or traveling.

HOW LONG IT TAKES:
10 minutes
WHAT YOU'LL NEED:
1 bowl
1 smoky quartz crystal
Dried mint
Comfrey root
1 4-inch square of blue fabric
White string

STEPS:

1. Place the bowl next to your open suitcases.

2. Hold the smoky quartz in your dominant hand.

3. Light the dried herbs.

4. Wave the smoke over the suitcase.

5. Zip the crystal into one of the inside compartments of your luggage.

6. Repeat steps 1-5.

7. Tie the crystal into the blue fabric.

8. Walk around your car three times with the crystal package, imagining a protective barrier around it and chant:

> *I am going there, as I am here;*
> *my travel is safe, my road is clear.*
> *I cast this spell to guard my car.*
> *It runs well and can travel far.*
> *As it is and should be.*

9. Put the enwrapped crystal in your glove compartment.

Mental Block Removal Spell

I want to issue a word of caution with this spell. There are several crystals that are very useful in removing mental blocks. It has been my experience that, sometimes, crystals can unblock issues that you may not be ready to deal with. Therefore, I would suggest beginning with a crystal that manifests in a more subtle manner, such as a rose quartz. This will only set free issues you are ready to accept and move beyond. Next in strength, perform your ritual with lapis lazuli to remove blockages that were hiding the truth from you. When you're ready, malachite unblocks deeper emotional issues and may leave you in tears. Lastly, obsidian can be used to blast through the rest of your blockages. This may leave you temporarily bewildered.

> HOW LONG IT TAKES:
> It varies
> WHAT YOU'LL NEED:
> 1 rose quartz
> 1 malachite
> 1 obsidian
> 1 lapis lazuli

STEPS:

1. Wait until sunset or midnight.

2. Create a sacred circle.

3. Focus on your intention to remove mental blockages.

4. As the sun goes down, chant:

As the sun goes down or as midnight reigns, my mind is free.
Clear all mental blockages from me.
As it is and should be.

5. Repeat the chant several times or until you feel the blockage is removed, and when you're ready move to the next crystal, repeat the steps.

Banishing Spell

Banishing should be considered an almost natural skill for any witch to cultivate. It is a cornerstone of spell practice and was the first thing I learned as a new witch. Whether you are banishing a situation, a person, negativity, or an unwanted spirit, this spell is an important one to have in your witch's tool kit!

HOW LONG IT TAKES:
15 minutes

WHAT YOU'LL NEED:
1 apple
1 small obsidian
1 mint leaf
1 knife
1 skewer
Black ribbon

STEPS:

1. Write what you want to banish on a piece of paper.

2. Horizontally cut the apple in half.

3. Dig out the core of each half.

4. Rub one half of the apple with the mint leaf.

5. Stick the crystal and the piece of paper in the apple.

6. Skewer the apple together.

7. Tie the apple together with black ribbon.

8. Bury the apple in your yard.

Give Me Courage Spell

At some point in everyone's life, fear takes over and we can act cowardly. If you have ever seen the *Wizard of Oz*, you may remember that the lion lacked courage. But, if you noticed, he was the one who always showed courage. He just needed to believe in himself, just like the scarecrow and the tin man needed to believe in themselves... just like you or me. It is always our intention to be courageous, but every now and then, we need a bit of a magical boost to summon our courage from deep within.

HOW LONG IT TAKES:
20 minutes
WHAT YOU'LL NEED:
1 moonstone
2 yellow candles

STEPS:

1. Light the candle on the left and chant:

Candle on the left,
Guide me through my quest.

2. Light the candle on the right and chant:

Candle on the right,
Give me courage and might.

3. Hold the moonstone in the palm of your dominant hand tightly.

4. With your palm facing downwards, wave your hand over the top of the candles (be careful not to burn yourself) and chant:

> *From these flames of fire*
> *and moonstone with desire,*
> *it is courage, I admire.*

5. For 60 seconds, with your eyes closed, imagine yourself in an act of courage. Play the scenario out in your mind to your desired result three times and chant three times:

> *I now have courage at the start.*
> *I now have courage in my heart.*
> *I now have courage in my walk.*
> *I now have courage when I talk.*
> *As it is and should be.*

Children are Sacred Spell

All parents', witches included, number one priority is protecting their children. Guarding children from physical, emotional, spiritual, and emotional harm is the single most important aspect of a parent's life.

> HOW LONG IT TAKES:
> 1 hour
> WHAT YOU'LL NEED:
> 2 small rose quartz crystals
> Super glue
> White cotton
> White cloth (approx. 1 foot)
> 1 lock of hair from the child or nail clippings/baby tooth
> 1 pen
> 1 piece of paper
> Rose essential oil
> 2 cups of caraway seeds
> White thread

STEPS:

1. Lay out your cloth and hand-draw a teddy bear on it.

2. It doesn't have to be perfect, but both sides should fit on the cloth because the front and back will be sewn together.

3. Write the child's or children's name on the paper.

4. Place two drops of rose oil on the rose quartz crystal.

5. Sew the front and back, leaving the top open for stuffing.

6. Fold up the paper and put it into some of the cotton.

7. Place the puppet to the side.

8. Put all of the items belonging to the child inside the puppet, then add the caraway seeds until it is full. It doesn't have to be stuffed to the seams. Caraway seeds have protective qualities.

9. Stuff the rest with the cotton.

10. Sew the doll closed.

11. Super glue the two small rose quartz to the cloth as the eyes. If you don't want to do that, place a rose quartz crystal on the inside of the doll.

12. Place your doll on your altar for three days. Three times a day, wave your hand or wand over it with your intention spoken aloud.

13. Put the doll in a hidden spot somewhere in the child's room but out of reach. Chant:

> *I hide you in (the child's name) room.*
> *Guard this child with great stealth.*
> *Protect this child from any dread.*
> *Bless his/her health from toe to head.*
> *As is it and should be.*

Ward Off Illness Spell

We are all working diligently to stay healthy and avoid any type of illness. We also want to shield and protect our loved ones, especially those most vulnerable. So on top of practicing regular preventive care, I thought of this spell's intention to protect and ward off illness from any new diseases, and remove any new diseases from anyone visiting or staying in our home. It is both preventive and protective. I was led by a bit of folk magic and pure intuition.

HOW LONG IT TAKES:
1 hour
WHAT YOU'LL NEED:
1 clear quartz crystal
1 rose quartz crystal
1 amethyst
1 purple candle
1 picture of yourself or the person for whom you want to ward off illness
Chamomile tea
Lavender essential oil
Eucalyptus essential oil
Abalone shell or fireproof container

STEPS:

1. Prepare a sacred space with all of your materials in front of you.

2. Put your photo into the abalone shell or fireproof container.

3. Place your clear quartz crystal atop the photo.

4. Place the other crystals in a circle around the container in the form of a triangle with the amethyst at the top point.

5. Put a drop of each essential oil on the clear quartz crystal.

6. Anoint each crystal with a drop of each essential oil.

7. Light the candle.

8. Look into the fire of the candle and visualize yourself turning away any and all illness and pain, turning dark to light.

9. Close your eyes and picture a glowing protective barrier coming from the crystals and flowing around you or the person for whom you are warding off illness.

10. Visualize a glowing triangle surrounding the photo.

11 Chant:

> *I cast this spell to turn away*
> *Any illness headed my way.*
> *I am strong and healthy now.*
> *I thank you spirits; I pledge my vows.*
> *As it is and should be.*

CONCLUSION

I hope you have enjoyed this exciting guide through the world of crystal magic. Crystals are powerful and versatile, loving, and mystical. They will protect you, bring you good fortune, and keep you company when you are feeling low.

With this book of crystal spells, you should be able to set your intentions and sharpen your magic in ways that will satisfy you and take to where you want to be as a new spell caster. If you were already experienced in the practice of magic, I hope that I have added wonderful new spells to your repertoire.

At this point, you have hopefully learned how to keep your crystals cleansed and charged, have some sacred moon water tucked away, and can cast spells ranging from love potions, good health and banishing to protecting your home and children and making more money!

Finally, it is my sincerest wish that you use this book to hone your own unique spell-casting styles using a wide range of crystals. I hope you learned how to keep your chakras balanced. Most of all, I hope that you have gained an understanding of the importance of intent and intuition. Like I always say, "as it is and should be!"

THE HERB MAGIC SPELL BOOK

A BEGINNER'S GUIDE FOR SPELLS FOR LOVE, HEALTH, WEALTH, AND MORE

INTRODUCTION

I was introduced to herb magic by a witch friend, and it took me a long time to learn how to use each herb correctly and how different herbs can work together. I wrote this book to make it easier for beginners to get started. As I learned what worked, I added to my Book of Shadows, from which the spells in this book are drawn. I now have an extensive collection of herbs in my pantry that I have grown or collected myself. I love spending time in my magic garden and walking in the woods to gather herbs. The walks and the garden make me feel much more connected to the world around me. This book will show you how to use herbs that you may already have in your kitchens for personal care, healing, rituals, spiritual practices, and spells. You will learn spells, notes of caution, recipes, their magical correspondences, and lore for each herb. Also, you will learn how to combine herbs with crystals, candles, colors, elemental energies, and more, for powerful magical workings. From arrowroot to turmeric and elixirs to incense, this valuable guide to herbal magic is designed to help you broaden your magic and spellcraft for a more magical and natural life.

The history of herbs, plants, and herbal magic is discussed to provide an interpretation guide for herbal magic. Various herbal spells, rituals, and methodologies are outlined, so you can incorporate them into your daily life and create a mystical herbal environment where your spells can be manifested. Each spell provides instruction on how to communicate your intentions within and throughout your use of herbs and using your intuition to interpret findings to discover the beautiful relationships we have with worlds beyond our own. Natural elements coupled with herbs are a considerable component of practicing witchcraft. Practitioners of herbal magic have been doing research and practicing the craft since the beginning of humankind. I am sure the plants and the elements were communicating with each other long before that.

A potion, ritual, charm, or spell is only as good as its ingredients. Many people have come to use herbal remedies, essential oils, and crystals for unblocking and balancing the chakras, raising spiritual vibrations, astral projection, and providing offerings to deities, along with the various intentions for each spell. Herbs and their oils are used to gain information from our subconscious mind and the spiritual realms. By using essential herbs in your spells, you can direct very specific energies towards your intentions for healing, love, prosperity, personal growth, luck, happiness, travel, retirement, and other rituals and magical traditions, of which there are too many to name.

Considering this is a book of spells, it's evident that many items, materials, and ingredients go into the art of magic. Rosemary, ginger, lemon balm, cayenne, sage, salt, garlic, and basil are just a few of the common herbal ingredients explained in detail for your information gathering. Essential herbs are used to amplify and enhance the magic of these spells. Herbs can be used in rituals, as talismans, incorporated into amulets and sachets, and even to anoint our physical bodies. In addition, they are also used to create powerful witchcraft goods. Our ancestors documented during medieval times that prayers were uttered for summoning guardian angels, and incantations were cast to ward off illnesses. Herbs such as rosemary have a long, rich history of being used to remember the dead and to enhance clarity and memory. So you will see many valuable rosemary tips as you read on. In fact, Shakespeare wrote of the memory-enhancing powers of rosemary in his plays *Romeo and Juliet* and *Hamlet*. Combining specific phrases, specialized rhymes, symbolic items, and herbs is far from unique to the Anglo-Saxon world. I consider my incantations the interlocutor of herbs acting together in a desired way to bring me my desired effects. To use the magic of herbs you need a knowledge of their properties, what they do, and how to use them properly. I wrote this book on herbal magic as a guide to connect you with the traditions, correspondences, and healing magic of various herbs and how they can bring better health and wellness, light, happiness, and love into your life. Please enjoy!

PART 1:

UNDERSTANDING HERB MAGIC

It is easy to underestimate the power of herbs in healing magic. People tend to go directly to over-the-counter manufactured medicines to treat inflammation, headaches, and indigestion because we have been conditioned all of our lives to depend on prescription or commercial drugs. The beautiful thing about herbs is that they are not formulated. They are provided by Mother Earth and nurtured by water, sun, and all that is natural in this world. You can choose an herb here and choose an herb there and have healing powers in the truest sense of the phrase. Each part of a plant has special and significant properties, so my primary objective in Part 1 is to teach you about them. Magic Herbs come from the leaves, roots, petals, and stems of special plants that can be used for healing magic, charging, and cleansing objects, or you can simply consume their magical properties. This half of the book is meant to explain how herb magic works, which is useful before jumping right into the spell work in Part 2.

1

THE MAGIC OF HERBS

Originally, there was no difference between "magic" and medicine. Now we recognize that medicine works on the physical, and magic works on the spiritual level. Without the lore of European magic, medicine and science could never have developed successfully. The evidence of the critical role magic has played in the origins of modern medicine is overwhelming. In order to understand the role magic has played in medicine, we have to be aware of the differences between the magic of a thousand years ago and what it has evolved into today. The magic at the beginning of the 20th century, referred to as natural magic, was predominately based on the belief that God created this world and that every individual component was not only connected but that correspondences between creatures in one part of the continuous chain corresponded to elements or creatures in another part of this unbroken chain in God's creation, with the purpose being the underlying belief. Nothing was done in vain by Nature or

God. Therefore, there is a purpose for everything. The belief was that God left clues as to those correspondences, such as the human brain and the flesh of a walnut in its shell. It was assumed that occult powers were part of these correspondences, and that was the reason they could affect each other. The magician's role was to identify the correspondences and their precise magical effect, so they could then be put to use.

Just as magic has been a part of scientific history, healing with herbs is as old as humankind itself. The relationship between humanity and our quest for medicine in nature dates back thousands of years. It is evidenced by historical documents, original herbal medicines, and preserved monuments (plants in their own right have become supreme documents that have to be preserved). Awareness of the use of herbs in medicine comes from years and years of fighting against illness and disease, which led man to pursue drugs in leaves, bark, seeds, fruit, and other plant parts. Present-day pharmacotherapy has accepted the active ingredients in herbs and has included many in modern medicine, including a broad range of medications of plant origin; information that was known to ancient peoples and used throughout millennia.

Herbal Magic on a Global Perspective

Herbal magic is an ancestral and traditional practice, especially for healing, and has many global origins. Witches and plants have converged naturally with provincial cultural beliefs and norms, seasonal patterns, health concerns, and community needs, gathering together to learn, discuss, and provide feedback to others about their magical experiences with herbs. Many people who live in plant-based cultures are natives. Also, in many developing countries, traditional herbal medicine is still the main source of healthcare, according to the World Health Organization (WHO).[1]

The use of herbs in healing cross-culturally has grown significantly in the past fifty years. It is now a very popular alternative medicine method and a profitable market for the health and wellness industry. Many people use healing herbs in their daily healthcare regimens through potions, elixirs, teas, culinary preparations, supplements, and tinctures. In addition, many mainstream medical practitioners add herbal medicines to their conventional protocols as a form of preventative medicine and treatment for chronic conditions. This magical renaissance has given way to an unprecedented relationship of herbalism as extensive historical lore, the world of healing magic, and a scientifically proven form of treatment in modern-day global capitalism.

Herbs and the Elements

Water, Air, Fire, and Earth are the four elements that make up the basic components of the Universe. All that is between the Earth and the spiritual realms is composed of one or a combination of these four elements. Many magical practitioners consider Spirit to be a fifth element that exists within the four elements. When it comes to incense burning in the Air or anointing with an herb, we draw directly upon the energies of the Elements to achieve our goal. To achieve the highest potency, get to know your element before working with something from its realm. The most basic manifestations of the elements come from nature. Earth can be a handful of soil, a leaf blowing in the wind for Air, a river flowing for Water, and an ember for Fire.

Many herbs correspond with the elements, and each element corresponds to a specific magical outcome:

EARTH promotes grounding, peace, business, stability, green growth, fertility, and employment. Herbs corresponding with Earth include:

Bisort	Honeysuckle	Fern	Mugwort
Oakmoss	Primrose	Rhubarb	Magnolia
Horehound	Patchouly	Vetivert	Vervain

AIR promotes freedom, divination, eloquence, intuition, travel, wisdom, intellect, and communication. Herbs corresponding with Air include:

Almond	Peppermint	Sage	Lemongrass
Lavender	Benzoin	Lemon Verbena	Mace
Marjoram	Star Anise	Marjoram	Acacia

WATER promotes peace, relaxation, psychism, healing, compassion, dreams, friendship, and reconciliation. The herbs corresponding with Water include:

Apple Blossom	Cherry	Lemon	Iris
Liquorice	Sweet Pea	Eucalyptus	Comfrey
Vanilla	Peach	Orchid	Sandalwood
Lilly	Elder	Tansy	Ylang-Ylang
Thyme	Coconut	Catnip	Lemon Balm
Camphor	Orris	Jasmine	Stephanotis
Spearmint	Plumeria	Violet	Hyacinth

FIRE promotes courage, passion, purification, magical power, defensive magic, and physical strength. Herbs corresponding with Fire include:

Basil	Dill	Nutmeg	Rose Geranium
Juniper	Lime	Marigold	Grains of Paradise
Sassafras	Peppermint	Fennel	Frankincense
Orange	Cinnamon	Carnation	Dragon's Blood
Garlic	Woodruff	Galangal	Angelica
Heliotrope	Coriander	Rosemary	Deer's Tongue

Why Herbs are a Great Place to Start with Magic

I am doing my happy dance when I blend spices and herbs and add a bit of magic! To start your own collection, all you need to do is gather some seeds, leaves, berries, bark, and a few bottles to concoct powerful ingredients to add to your spellwork. As a real-life practitioner of herbal magic, I am happy to provide you with great recipes, great spells, and overall great magic as you continue your journey through this book. Here are some steps for you to start on your path toward herbal magic:

TOUCH, SMELL, TASTE:

Crush your herbs and then rub them together and smell. Practice naming herbs and spices without looking at labels, or blindfold yourself and get together with family and friends and take turns guessing what the herb is using only smell and touch. Envelop yourself in the experience of the aroma. Create a collection of sacred tins and jars. Put your magic into selecting the container for each herb. Cleanse with sage (of course, you want to cleanse with an herb). Design and creatively enhance your labels, making some for whole herbs and some for your magical blends.

TWO HERBAL MAGIC RULES:

1. The oils in spices and herbs dissipate or can go bad after a while, so it is best to start with whole spices and grind them yourself as needed. You can buy the following pre-ground: garlic, cinnamon, turmeric, and sumac. Throw away any old spices you have that were pre-ground.

2. When starting out, use tried and true recipes and experiment with your own later, after learning how to combine your herbs and in what ratios. After making some blends from expertly written recipes, start using your own creativity, and herbal blending will soon become second nature.

PRACTICE:

The classic method for grinding herbs and making your own spices is by using a mortar and pestle. However, you can use an electric spice grinder for wizardry results. Here are some excellent methods for you to play with:

- Toast your spices before grinding.
- Smell after you grind your herbs.
- Add a little salt to your blend (great for popcorn).
- Don't rush. Enjoy the process; make sure you have allotted extra time for concocting.
- Keep your ground herbs and spice blends where you can see them so you remember to use them.
- Use them up within a couple of months.

2

HERB MAGIC BASICS

When we talk about herb magic, we may be referring to herbs, flowers, or even roots. All witches honor wild things and use ingredients given to us by the Earth. It is believed that herbs are probably the oldest known instruments of magic. Before the separation of medicine and magic, most healing practices were accomplished with herbal concoctions, prayer, and rituals. In modern times, a steaming cup of tea concocted with herbs can have emotional, spiritual, and nutritional benefits. Herbs are symbolic of the magical powers of the Elements. They begin as seeds of the Earth, where they are provided with nourishing minerals, and then interact with Fire (sunlight). From this phase, carbon dioxide is converted to oxygen by consorting with Air. Air in the form of breezes and wind scatters the seeds and continues the circle of life. All of these phases cannot take place without Water. Plants are critical to the Earth's water cycle as they purify and help the movement of the soil into the atmosphere.

Here lies the great illustration of how the Elements correspond with herbs. Plants are living beings and communicate with their plant neighbors through their roots, pollen, exchanging minerals, vibrations, and in other mystical ways. Plant intelligence is the subject of many research projects these days. Growing your own herbs, berries, flowers, and plants will help you commune with the Elements and the insect and animal world. Herbs are versatile and very useful in the practice of magic. Keep them in sachets, spell jars, as talismans, and other charms used for your magical workings. Spellwork transfers the energy of the herbs into a form we can use to bring our intentions into the world!

Doctrine of Signature

We can learn a great deal just by looking closely at plants. Learning about the climate, local habitats, hydrology, soils, and wildlife will enrich your magic in many wonderful ways. For instance, rich dark leaves indicate that a plant may do well in soil that is sandy or may be able to endure periods of drought. Plants that are picky about access to their berries grow thorns. And flowers that smell badly rely on insects that feed on carrion to spread their seeds. For millennia, people have used the appearance of plants to divine their magical properties. The "Doctrine of Signatures" is a broad concept depicting the plant's features resembling a body part or condition that the herb can treat. Hence, scarlet roots can heal problems of the heart or blood. Ginseng root is used to aid male sexual vitality because it resembles male genitalia. The spotted leaves of lungwort are thought to resemble a diseased lung; these are all examples of the Doctrine of Signature. The herbs' common names are often associated with their signature. In medieval times, magicians believed that God created signatures when creating plants to communicate to people how to use them.

Creating Your Altar

You don't have to be at an altar to cast a spell, but creating sacred space with your altar is a great place to focus your intentions, energy and practice your craft. You can set your altar up anywhere your intuition tells you. I was drawn to a window in my bedroom, facing the west, where the sun sets. I also have one in my office next to my desk. Having an altar somewhere it cannot be disturbed is important because spells work for as long as you have corresponding items in a sacred space. Every witch has their own unique journey, so be sure you feel connected spiritually to your altar and anything that comes into contact with it. Cloths are placed on an altar (usually) to keep them clean. Choosing an altar cloth is also part of your craft. It is a magical procedure, and you can use anything to which you feel drawn. I believe in using natural items, such as silk or bamboo. Here are some ideas for the color you may want to choose for your cloth:

- Red corresponds with Fire, and its magical properties include passion, courage, willpower, love, and desire.
- Green corresponds with Earth, and its magical properties include money, health, fertility, luck, abundance, and nature.
- Yellow corresponds with Air, and its magical properties include happiness, intelligence, clarity, and memory.
- Blue corresponds with Water, and its magical properties include spirituality, wisdom, calmness, and relaxation.

- Pink corresponds with Fire, and its magical properties include nurturing, romance, friendship, and healing.
- Orange corresponds with Fire, and its magical properties include justice, sexuality, buying property, emotions, and intellect.
- Brown corresponds with Earth, and its magical properties include cooking, animals, grounding, gardening, and nature.
- Purple corresponds with Spirit, and its magical properties include sexuality, balance, love, and acceptance.
- White corresponds with Air, and its magical properties include clarity, light, peace, cleansing, and inspiration.
- Gold corresponds with Fire, and its magical properties include wealth, enlightenment, fame, and fortune.
- Silver corresponds with Water, and its magical properties include dreams, intuition, telepathy, and astral projection.

Include items or symbols attributed to what you are honoring. I have five candles, one for each of the four directions and one in the middle. They can also be representing the Elements. I fill a clear crystal bowl with blessed water. When I first started, I had a glass bowl with spring water, and it was fantastic magic. As time went on, my interests and intentions grew. Here are some suggestions as to how you can honor the Elements on your altar:

- *Air - East:* Windchimes, feathers, incense, magnifying glass, knife
- *Water - West:* Rocks, crystal ball, water bowl, driftwood, seaweed, salt

- *Earth - North:* Herbs, seeds, bones, soil, bonsai
- *Fire - South:* Candles, orange, yellow, red crystals and flowers, lava stones, cactus, spicy foods, lighter or matches

When getting ready to start working magic in your kitchen, an altar is the best place to begin. While the kitchen itself is a sacred space, having an altar for spellwork can be useful. It is totally up to you how far you want to go with your kitchen altar, and it depends on the amount of space you have and how extensive your magic methods are. Some practitioners have a special place on their countertop, which is helpful unless you have limited counter space. You can make hanging altars, place crystals and tea candles on the back of your stove, or hang wall decorations with small shelves. Wall shelves come in handy in small kitchens. Once you get into it, you will find your whole kitchen is somewhat of a functioning altar, with magical tools, a blessed stovetop, and magical herbs lighting up your life.

Creating a Workspace in Your Kitchen for Herbs

Whether you grew up in a small family or a large family, the kitchen is usually the heart of the home. In my family, people seem to gravitate towards the kitchen. It seems to be where people bond and socialize while smelling the aromas of what is about to bring them together. This sense of togetherness is part of the magic that happens in the kitchen. It can take on a life of its own and lead to traditions and rituals that spring from daily living. These traditions and rituals often form the foundation of a witch's energy when it comes to herbal magic. Some people scoff at traditional domestic folk magic in a kitchen setting, but this type of magic has deep power woven into the fabric of our lives. After all, what could be more important than family, community, food, and a sacred place that provides all three?

Since we use herbs in almost every dish we make, it is important to realize how their potent energies match their potent flavors. Adding a few herbs to anything takes it up a notch in beautiful ways while at the same time intermingling your magical intent into your dish. As previously discussed, start by adding basic herbs, then as you learn more, start pairing energies and flavors together. Look to the corresponding colors and elements list provided and match them to your intentions and your herbs or blends. The spices and herbs work differently for different people because everyone has their own unique vibrations. Some herbs work better for me than others. For instance, I always have great luck with basil, while sometimes my spells fall flat with rosemary. Needless to say, I use a lot of basil. Figuring out which herbs work best for you can greatly improve your spellwork. While it isn't mandatory, growing your own herbs, knowing the seasons that are best for growing each particular herb where you live, and learning how to work conjointly with your kitchen's spirits, as well as the spirits in your hometown, can add a great depth to your herbal magic. Spellwork transfers the energy of the herbs into a form we can use to bring our intentions into the world.

How to Grow Your Own Herbs

Step 1: Choose your containers. Choose pots or containers that you can move from your kitchen to your porch or outside and back to your kitchen and altar. Clay, metal, resin, or wood; it is up to your intuition. Just make sure there is an escape route for water drainage.

Also, size matters! Pick a pot that matches the size of the herb's growth you want to achieve. If the plant is in too big of a container, it will spend too much energy growing its roots. If a plant is cramped in a planter, it can become stressed out and die.

Step 2: Picking your herbs. If you are new to growing herbs, start simple. Basil, parsley, and mint are perfect for the new herbal magician. They lend themselves perfectly to frequent harvesting. Here are some other examples of herb choices and their properties:

- Mint: Grows aggressively, so it should be in an above-ground pot and does well with direct sunlight, but can do okay with some shade.
- Basil: Grows easily and needs to be well-watered. Use rich soil and provide direct sunlight.
- Parsley: Can grow with partial shade and does best in soil that is moist but well-drained.
- Oregano: Needs good drainage and full sunshine but does not do well in cold temperatures.
- Thyme: Needs less water, just moistened soil, and direct sunlight.
- Rosemary: Moisten the soil for the highly aromatic leaves of your rosemary plant. Do not leave it outdoors during winter months.
- Sage: Avoid planting it near cucumber (it affects the taste), but you can plant it near rosemary and cabbage. It needs well-drained soil and full direct sunlight.

Step 3: Start your herbal garden with starter plants. It will save you weeks of growing time and gives you a better chance of having a successful harvest.

Step 4: Choose the right soil, such as potting soil. Potting soil makes for better drainage than garden soil. Potting soil is porous and lighter, and gardening soil traps in moisture and is dense.

Step 5: Harvesting and caring for your herbs means watering them regularly. Harvest them sooner rather than later, as it will prime them for new growth.

Tools You'll Need for Your Herb Garden

1. Planters
2. Watering can
3. Fertilizer
4. Transplanter
5. Pruner
6. Labels
7. Grow light
8. Starter plants
9. Potting soil
10. Trowel

Enchanting Your Herbal Garden Tools

Enchanting or consecrating your herbal garden tools is the same as blessing your altar, crystals, candles, water, etc. Don't stop with just your garden tools. Enchant your cast iron skillet too. Just make sure to include your intent in all of your enchanting spells. Here are a few suggestions about how to make your garden tools magical:

- Get yourself a wood burner for a variety of magical needs. Burn symbols, sigils, words, and names into your spoons or potters.
- Draw a corresponding sigil with white chalk on the bottom of your cauldron or cast-iron prior to seasoning them.
- Burn your herbs like incense to enchant the whole kitchen and all of the utensils.
- Enchant your knives with protection spells and for sharpness.
- Keep clear quartz crystals near your herbs for overall powerful magic.

3

THE WHEEL OF THE YEAR

The Wheel of the Year represents the eight Wiccan and Neo-Paganism religious celebrations. It includes a celebration for the four solar festivals and the changing seasons: Fall equinox, summer solstice, spring equinox, and the winter solstice. The ancient Celts considered time cyclical. People are born and die, seasons change. However, everything comes again in some form or another, and naturally, the cycle repeats. In modern times, the Wheel of the Year helps pagans and witches keep balanced in an uncertain world. A scholarly mythologist named Jacob Grimm (1835) coined the term, and the Wiccan movement fixed the term in the 1950s. A core value of all pagan religions is to become aligned with nature. Celebrating the dates in the Wheel of the Year is meant to encourage a harmonious lifestyle with nature, not against it. In order to not depend on a predetermined beginning and end, the Wheel of the Year is a nonlinear arrangement of time. It's important to be in tune with what grows when in your local area and how that connects you to the earth and grounds you. Herbs and their folklore are an essential part of almost every pagan religion. Specifically, many of the Sabbats correspond with the magical properties of different herbs. The Wheel of the Year holy days include:

SAMHAIN

Samhain is a pagan religious festival to welcome the dark half of the year and hail the harvest's coming. Samhain celebrates the breaking down of the barriers between the physical world and the spirit world, bringing forth better interactions between humans and residents of the Otherworld.

Holiday: Halloween

Herbs:

Rosemary: Rosemary is a fantastic smudge for clearing and protection of all things sacred. Burn it for good health and vitality in the new year. Create a rosemary charm sachet to bring good people to you, and then blend it with thyme for the power to see them. It is also traditionally used at funerals to honor death as the great renewal of life. It has been said that rosemary is associated with women's culture and that it grows by houses where women are in charge. So, it should be no surprise that I have rosemary growing in front of my home! A ritual rosemary bath is a great way to prepare for Samhain.

Mugwort: Mugwort provokes visionary states by trance or dream. Use in teas and sachet charms for a ritual for the rites of Artemis. This charm will bring justice to wrongdoers and healing to those who have been harmed. I use it infused in water with wormwood to wash my crystal balls and scrying mirrors for blessings. Put a bit in your shoes to protect you from weariness.

Sage: Sage protects during Samhain and works to enhance wisdom for the new year and bring prosperity. Its magical properties also include longevity, fertility, and protection for pregnancy.

St. John's Wort: Removes negativity, protection, alleviates anxiety and depression. Worn to protect against mental illness and dried over fire and placed in windows to ward off necromancers, ghosts and to protect the family from lightning, fire, and misfortune. Drives away all that is evil in preparation for Samhain.

Chamomile: Used in teas to promote sleep and reduce anxiety. Drink before a spell casting or ritual to break curses and bring prosperity. Chamomile will entice a lover, promote well-being and happiness, bring sweet dreams, and regenerate spirituality.

Crystals: Bloodstone, Black Obsidian, Carnelian, Jet, Crystal Quartz, Onyx, and Jet.

Earth Event: Scorpio

Date: October 31

Occasion: Celebration of the dead; cleaning and releasing

YULE

The rebirth of the sun follows the longest night of the year. Yule symbolizes the newly-born solstice sun or the "Great God." What could represent Yule better than hauling an evergreen in from the woods and adorning it with ornaments and lights? Fir, cedar, juniper, and pine trees offer protection, prosperity, the life cycle, and rebirth as magical properties. Maybe you have noticed, when all of the trees lay down for the winter, the evergreen remains green. What better portrayal for the continuation of life?

Holiday: Christmas

Herbs:

Cinnamon: During ancient times, cinnamon was used as a preservative and an expensive flavoring agent in meats. During the 1st century A.D., it was worth ten times the equivalent weight of silver. Cinnamon sticks are made from evergreen bark. Very often, what you are buying in the store is not "true" cinnamon, but cassia. They are both from the same species. Use it in incense, teas, and potions for increased clarity and magical powers. Cinnamon correspondence with Yule is evident by its warmth. Use it to anoint your broom and use it for cleansing as it has antimicrobial actions.

Ginger: Ginger is my favorite! Nothing speaks Yule like gingerbread. It makes a wonderfully magical tea, too! Basically, this particular plant has one thing directly in common with Yuletide. It was not a Christmas herb until the 1700s. Ginger corresponds with the sun and Mars, and its magical properties include love, health, money, grounding, and creativity. It also is great for digestion. Ginger symbolizes the promise of beginnings; the new year. Make some gingerbread cookies, and the whole world smiles.

Peppermint: Peppermint is a hybrid of spearmint and watermint that occurred naturally in the mid-1600s. Obviously, the world is familiar with the correspondence between Yule and peppermint as it is symbolized around the world in the form of candy canes. Originally, they were given to children in the 1800s to keep them quiet during Christmas church services.

Nutmeg: Nutmeg comes from the evergreen tree, which also produces mace. Until recent times, both were very expensive. Back in the 1300s, one pound of nutmeg had the same value as one cow. It was only available from one South Pacific island until the British began growing it in other regions. Believe it or not, nutmeg, along with cinnamon and clove, was the source of wars being fought, as it was used in mincemeat preparations during the 12 days of Christmas. It corresponds with the element Fire, and its magical properties include fidelity, luck, money, and good health. Consider using nutmeg for your oaths rituals. ***WARNING: Nutmeg can be toxic in very large quantities, so season with good sense.

Crystals: Blue Calcite, Garnet, Fuchsite, Moss Agate, and Clear Quartz

Earth Event: Winter solstice: Capricorn

Date: December 20-25

Occasion: Fellowship, song, candlelight, and lighting the sacred fire

IMBOLC (BRIGID'S DAY)

Imbolc symbolizes pregnancy, the start of the lambing season, and the beginning of spring. It is associated with the earth awakening, hidden potential, the stirring of life, and the promise of renewal. It is a time to look forward and let go of the past. Spring cleaning is in the air, making room for new beginnings. This can be manifested by clearing your heart and mind, making wishes and making commitments, as well as cleaning your home. Brigid was the Celtic Goddess of poetry, smithcraft, and healing, and was such a part of the Christian faith, she was entitled St. Brigid. As the Fire Goddess of the Sun, she offers fertility to the people and the land. She is deeply connected to newborns and midwives. In the Wiccan religion, she is the Triple Goddess, but in her Maiden aspect at Imbolc.

Holiday: Candlemas

Herbs:

Angelica: Angelica is associated with the angels Gabriel and Michael. It corresponds with the sun and the element Fire. Magically it is used for protection against evil and for breaking hexes. It also has blessing properties, and you can grow it yourself to protect your garden and home. Added to a sachet or amulet, it will ward off evil spirits and illness, thereby increasing longevity. Take it with you as a talisman if you want to gamble. Added to a ritual bath, it is a great spell breaker. If your home needs to be exorcised, Angelica is the herb for the job. Burning the leaves is known to stimulate visions and enhance clairvoyance.

Heather: Heather provides us with the ability to see reality for what it is and to do so objectively. Bees love heather, symbolizing positive community living. Bees have long been associated with social order and communal living, with each bee having a clearly defined role, but the hive is viewed as a single organism rather than as thousands of individual bees. It symbolizes sacrifice and self-control. Heather's magical properties include enthusiasm, conjuring ghosts, making rain, sensuality, self-expression, and the possible consequences of unbridled passion. Heather's association with Imbolc helps us to understand the magic behind the holiday. Wear it for good luck. If you want to be visited by a loved one who has passed, at midnight, pick a sprig of heather and place it in some blessed water, and put it in the darkest corner of your home. Meditate on your lost loved one, and it is said their shadow will appear.

Celandine: Celandine represents a time for planting the first seeds, a time of hope for warmer days to come. Sheep, while impregnated, began to produce milk, which was a sign of spring approaching. Celandine aids in getting you out of a bind and in escaping any type of unwarranted imprisonment or entrapment. Every three days, place a new piece next to your skin, and any depression will be lifted. It is also a court-spell herb, in case you need to win the favor of a jury or judge. Celandine's power frees the mind of depression and will detoxify the liver and blood. It is also suggested to those suffering from cataracts.

Blackberry: The berries and the leaves of the blackberry bush are sacred to Imbolc and are used for healing and prosperity. One method for enhancing your spellwork is to sprinkle blackberry into a candle flame during your ritual. This adds more power to your spells. Use the leaves in your rituals for prosperity or add to an elixir for protection. I carry it in a charm pouch for its healing properties, and I love adding blackberry to my bathwater.

Crystals: Amethyst, Peridot, Moss Agate, Onyx, Selenite, Moonstone, and Sunstone

Earth Event: Midway between the winter solstice and the spring equinox: Aquarius

Date: February 1

Occasion: Celebration for the Earth Goddess's recovery postpartum, Lunar Fire Festivals Day of Feast, Earth Goddess gives birth

OSTRA (LADY DAY; BACCHANALIA)

The Wheel of the Year's second spring festival (in between Imbolc and Beltane) is a celebration of the equilibrium between extremes that happen during the seasons. It is the official start of spring and the exact moment of balance between the dark and the light. The days growing longer is symbolic of the transition of God from infancy into maturity. As the temperature warms upon the Earth, it becomes more fertile, and with that, greener, and buds start to blossom. Just writing about the buds starting to blossom gives me goosebumps. The bees start to pollinate as winter is past and being outside is enjoyable again. The heat of summer is yet to come, so this is the time for enjoying the equinox and its balanced energies.

Holiday: Easter

Herbs:

Lemongrass: For centuries, this herb has been used for healing. Lemongrass has been used historically for its oils. In the 1600s, it was shipped as a perfume around the world. People of great wealth anointed themselves with the precious oil to cover their own bodily smells. Medicinally, it helps relieve digestive issues, lower fevers, and provides antimicrobial and antibacterial properties. Magically, it aids in openness and communication, protection, love, and luck.

Spearmint: This is used for healing, love, and protection while sleeping. Burning spearmint works magically for healing respiratory illness. Carry it in a sachet for overall health and wellness, or use it in a ritual bath while enjoying its aromatic qualities. For wishing spells, write your intention on a piece of paper and wrap it in spearmint leaves. Wrap in a piece of red material, sew it closed with red thread, and keep it in a sacred place. Your wish will be granted by the time its smell has dissipated. Its magical properties affect dreams, relaxation, transformation, exorcism, animals, spirit offering, and protection against intruders and dangers. Spearmint is also advantageous to use in lust spells and as a good luck travel spell.

Dogwood: Some believe Jesus was crucified on a dogwood cross. It is associated with comfort, happiness, ancestor work, banishment spells, fertility, lust, love, and will protect your secrets. If you need to protect anything written down, use the oil and the flowers, and it will ward off any prying eyes. The sap of the dogwood is thought to grant wishes, and carrying a piece on your person will ward off rabid dogs. As the name implies, dogwood is as loyal as a dog! It will help you determine which things you should exclude from your life and grant you protection from those things. Plant it around your home for protection. My grandfather planted three dogwoods around his home. Clearly, he understood the power of three. He even brought sticks from all three when he moved.

Catnip: If you want to have a psychic bond with your cat, give her a bit of catnip (it will also give your kitty a nice buzz). Combined with rose petals, catnip makes a powerful love sachet. Hold it for a while in your hand until it warms up, and then hold hands with a friend to tighten your bond. Keep the catnip you had in your hand in a safe place. Hang it over your door or grow it near your home, and it will attract great luck and good spirits. It is also used to enhance happiness and beauty spells. Boxers have been known to chew catnip before a match for increased aggressiveness and good luck.

Crystals: Ocean Jasper, Azurite, Citrine, Lapis Lazuli, Chrysoprase, and Amazonite

Earth Event: Spring equinox: Aries

Date: March 20-23

Occasion: Spring cleaning, planting seeds

BELTANE

Beltane symbolizes the full exhilaration of spring. With winter months past, nature comes alive with warmer air and vibrant shades of green bursting free. The skies are full of singing birds, and spring flowers are blooming. It is a time of renewal and passion as the Goddess is impregnated with new life. Bonfires celebrate Beltane, and the maypole is dressed with ribbons as people, young and old, dance around it. For some covens, witches celebrate coupling, or the "great rite." Altars and other sacred places are decorated with branches and spring flowers and the hair of worshipers with wreaths of flowers.

Holiday: May Day

Herbs:

Dill: Powered by magic, dill helps with romance, protection, prosperity, and more. Whip yourself up a wonderful love potion along with creating a delicious fish dinner, and romance is in the air. Use dill leaves in a ritual bath to attract romance or ward off bad dreams by hanging a sprig of dill over your bed. Wear dill on your person and keep hateful, jealous, and hurtful people out of your location. Sniff the aromatics of dill to help you through emotionally difficult times. Create a powder out of your dill and dust your purse or wallet for good luck with money. Infuse it into a cool glass of lemonade for a love potion.

Lemon balm: This beautifully aromatic citrus-scented herb added to your spellwork is truly magic. Use it for success spells and carry it on you to attract romance, relieve anxiety, and bring calmness and balance to your life. I frequently love to drink lemon balm tea to relax and calm my thoughts, and ready myself for a good night's sleep. Use it for a night of lust and romance as an aphrodisiac to increase your and your lover's desire to have intercourse. Since ancient times, sorcerers have used it as a love mixture for couples whose relationship lacks enthusiasm and romance. Use it in a love spell to draw the one you are attracted to, or float it in a glass of wine and drink it as a love potion. It has been said that lemon balm's powers are so strong that it would help someone recover from a sword slashing!

Coltsfoot: The yellow flowers of the Coltsfoot plant only open on sunny days. Its appearance is similar to a dandelion, and it belongs to the same family as the sunflower. It is one of the first plants to flower in the springtime, sometimes as early as February. It's the perfect herb for springtime rituals welcoming the return of Imbolc, Ostara, and

Beltane, depending on when they blossom that particular year. Use their long stems to weave into wreaths and place them on your door for healing, money, love, and tranquility to blanket your home.

Crystals: Malachite, Magnetite, Moss Agate, Garnet, Carnelian, and Tiger's Eye

Earth Event: Taurus

Date: April 30-May 1

Occasion: Fertility, Fire celebration; Couples dance around the fire

LITHA

Midsummer and the shortest night and longest day of the year is Litha. The Sun God is at the peak of his virility, and the Goddess is pregnant, symbolizing the solar year's life-giving powers. When the Earth is engulfed with fulfillment and fertility, it is time for celebrations of joy, achievements, and expansiveness. It is a tradition to light a bonfire on Midsummer's Eve and stay up all night to watch and welcome the rising sun. The bonfires symbolize the sun's reflection at its peak strength. Oak is the chosen wood, and aromatic herbs are tossed into the fire. Witches dance around the bonfires, leaping through them. Torches set ablaze are carried around the fields and houses in a sun-wise direction. Coals from the bonfires are littered about the fields, magically ensuring a good harvest. From here on, the nights grow longer and the days shorter, and we are taken back into the dark, completing the Wheel of the Year.

Holiday: Midsummer

Herbs:

Chicory: Known as a substitution for coffee, chicory has a rich history dating back thousands of years, where it was grown along the banks of the Nile River in Egypt. Among its magical properties are strength, removing curses, unlocking doors, divination, invisibility, obstacle removal, and good luck. The ancient Egyptians used chicory for invulnerability and to bring success. If it is pressed up against a lock, the lock will open. It was once thought to make you invisible. Using chicory oil to anoint your body will grant you favors and attract good people. While it is believed to remove curses, it is commonly used to cast a curse. When carried on your person, chicory promotes a lack of wastefulness (frugality), and when burned as an incense, it will purify and cleanse your sacred items.

Chickweed: This marvelous herb grows in groups, ever reminding us how to survive and live in balance with others and ourselves. Once when I came across a patch of chickweed, I noticed that within the group of herbs, each one had plenty of room to grow while still sitting comfortably and in close contact with the rest of the patch. It goes to show you that chickweed promotes structure and individuality within the bounds of a balanced group. With chickweed in your realm, you may want to closely examine the space you provide to others as well as your own space. Chickweed reminds us to move on if the qualities we need for a good life are not present. Chickweed teaches us not to "judge a book by its cover" and to look beyond the surface and into the people we want to grow a relationship with and to be picky as well.

Mistletoe: Mistletoe has always been thought of as magical. Two people kissing under the mistletoe promotes everlasting happiness.

Carrying mistletoe on your person will bring you fertility, good luck, and protection. It has always been considered a magical, good luck plant. Lovers who kiss beneath it will have lasting happiness, and carrying a sprig on your person will ensure good luck, protection, and fertility. Hanging it in the home was supposed to protect from disease, lightning, werewolves, and having your children switched with faerie changelings.

Crystals: Citrine, Ruby, Carnelian, Garnet, Sunstone, and Tigers Eye

Earth Event: Summer solstice: Gemini

Date: June 20-22

Occasion: Gratitude for life and light; honors the Sun God

LUGHNASADH

Modern day witches celebrate the first harvest of the year as a Lughnasadh festival. Lughnasadh, also known as Lammas, acquired its name from the Old English term for "loaf mass." It originated from celebrations in early English harvest times, where loaves of bread were blessed as sacred. Many polytheists and pagans celebrate Lughnasadh by singing songs, playing games, and feasting on bread and baking cakes. At Lughnasadh, the fields of corn are being harvested, and for some, this is considered the true essence of the festival. The lore is that John Barleycorn, the character who on Beltane laid with the Lady in the woods, has now become old and stands bearded and bent over with a crooked cane. He gazes at the sun and has now turned from green to gold, and he knows it is time. His sacrifice is honored at Lughnasadh and will feed all of the people.

Holiday: First Harvest

Herbs:

Elderberry: Vibrant, juicy, wise, and protective, elderberry is encoded with celestial divinity and the ancient wisdom (Gnosis) of self-care. Since ancient times, this herb has been used for healing to treat ailments ranging from skin irritations to colds and flu to bruises and sprains. It is known in some cultures as the Holy Tree and is cherished for its magical properties and correspondence to the cycle of life, death, and rebirth. I use it in my protection, healing, and love spells.

Goldenrod: Wearing a goldenrod flower shows you on the next day your one true love. Grow around your home for prosperity. Washing a child in a goldenrod spiritual bath ensures a pleasant disposition and a good sense of humor when they are grown. Serve it in a tea to seal the emotions of your lover. If you have lost something, hold a stalk of goldenrod flowers in your hand, and it will point you in the direction of your lost item. Carry it in your purse or wallet for good fortune. As the main source of nectar, goldenrod offers a seasonal snack for butterflies, moths, bees, flies, beetles, wasps, and many more insect and animal kingdom residents. The larvae of many insect species feast on the leaves of the goldenrod. It encourages us to bring forth offerings and stand tall against adversity, mistruths, and old stories.

Sunflower: Nothing symbolizes the innate wisdom given by the Great Sun like the sunflower. Beautiful, fleeting, and bold, sunflowers show off their vibrancy and their magical empowerment. The striking resemblance of a lion's mane to the sunflower's head provides the perfect essence for spells about courage. Grab some sunflowers while they are in season to dispel shyness, and stimulate you into taking bold steps towards times of uncertainty. Bring this flower to your solar rituals for fertility spells and friendship blessings. Place a bouquet of sunflowers in any room where someone is ill, and the negative energy will be chased away. Because of their rewarding solar vibes, they are the perfect spiritual "disinfectant."

Crystals: Clear Quartz, Pink Quartz, Amber, Jasper, and Sunstone

Earth Event: Halfway between the summer solstice and autumn equinox: Leo

Occasion: Symbolic gifts of the first fruits as offerings to a deity; honoring hard work that pays off

MABON

Mabon is named after the Welsh God. He is the son of Mother Earth Modron and the Child of Light. This is another example of the journey of perfect balance through the Wheel of the Year. Day and night are equal once again - masculine, feminine, outer and inner, all in balance. At this point, the year is beginning to wane, and from here on out, darkness defeats the light. The natural cycle of the world is heading towards completion. The power of the sun is waning, and the days are shorter and cooler. The tree's sap returns to its roots, and the summer green changes to the fire of autumn.

Holiday: Thanksgiving

Herbs:

Yarrow: Revered for its physical, spiritual, and magical properties, yarrow has a plethora of medicinal benefits. It is an ancient herb named after the great legendary hero Achilles. It is used for love, healing, and courage spells. It was written that Achilles used yarrow to soothe the muscles and for healing other injuries on the battlefield. I use it to clean my skin, and I love it. If you are ever feeling a bit melancholic, call upon the magic of yarrow to heal your mind, spirit, and body when it seems to be unmovable. Let it ground you in times of strife and help you to renew your foundation. Yarrow will ground you without weighing you down and will give you discernment and clarity.

Rue: From the stealthy evergreen shrub with its yellow blossoms and woody stems arising during the summertime, rue is an herb of purification, balance, and protection. According to the Bible, it was given as a tithe, and in the days of antiquity, this herb was quite popular in Roman cuisine, even though it has a bitter taste. Burn it as an incense to promote clarity and reduce anxiety. Often utilized in health and protection spells, rue also comes in handy for breaking curses and hexes. It was considered the witches' herb during the middle ages. From my research, I have learned that witches seem not to like the smell of rue, but neither do disease-carrying rats! It was used in ancient times by wise people in potions against other witches. I read that Michelangelo and Leonardo DaVinci used rue in small amounts to enhance their creativity. The one thing I know it is good for is insect repellent. WARNING: NOT FOR HUMAN CONSUMPTION!

Crystals: Tiger's Eye, Clear Quartz, Citrine, Ruby, Topaz, and Moss Agate

Earth Event: Autumnal equinox: Virgo

Date: September 20-23

Occasion: Time for resting after the hard work of the harvest; a time to reap what was sown; time for finishing up projects

4

ESSENTIAL HERBS

Nutmeg does more than make fantastic eggnog, and cayenne pepper does more than put heat into your chili! The spices you have in your kitchen pantry are brimming with magical properties just waiting for you to tap into! Not only will this list of commonly used spices and herbs add power to your spells, but it will also allow you to connect your spiritual and magical practices together and use them both in your daily life. The following are the 31 most commonly used herbs in magic:

ALLSPICE

Allspice was used to embalm the dead by the ancient Mayans and to cure meat by the Arawak. South Americans also used it to add flavor to chocolate. Allspice got its name in English because of its aromatic qualities of multiple spices, such as cloves, cinnamon, pepper, juniper berries, and nutmeg. Allspice has been known to soothe a toothache, act as a breath freshener, and aid digestion. It is useful to many healing spells.

Latin Name: P. dioica

Folk Names: Pimenta, Jamaican Pepper

Element: Fire

Magical Uses: Money, positivity, luck, uplifting mood, increases energy, and determination

BASIL

Starting in India over 5000 years ago, basil has become a staple herb in magical, medicinal, and culinary practices. The word basil means "fragrant" and stems from the Greek word meaning "King," associated with royalty and wealth. But, it is more associated with romance and love than it is royalty and wealth. The correspondence between love and basil is so powerful that in the past, men wore basil in their hats when preparing to court a woman. Offer a sprig of basil to someone to whom you are attracted to divine a future lover. Sprinkle some basil over your lover's heart to ensure that they will remain faithful.

Latin Name: Ocimum spp.

Folk Names: King of herbs, Witches herb

Element: Fire

Magical Uses: Love spells, protection rituals and spells, prosperity spells, hedge riding (astral travel), purification, peace, and banishment

BAY LEAVES

(DON'T CONSUME IF PREGNANT)

The aromatic bay leaves of the laurel have a deep history in mythology and folklore. Mentioned in Homer's Odyssey and the Bible, bay leaves are most commonly known for their culinary properties but also for their attendance in wreaths given to triumphant Olympic athletes. However, in ancient mythology, Daphne was a nymph who was transformed into a laurel tree to protect her virginity from the hot pursuit of Apollo. To the ancient Romans, the bay leaf symbolized glory and was viewed as protection against thunder, lightning, evil, and the plague. Roman soldiers cleaned the blood off of their weapons with bay leaves. In ancient Elizabethan times, it was believed disaster would follow the death of a laurel tree.

Latin Name: Laurus nobilis

Folk Names: Bay, Bay Laurel, Bay Tree, Daphne, Grecian Laurel, Laurel, Laurel Común, Laurier d'Apollon, Laurier Noble, Laurier-Sauce, Laurier Vrai, Mediterranean Bay, Noble Laurel, Roman Laurel, and True Bay

Element: Fire

Magical Uses: Exorcism, banishing, fidelity, empowerment, luck, wealth, psychic development, and wishing

BLACK PEPPER

Black pepper is earthy, spicy, and amazingly grounding. It has an incredible ability to create endurance and strength to express yourself freely. Grown in Southern India, pepper has been used in magic for more than 2000 years. It is considered in Asian cultures to be a powerful herb thought to support healthy aging, detoxify the liver, and aid in digestion and circulation. As the story goes, during the 5th century, Attila the Hun demanded 4,000 pounds of black pepper be paid in ransom for the city of Rome. It was heavily used in the Middle Ages and by the ancient Romans and became a staple of fine cuisine.

Latin Name: Piper nigrum

Folk Names: Benin pepper, Uziza seeds, Ashanti pepper, and False Cubeb

Element: Fire

Magical Uses: Protection, exorcism, jealousy, negativity, strength, confidence, and gossip

CAYENNE

Cayenne peppers have a history spanning over 8000 years and started out as a ritualistic and decorative item, later finding their way into the culinary world and the world of medicine. I read an article that said they found seeds on the grounds of cave dwellings of the ancient primitive peoples in Mexico[1]. In the 1500s, cayenne was valued in trade in areas where it did not grow, and some of the ancient Indians used it as offerings to their gods. They were also used in South America in smoke form, as a weapon against invading troops. Cayenne is usually used in powder form for spicy dishes. Some pickle them, and some eat them whole! These peppers are commonly harvested in Mexico, India, East Africa, and the U.S. They are named after the cayenne region of French Guiana. The Tupi Indians gave cayenne its name. It has many beneficial health attributes, especially for the cardiovascular system. It lowers your cholesterol and your triglyceride levels. It has been used for centuries and is also sold as an herbal supplement. Cayenne is also known as "the healing spice." Please do not use cayenne in equal amounts to paprika, not that you don't know better, but just in case.

Latin Name: Capsicum annuum

Folk Names: Africa peppers, Bird pepper, Zanzibar pepper, Goat's pepper, Spanish pepper, and Cockspur pepper

Element: Fire

Magical Uses: Spiritual connection, strengthens the magical powers of other herbs, purification of water and home, rids the home of negative energy, removes obstacles, and helps you reach your goals

CINNAMON

Cinnamon dates back to 3000 B.C. in documented Chinese writings and is still known today in Cantonese as kwai. When used as an incense, cinnamon can create elevated spiritual vibrations and aid in attracting positive energies such as money, healing, and protection from evil. Sprinkle some around your home to protect and purify it. Add a bit of cinnamon to your plant water, and they will be purified of all negativity. Cinnamon has been known to have antiviral, bactericidal, and antifungal properties. It has been used medicinally to prevent the spread of certain types of bacteria and viruses. During medieval times, healers or doctors used cinnamon medicinally to treat sore throats, coughing, and hoarseness. Most interestingly, Roman Emperor Nero, out of remorse for murdering his wife, ordered a year's supply of cinnamon be burnt in her honor.[2]

Latin Name: Cinnamomum verum

Folk Names: Kwai, Sweet Wood, and Ceylon

Element: Fire

Magical Uses: Esotericism, white magic, healing, protection, love, success, power, and sexual desire

CLOVES

In 200 BC, convoys carried cloves from Java to the court of the Han dynasty in China. Believe it or not, it was used as a breath freshener. There were even clove battles in the 17th century, where the Dutch decimated cloves on all of the Spice Islands to keep the prices high by creating scarcity - the whole "supply and demand" concept. Cloves were an important herb in the early days of the spice trade. They are indigenous to the Spice Islands of Indonesia. Their aroma is hot and strong in taste but they are used to flavor meats and bakery items. In the U.S. and Europe, it is known as the holiday spice in such fare as mincemeat, fruitcake, and wassail.

Latin Name: Syzygium aromaticum

Folk Names: Mykhet, Carenfil

Element: Fire

Magical Uses: Enhances spiritual vibrations, purification, prosperity, wards off negative and hostile forces, clarity, empathy, healing, and memory

CUMIN

Cumin has been chronicled since the dawn of written history and has been popular for just as long. For centuries it has been a staple in love spells. One very interesting fact about cumin is that it is the only word in the English language that can be traced back to the first language ever written, Sumerian ("Gamun"), 4000 years ago. Another amazing fact about cumin is that it is an ingredient in the oldest recipe in human history (1750 BC) on the Mesopotamian tablets. It was placed as an offering at the tombs of ancient Egyptian pharaohs.

Latin Name: Cuminum Cyminum

Folk Names: Cumino, Cumino Aigro, Kamûnu

Element: Fire

Magical Uses: Fidelity, repels evil, love, peace, exorcism, passion, aphrodisiac, and protection against thieves

CURRY

There are many magic herbs grown on Indian soil. A close friend of mine grew up in India, and she told me that curry is not just an herb; it is a sentiment. She grew up savoring many different curry dishes as a staple meal for years. She and I shared a love for the distinct flavor of these savory and spicy curries that seem to dance on our taste buds. Needless to say, I use curry in many of my spells. It is important to use actual curry in your spells and not a spice blend, because all spices have their own magical properties. Curry leaves are one of the many magic herbs that are found and grown on Indian soil.

Latin Name: Initam volebant

Folk Names: Krishi Jagran, Kadi Patta

Element: Fire

Magical Uses: Protection, burn at nightfall to ward off evil energies

DANDELION ROOT

Every spring, I look forward to seeing my yard suddenly blanketed with the bright and sunny yellow faces of the dandelions. Some people I know spend loads of money trying to eradicate these magical little flowers. The truth is that dandelions have a rich and long history in folklore, both from a medicinal and a magical perspective. Do you remember when you were a kid, and you would make a wish and blow on a dandelion, and when you did, the little seeds would carry your wish in the wind to fruition? Even today, I hold a dandelion under my chin to see if it reflects yellow. If it does, I know I am coming into some money! This magic dates back to before medieval times.

Latin Name: Taraxacum

Folk Names: Blowball, Cankerwort, Lion's Tooth, Priest's Crown, Puffball, Swine's Snout, White Endive, and Wild Endive

Element: Air

Magical Uses: Growth, transformation, ridding yourself of a bad habit, overcoming adversity, wish granting, psychic abilities, dreams coming true, and second sight

DILL

Dill's rich history dates back to 3000 BC, as well as the Middle Ages where it was known to have the power to destroy evil and break any evil spells cast against someone by a witch. It is native to the eastern Mediterranean region and western Asia. It was documented in ancient Egyptian medical works thousands of years before Christ. Just the word dill brings to your mind pickles! Believe it or not, Americans eat more than 2 ½ billion pounds each year! Dill has been a staple herb used widely in Nordic countries to flavor seafood.

Latin Name: Anethum graveolens

Folk Names: Aneto, Aneton, Dill Weed, Dill Seed, Dilly, and Garden Dill

Element: Fire

Magical Uses: Lust, protection, money, luck, love, warding off dark forces, blessing your house, keeping you informed about the difference between superstition and magic, and attraction

DOGWOOD

Cultivated first in 1730, the dogwood tree is native to Asia, North America, and Europe. Use of the dogwood was documented by Native Americans long before settlers came to America. The flower of the dogwood became the state flower of North Carolina in 1941 and the state tree in Missouri in 1955. The dogwood holds a profound meaning to some people based on a legendary story from 2000 years ago. Folklore has it that the dogwood felt great sympathy and anguish for the suffering of Jesus Christ, crucified on a cross made from the dogwood tree. It is said that Jesus felt the tree's sorrow and transformed it so that it could never again be used for crucifixions, and this is why the dogwood is now a shrub-like tree with twisted limbs[3].

Latin Name: Cornus

Folk Names: Boxwood, Squawbush, Budwood, Flowering Cornel, and Green Osier

Elements: Air, Water, and Fire

Magical Uses: Protection, stability, kindness, confidence, guards journals, diaries, letters, and Books of Shadows

DRAGON'S BLOOD

Off the Horn of Africa is an island that carries a tree's root with a menacing crown with vein-type branches that trickle a deep-red resin. The Dracaena cinnabari has earned its name in blood throughout history with legends of magic and dragons. By carefully cutting small incisions, locals collect the blood-colored resin and let it dry. Dating back to 17th century Europe, dragon's blood was valued as a cure-all. Medical practitioners prescribed dragon's blood for serious health conditions. We know now that it has anti-inflammatory and antimicrobial properties. It was also used in ancient times as a breath freshener and for magic in love potions.

Latin Name: Dracaena cinnabari

Folk Names: Blood, Blume, Calamus Draco, Dragon's Blood Palm

Element: Fire

Magical Uses: Protection, spell potency, banishing, preventing impotence, protects your business, luck, purification, and magical ink

ECHINACEA

Native to North America, Echinacea is known by many different Native American tribes. It is called "elk root" by the Ute, a Western Indian tribe. They hold the belief that if an elk is injured, it seeks out the Echinacea as a medication. It has been a traditional healing herb used by many tribes from the Midwest to the Great Plains to treat burns, swelling, and pain. It is also known as Coneflower and has been part of Sun Dance rituals throughout Native American history. The Navajo consider it sacred and chew it while they dance during ceremonial rituals.

Latin Name: Echinacea purpurea

Folk Names: Purple Coneflower, Coneflower, Black Sampson, Rudbeckia

Element: Earth

Magical Uses: Money, offerings, protection, power, exorcism, added strength for spells and charms, fertility, healing, clairvoyant and psychic abilities

ELDER

In Scandinavian and English folklore, Hyldemoer or Sambucus or "Elder Mother" was believed to inhabit the Sambucus or Elder Tree. Hyldemoer is the nymph or goddess of vegetation, life, and death and has the dual power to harm or protect. Legend has it that one should ask permission of the Elder to use part of her tree for its magical and protective qualities or be prepared to be cursed. One method for asking the Elder Mother for her permission is to give offerings to her and speak aloud, "Elder Mother, may I have your wood, and I will give you mine when I become a tree?" NOT FOR HUMAN CONSUMPTION.

Latin Name: Sambucus

Folk Names: Tree of Doom, Pipe Tree, Witch's Tree, Old Lady, Devil's Eye

Element: Earth

Magical Uses: Wisdom, home and business blessings, protection, death and dying transportation to the Otherworld, dream pillows

EUCALYPTUS

The Eucalyptus is native to Australia and stems from the Greek words "eu" and "kalyptos," meaning beautiful hat, because the pistils and stamens together look like a hat. Eucalyptus is the Aboriginals' holy tree. It symbolizes, for them, the division between the Earth and Heaven, or the Underworld. Its leaves, when burned, ward off negative energy.

Latin Name: Eucalyptus globulus

Folk Names: Blue Gum, Curly Mallee, River Red Gum, Mottlecah, Maiden's Gum, Fever Tree, Stringy Bark Tree

Element: Air

Magical Uses: Protection, healing, purification, reconcile relationships, health and wellness, clarity, raises positive vibrations, repels enemies, overcome jealousy, and ward off evil

EVENING PRIMROSE

Considered by some to be a weed and others a wildflower, Evening Primrose comes in colors of yellow, purple, pink, and white with lance-shaped leaves that spiral, beginning on the ground and moving up and around the stem, into a cup-shaped flower. It only blooms at night, hence the name Evening Primrose, and closes the next day before the noon hour. Make sure to pick your starter plants based on their scientific name, because not all species have this trait.

Latin Name: Oenothera

Folk Names: Fever Plant, Field Primrose, King's Cureall, Night Willow-herb, Scabish, Scurvish

Element: Water

Magical Uses: Altar decorations, ritual baths, desirability, beauty, luck for a new job, hunting, and goal success.

FENNEL SEED

Ancient folklore called the fennel plant the snake herb, as it is believed that snakes sharpen their eyesight by rubbing against it. The Puritans would chew fennel seeds at church, giving them the name "meeting seeds." It has a part in European history, as it has grown wildly around the Mediterranean basin for millennia. The Old English word for fennel is "hay."

Latin Name: Foeniculum vulgare

Folk Names: Snake herb, Large fennel, Sweet fennel, Wild fennel, Finocchio, Carosella, Florence fennel, and Fennel seed

Element: Air

Magical Uses: Sexual virility, protection, purification, healing, courage, vitality, increase the length of incarnation, and ward off evil

FEVERFEW

Feverfew grows, albeit short-lived, in Greece, Egypt, Australia, and North America. It was used in Ancient Egypt and Greece by medicine practitioners for ailments such as inflammation, pain management, and menstrual cramps. Folklore says you can protect your family from disease by planting feverfew flowers by the door of your house. It was used in medieval times during plagues to ward off illness. It is documented that rats carrying the plague hated the smell and taste of feverfew, so they avoided eating it. Because of its connection to curing pains and aches, it is also known by some to cure feelings of rejection in love and heart-sickness. Folklore also has it that feverfew protects against elf shot, which was thought to be a sudden stabbing pain caused by the arrow shot by an invisible elf. Today this pain is thought of as a charlie horse or even arthritis.

Latin Name: Tanacetum parthenium

Folk Names: Featherfew, Rainfarn, Wild Quinine, Featherfoil, Prairie Dock, Missouri Snakeroot, Flirtwort, Parthenium, Febrifuge, Devil Daisy, Bachelor's Button, Maid's Weed, Midsummer Daisy, Nosebleed, Vetter-voo, Wild Chamomile, or Matricaria.

Element: Water

Magical Uses: Protection when traveling and against accidents, health and wellness, and spirituality

FIG

Fig trees are featured in origin stories around the world. The best-known origin story is that the leaves of the fig tree clothed Adam and Eve. Another story about the great fig is that it provided shelter for a she-wolf whom a baby boy suckled and who later went on to found Rome. Yet another story of the great fig tree is that its leaves created the tongues of the first people, as well as provided their food and shelter.

Latin Name: Ficus carica

Folk Names: Common fig

Element: Fire

Magical Uses: Travel, answering questions (if its leaves dry slowly, it's a "yes," otherwise, it's a "no,"), divination, love, and fertility

FLAXSEED

Latin Name: Linum usitatissimum

Folk Name: Linseed

Element: Water

Magical Uses: Healing, money, protection when mixed with red pepper, divination, future telling, and keeps away poverty

FRANKINCENSE

One of the oldest known magical resins is that of frankincense. It has been an item of trade in parts of the Arab world and Africa for more than 5000 years. It is mentioned in the book of Matthew as a gift given by the Three Wise Men after the birth of Jesus Christ. Frankincense is also mentioned many times in the Talmud and the Old Testament. It has been a staple in many Jewish and Christian rituals and ceremonies.

Latin Name: Boswellia sacra

Folk Names: Frankincense Tears and Olibanum

Element: Water

Magical Uses: Consecration, protection, success, meditation, self-control, manifestation, brings success, offering at Yule, Beltane, and Lammas, and elevated topaz power

FUMITORY

Fumitory is believed to be a protective herb since ancient times. It is documented as far back as the Stone Age, 9000 BC. It can slowly grow at almost freezing temperatures, so it was one of the first emerging weeds. It fertilizes itself and can take over gardens and crops. Because it grows in lighter types of soil, it has earned the name of "beggary." It was thought to protect against evil spirits and witchcraft. NOT FOR HUMAN CONSUMPTION.

Latin Name: Fumaria officinalis

Folk Name: Earth Smoke, Drug fumitory, Hedge fumitory, Beggary, and Wax Dolls

Element: Fire

Magical Uses: Consecrating tools for rituals, purification, use at Samhain, new home blessings, money draw, protect your property, and attract love spells

GINSENG

For thousands of years, ginseng has been thought to be a necessity for life in China. This strong cultural belief is that it slows the aging process, prevents illness, and stimulates sexual arousal. Ginseng's history dates back to before the Declaration of Independence in America. Native Americans used ginseng for spiritual rituals, and the medicine man prescribed it for digestive health and to treat fevers. It has also been used worldwide as an aphrodisiac.

Latin Name: Panax ginseng

Folk Names: Sang, Wonder of the World Root

Element: Fire

Magical Uses: Lust, beauty, love, money, wishes, healing, protection, sexual potency, health and wellness

HAWTHORN

The tree most likely to be protected or inhabited by the Wee Folk is the mighty hawthorn tree. Most of the lone bushes or isolated hawthorn trees in Ireland are said to house fairies. You can't hurt a hawthorn tree without incurring the wrath, often deadly, of the faeries. The Faery Queen next to her hawthorn is believed to represent a pre-Christian archetype. I always picture myself worshiping the Faery Queen as a goddess during a ritual in a sacred hawthorn grove! It is also known as the May tree because it blossoms during May.

Latin Name: Crataegus

Folk Names: Haw, May bush, May tree, Mayblossom, Mayflower, Quickset, Thorn-apple tree, Whitethorn, Bread and Cheese tree, Quick, Gazels, Ladies' Meat

Element: Fire

Magical Uses: Faeries, chastity, fertility, fishing, happiness, protection against lightning, ghost repellent, wards off evil spirits, removes negativity, profession, employment, and celibacy

HYACINTH

Hyacinth was named after the Greek hero, Hyakinthos, who Apollo beloved, and for this reason, it is considered the protection herb of homosexual men. According to Greek mythology, Hyakinthos gave hyacinth the divine attributes known to the plant. It was believed the herb was created from Hyakinthos' spilled blood when he was killed by Zeypherus, the NorthWind God, because of his jealousy for Apollo's love for him. In Apollo's grief, he wouldn't let Hades take Hyakinthos to the Underworld, so he resurrected him as the hyacinth plant.

Latin Name: Hyacinthus

Folk Names: English Bluebells, Wood hyacinth, Endymion, or Nodding Squill

Element: Fire

Magical Uses: Love, money, homosexuality, dreams, peaceful sleep, eases the pain of childbirth, and good fortune

JUNIPER

Juniper has been used throughout history as an herb to ward off disease. It has been tied to magical practices for the workings of fire and for its herbal wisdom. Traditionally, magicians have used juniper in spells to retrieve stolen items. Its history dates back to ancient times, where its documented use in rites of purification and to drive away evil spirits is listed in the Key of Solomon, a 14th century Book of Spells.

Latin Name: Juniperus

Folk Names: Juniper berries, Ginepro, Enebro, Wachholder, Eastern Red Cedar, Red juniper, Baton Rouge, Pencil cedar, and Savin

Element: Fire

Magical Uses: Potency, attract love, safeguard against thievery, prosperity, healthy energies, banishing harmful things toward good health, attract positivity, healthy energies

MANDRAKE

The ancient Greeks used mandrake as an aphrodisiac, and it was known as the "love-apple of the ancient peoples." The ancient Hebrews believed mandrake induced conception. The roots of the mandrake are said to look weirdly like a human body, and legend says it reveals itself in female and male forms. One legend holds that mandrake springs from the blood, semen, and fat of a hanged man and that if you pull it from the ground, it lets out a blood-curdling scream, projecting pain and death to anyone within earshot. I have been near many mandrakes. Thank heavens I never tried to pull one out of the ground! NOT FOR HUMAN CONSUMPTION.

Latin Name: Mandragora officinarum

Folk Names: Mandragora, Satan's Apple, Manroot, Circeium, Gallows, Herb of Circe, Mandragora, Raccoon Berry, Ladykins, Womandrake, Sorcerer's Root, Wild Lemon

Element: Fire

Magical Uses: Protection, prosperity, fertility, exorcising evil, attracting love, and preserving health

PATCHOULI

Patchouli was a favorite among the hippie movement of the 1960s and 1970s. The word patchouli comes from the Hindi word for "scent." Its history spans thousands of years. It is documented that King Tut had patchouli oil buried with him in his tomb. Europeans historically traded patchouli for gold, and it has been the standard of many fabrics such as silk to act as a protectant against insects.

Latin Name: Pogostemon cablin

Folk Names: Patchouly, Pucha Pot

Element: Earth

Magical Uses: Fertility, grounding, drawing money, love, spiritual bathing, business growth, return from other realms to the spiritual world

SAFFRON

The origin of saffron is in Asia Minor, where the trade industry used the stems to dye fabrics imported from Phoenicians. It was then spread by the Arabs in their conquests against India and Spain. Already precious to the Romans, saffron was described by the famous poet Ovid in the 1st century. Towards the latter part of the 1300s, during the Spanish inquisition, saffron cultivation began, and there started its production.

Latin Name: Crocus sativus

Folk Names: Kum Kuma, Zaffran, Kesar, Autumn Crocus, Spanish saffron, Dyer's saffron, Thistle saffron, Bastard saffron, American saffron, and Parrot's Corn

Element: Water

Magical Uses: Happiness, strength, healing, love spells, lust, raising the power of wind, increasing psychic awareness, controlling the weather, and aphrodisiac

VALERIAN

The word valerian comes from the Latin word "valere," meaning to be healthy and strong. In this case, "strong" may mean its powerful healing properties or may mean "strong" in odor. The ancient Greeks referred to this herb as "Phu" as in "Phew!" Throughout history, it has been believed that valerian has the ability to turn anything bad into something good.

Latin Name: Valeriana officinalis

Folk Names: All-Heal, Garden Heliotrope, Graveyard Dust, Phu, Setwell, Vandal Root

Element: Water

Magical Uses: Protection, harmony, substitution for graveyard dirt (as long as all involved agree), repairs relationships, dream magic, purification, calmness, reconciliation, and settles arguments

5

GATHERING HERBS IN NATURE

Of all of the wondrous things to do in this world, one of the most spiritual and enjoyable activities I do is gather herbs in nature. Learning about them, picking my own delicious berries, and finding gems on the land after I just looked them up online is monumentally rewarding. I use them in teas, cleansing bundles, culinary creations, to charge my crystals, spiritual baths, my spells, and so much more! Some gardeners have their own unique take on handling herbs. Rather than dismissing them as maddening or mundane, I have chosen to embrace wild herbs with all of their magic, deliciousness, and enchantment. Some call it "foraging." I prefer "wildcrafting." Either way, collecting your own herbs is one of the most empowering and spiritual practices one can undertake. It means taking the time and putting in the effort to educate yourself about the plants' virtues, properties, and benefits. The process of learning how to identify herbs and their habitat, how to cultivate them in your garden, and how to use them in magic means you have chosen a life of self-care and oneness with the Elements.

Before we get started, it is essential to mention that self-care and self-treatment are two different things. There are always cases when it is advised to seek a medical professional, so remember while holistic forms of healing are very helpful, they do not take the place of conventional medicine when necessary. Besides, chances are, your doctor might prescribe a complementary treatment with herbs anyway. That being said, it is also important to know how to gather your herbs in a way that does not harm the plant populations themselves or needlessly take the life of a plant.

Rule #1: Ensure the herb you are gathering is the herb you think it is.

Rule #2: NEVER ingest an herb you have not identified with certainty. That means knowing what it looks like and which herbs look like the one you are looking for.

Two of my buddies were wildcrafting one day and thought they would chew on the roots of a cattail they picked from the edge of the pond near my house. I wasn't with them because I was making salads so we could add their wonderful finds. Before I even finished preparing lunch, the two of them were in the bathroom vomiting and pooping. The herb they decided to chew on was an iris, not a cattail! Cattail is edible, and iris is not! So be very careful you identify what you forage before you put anything in your mouth. This was a mild case of poisonous look-alikes, but it could have been much more serious or even deadly with other herb imposters.

If you are picking up your basket for wildcrafting for the first time, make it a ritual because this is truly a special moment. Getting to know your locally-grown herbs and then bringing them home to your apothecary and kitchen will be one of the most spiritual life experiences you have ever had. When I first started wildcrafting, I focused on a specific range of generous, plentiful, and beneficial herbs, so I looked to the common flora, wild weeds, and those that quite frankly were invasive. I strongly suggest you do the same. These particulars also happen to be some of the most nutrient-dense and medicinal allies of wild foods. Remember, we also want to practice sustainability by honoring Mother Earth. Many of these feral plants are my main choices because they are the most sustainable wild food options out there. Plus, they are not difficult to find and become friends with. Believe me, just connecting to these wonderful botanicals is spellwork at its finest.

Tools You Need

I had no idea what tools I needed when I first started. I only brought a basket, which seems funny now. All wildcrafters have a set of sacred tools. Plus, you can also use them for your gardening.

1. Sunscreen
2. Hat
3. Gardening gloves
4. Books to identify plants (I didn't think of these the first time I went collecting and then realized I didn't know what anything was!)
5. Pruners are the tool you will use most often when gathering

and processing your wild herbs. They will snip their way right through twigs, roots, small branches, and herbaceous stems. I use them so often that I keep them in a holster on a leather belt so I can reach down to my hip when I need them.

6. Weeding knife, or Japanese garden knife called a hori-hori: having a sturdy knife is an excellent wildcrafting tool and a great weeding instrument. I use mine to dig small roots from the earth and break up soil or pry up rocks. They also come in handy for transplanting roots. I keep mine in my leather holster. I suggest getting tools with wooden handles because they are sturdier than plastic. If you tend to lose things, get tools with orange or red handles so they will be easier to find.

7. Digging fork: This is the best tool for digging up roots. The fork tines are effective in loosening soil and lifting roots from the ground. I also use mine to weed my garden and harvest roots I use in my spells.

8. Gathering baskets: I love picking my basket for the day. They come in handy for gathering and drying herbs, and they are beautiful to look at. It's helpful to have an assortment on hand. You can typically find used baskets in thrift stores. Look for a few with an open weave that are broad and flattish (helpful for increasing ventilation when drying loose herbs). The bottom line is to enjoy your baskets.

9. Pruning saw: This tool is good for cutting small branches and gathering medicinal barks from wild cherry and birch trees.

10. Bags, labels, and markers: Don't keep your herbs in plastic

bags unless you refrigerate them. Label them with different color markers and date them.

Learn your Latin names: Don't always depend on common names because they can apply to different plants, and some edible plants share the same common names as toxic plants. Hemlock is a good example, as poisonous hemlock is Conium maculatum, and the edible Eastern hemlock is Tsuga canadensis. The Latin names were used to title plants because there is no chance of the language evolving or changing, since it is a dead language.

Use your senses: Lots of plants, including edibles, have look-alikes. So use your sense of smell and texture. While not always the case, many toxic plants smell awful and are unpalatable. However, don't go around tasting plants. Obviously, some, even in very small doses, are deadly.

Learn your habitats: Learn about your habitats. A plant's habitat must have enough space, water, and food. Each habitat has identifying characteristics that correspond with different types of herbs. Not every herb can live in the desert, nor in the marshlands, nor the woodlands. You won't find ramps in the marsh nor cattails on high slopes. There are many types of woodlands and forests, depending on the climate. I love to use journaling and I write down things I learn from living books or encyclopedias and diagram them with each habitat I explore.

Know your seasons: Journal how they change with each season. Learning to follow your herbs through the seasons is a way to identify changing plants. Sometimes by the time they are identifiable, they are past the point where you can use them. If you start taking notes early, such as in summertime, you will know where to find your herbs when they first sprout in the spring. If you are steadfast with your journaling, as the months and years go by, you will have created a calendar that tells you what to look forward to harvesting. Foraging in the spring is all about the cornucopia of wild greens that are nutritious and abundant. It is a traditional ritual for cleansing your spirit and your body after a long winter. Chickweed, dandelion, wintercress, daylilies, and stinging nettles are all out there for spring-picking.

Summer's herbs are full of antioxidant mushrooms, berries, and flowers. This is the season of colorful herbs and, most of all, the best time of the year for drying and preserving your herbs. You can dry them, freeze them, ferment them, make jam, or infuse them in your favorite beverage. Others can be dried and stored for your spellcrafting year-round. On the other hand, fall brings earthy, sweeter, and softer herbs to your baskets. Fall is the time for savory nuts, sun-toasted seeds, edible roots, and ripening fruits. This is the time to gather as much as you can before the months of frosty winter.

Know which parts of the plants are safe: Just because you know certain plants are edible doesn't mean all parts are edible. For example, the roots, bark, and stems of elderberries are poisonous, even though ripe, cooked elderberries are safe to consume.

Dos and Don'ts

1. No trespassing.
2. Watch your footing. Sometimes you may be tempted to scale a hill that is too steep, or you may find yourself on a slippery slope. SAFETY FIRST.
3. Watch out for poison ivy and poison oak. The first time I got poison ivy, it was like watching myself touch it in slow motion. No sooner did I see it than I knew I would soon be looking for the calamine lotion.
4. Wear boots and gloves.
5. Watch out for snakes.
6. Don't carry more than you need.
7. Express your gratitude. "Spirits of these herbs, I give thanks, from the hillsides to the banks, may you nourish and heal us, I give you all of my trust. So it is and should be."
8. Know the foraging laws in your areas. For instance, it is illegal to harvest herbs or pick flowers in a National Park. Each public area has different rules, so check first. Even if you think you won't get caught, you don't want to give wildcrafters like me a bad name. Besides, some of the rules are to protect our ecosystem, so check your local guidelines.
9. Harvest at the most 25% of the plant to avoid overharvesting. I read that sage and ramps are becoming more scarce due to overharvesting. Learn about what herbs are rare because they may seem plentiful in your area but are diminishing overall. This is also happening because habitats are growing smaller.

10. Don't forage near busy roads. Many leaves absorb metals and lead from toxic exhaust. The toxins from the highways tend to settle in the soil. Also, make sure you check on the pesticides in the areas you are wildcrafting.
11. The same goes for foraging in any water source. Unfortunately, most water sources are polluted or are becoming polluted. Eating a plant from polluted water is the same as drinking contaminated water. You also don't want these chemicals mixed into your spells and rituals. Heavy metals do not cook away.
12. Ask permission to forage. It is the courteous thing to do if you think you may be on someone's property. I always do. The one time I didn't (because I didn't know I was on private property), the owner came up to me on a four-wheeler and told me I was trespassing. I was embarrassed and never made that mistake again.

6

GROWING YOUR OWN HERBS

As much as I enjoy growing my own vegetables, I really believe starting with an herb garden is the best choice. It doesn't take a great deal of effort to reap the benefits of being able to sense their magic all around you while at the same time doing something healthy. It's easier to grow your own herbal garden than growing vegetables or flowers. You can grow them in pots indoors, or if the soil in your yard is nutritious enough, you can grow them in your yard. There are even hydroponic kits, like the AeroGarden, for your indoor herbal garden, but I chose to learn about each species and do it myself. I grow mine in pots that I can put on my patio where they always get the morning sun. Most can handle a broad range of temperatures. Just a couple of steps in the morning, and I have fresh basil for my omelet. While they are a great addition to my eggs, I also use them in salves, teas, essential oils, and tinctures.

I first started with transplants, and then as I learned more, I used seeds. You can even have different herbs in the same pot, but you have to be careful because some, like mint, will take over. Having your own organic herbs from your garden is so self-fulfilling and benefits your health in many ways. Detoxifying and strengthening your immune system helps prevent the common cold, aids in digestion, lowers your stress levels, and so much more. Just about every morning, as soon as I get up, except during the hottest months, I step out onto my patio and pick a few leaves of basil for my breakfast. This easy and quick access to fresh organic herbs is far above anything I can get at the grocery store. By having your own herb garden, you can grow what you want for your taste and magical preferences.

Some of the medicinal or healing herbs I grow include:

- Chamomile is not only delicious but helps to relax me and promotes a good night's sleep.
- Peppermint eases nausea, provides clarity, boosts your mood, and eases digestion.
- Lavender helps improve sleep, remedy pain, lowers heart rate and blood pressure, eases hot flashes from menopause, promotes hair growth, and relieves congestion.
- Echinacea I keep around to fight off the cold season. It has many medicinal properties, including helping relieve and cure urinary tract infections.
- Oregano is loaded with antioxidants, has antifungal and antibacterial properties, and boosts your immune system.
- Rosemary has anti-inflammatory compounds that improve your circulation, is a cognitive stimulant, enhances the

quality and performance of your memory, and raises your focus and alertness.

Spending Time in a Garden is Healthy

While enjoying the improved physical health your herb garden provides, actually tending to them welcomes in their magical properties. Tending to your herbal garden provides you with the opportunity to live a more healthy and active lifestyle. Being one with Mother Nature puts you in an atmosphere of fresh air rich in vitamin D, and offers some good exercise at the same time. All of the qualities of home gardening lead to a higher quality of life, allow you time to unplug from your smart devices, and lower your stress. It is proven to be therapeutic for your mental and spiritual health. Spending time outside visiting with your herbs, watering them, singing to them, all of it is healthy for both. Working with dirt physically puts you in touch with microorganisms, minerals, and bacteria that boost your immune system. Exposing yourself to these small quantities of bacteria allows your immune system to strengthen and protect you against diseases and potential allergies later in life.

Earthing

Earthing, also known as grounding, is the act of being in direct contact with the earth. This means having your body or skin touching the grass, water, sand, soil, or raw conductive materials covering the ground. This means, take off your sneakers! Rubber soles prevent you from earthing. So do plastic and asphalt, and treated woods. The earth is rich in electrons, so it has a negative charge. Free radicals have a positive charge. Your body is infiltrated by free radicals from the electromagnetic radiation coming from your cell phone, microwaves, computers, WiFi, and Bluetooth devices. They are by-products that are toxic to our body and that build up. However, when earthing, they are neutralized by the negatively charged ions created by the earth. The earth grounds our bodies, just like it does the electrical outlets in our homes, where it lessens any extra positive charges. Earthing improves circulation, reduces inflammation, improves sleep, and balances your cortisol rhythm. So, next time you're out in your garden, kick off your shoes and reap the benefits of a few negative ionic energies.

In a world where expectations are diminishing and hopelessness is rising, gardening brings forth expectation and promise. Growing your herbs is an act of faith. Taking a tiny plant of the tiniest seeds and planting those seeds in the healthiest soil, tending and caring for them while they grow, and experiencing the awe in the changes that occur gives us great pause while we stand rapt in the poetic symbolism of transformation. It's like watching a child grow up and become themselves. On whichever side of the solstice we are sitting, and whichever holidays converge from the many different cultures and religions, themes of brotherhood and peace rise in the air, and you and I can think of the joy our magical gardens give us.

Our sacred places where we grow our herbs are where expectations, faith, and hope are planted. If we work hard and nurture and learn the techniques, it symbolizes our love and care, not just for our plants but also for our family, friends and neighbors. It's a reminder of our heritage, grandparents, and how much we love our family and want to provide organic, fresh, sustainable goods. It reflects our personality and character. When the daylight hours start to grow longer, we can joyfully anticipate the greenery ahead of us. Sometimes on a clear night, I go out and stand in my garden covered in snow, under the millions of stars, barefoot, and think about the herbs of happiness to come. I practice my garden rituals of thanking the Elements and express my gratitude for what is to come.

Outdoor Gardens

Whether you plan on a cottage garden, small garden, courtyard garden, or a long and narrow garden, you should plan what times of the day and where each part of the garden gets light and sun. Consider what your plans are for your garden and how you will access each part. Will you be growing vegetables with your herbs; will you have a spot nearby to enjoy a cup of coffee? Take a seat by a window or on the porch or patio and ponder the size of your lawn. Then think about the size of your garden. It doesn't have to be square or rectangular. It can be a circle, oblong, or oval shape. Herbal plants hold their own in a formal garden design or live happily in areas where plants already exist. While you are planning the size of your garden, think about how you plan to use them. For cooking, rituals, spells, teas, etc.

You might intend to make herbal blends for gift-giving or bath favors, or maybe you have always wanted to make your own herb wreath. Whatever your dreams are, you will need to design a garden that will accommodate multiple plants. Herbal plants yield surprisingly large amounts. For regular culinary use, you may only need one tarragon, rosemary, or oregano plant. But if you plan to dry your herbs, or make a year's worth of parsley pesto, you will need more like a dozen plants. One way to narrow the playing field is to think about your spells and your cooking. If you make lots of salads, pasta, or pizza, consider multiple oregano, basil, sage, and thyme. Then again, if you love tacos, grow mint, cilantro, oregano, and marjoram. If you are a tea lover, grow some lemon balm, chamomile, mint, and pineapple sage! The ideas are endless.

Start with the Soil

Most herbs need well-drained soil. Do your research for this. You can amend the soil you already have by making a raised garden bed design. This way, you can customize the type of soil you use to suit the herbs you plan on growing. Know this: different herbs require different types of soil. For instance, rosemary, lavender, and thyme do well in alkaline soils that sharply drain. Mints and basil prefer loads of moisture and richer dirt, so you can plant them near your hose if you want.

When you start thinking about how you will arrange the herbs in your garden design, there are some basic garden fundamentals: shorter plants should be planted along the edges of the garden with the taller plants in the back. Rosemary, tarragon, dill, and fennel are examples of taller herbs, where lavenders, chives, and mints are in the mid-range category for height, and parsley, oregano, and thyme are a bit shorter. If you are grouping herbs together, remember to pair them with herbs with the same soil, sun, and water needs. So, plant your dill, lavender, rosemary, cilantro, and oregano where the most direct sunlight falls, whereas mints, sage, and parsley can handle partly shady areas. There are no other groups of plants that offer such diversity in usage as herbs. Whether for healing, spellwork, cooking, or landscaping, herbs have been grown and harvested all over the world for as long as humankind or animals have walked the earth. For me, it has taught me how to be more patient and to never give up. It's incredible how one can have total faith that something you have planted or cared for will bring such joy.

Gardening Tools

Every gardener needs to be all about hands-on work, but equipment and tools exist to help garden more efficiently, reduce calluses on our hands, and create holes in the ground for our herbs to grow much easier than digging by hand.

Important Gardening Tools Include:

1. Hand trowel
2. Garden hand fork
3. Shovel
4. Spade
5. Watering can
6. Rake
7. Garden hose
8. Garden knife
9. Wheelbarrow
10. Weeder
11. Pruning saw
12. Pruning shears
13. Mattock
14. Moisture meter
15. Hedgers
16. Hand sprayer
17. Lawn mower

7

USING HERBS IN YOUR MAGIC

Herbs are one of the most magical tools to use in your witchcrafting! Power is the foundation of herb magic. Power is generated and cared for by the universe, from single seed germination to the energy that rotates our planet, the energy of all living things, of birth, life, death, and rebirth. Like each crystal, each herb has its own unique vibrational energy, which, again like crystals, is determined by its chemical density and composition. These herbal powers and properties are dictated by their habitat, color, scent, design, and other aspects. The magic of herbs, therefore, is to cause needed or desired change. For maximum herbal powers, you should choose the herbs with the vibration corresponding to your specific ritual or spell. For instance, cedar will help with fertility spells but also powerfully enhances money-drawing spells.

Contrary to what many believe, a full moon is not necessary for herb rituals or spells. They can be used for magic 365 days a year during any type of weather, at any time of day or night! The only real necessities for herb magic are the seeds, herbs, flowers, and a few previously mentioned tools for gardening and grinding, including a mortar and pestle, a large bowl (wooden not metal), candles, jars, charcoal, and an incense burner, a large glass or ceramic bowl for infusions, and, of course, your sacred altar or spell table. Your herb spells are cast, and your herbs enchanted at your altar. If you are spell-casting or performing rituals outside, use a tree stump or flat rock.

Preparing yourself before engaging in herb magic is very important. Get yourself clean and relaxed in loose clothing. I always take an herbal ritual bath or add an herbal sachet to my bathwater. Then I begin creating my vision. Visualization is the essence of spell magic. I picture my intent of what I need in my mind's eye. I suggest you do the same. For magical purposes, visualization is used to form a clear picture of your intent and then direct your powers towards it, as if it has already manifested. For example, visualize that you are dating the person you are attracted to. Never forget to get the permission of others onto whom you cast spells unless the spells are in the form of gifts.

How to Create Magic with Herbs

Enchanting your herbs aligns your magical intention with the plant's vibrations. Sometimes, this calls for a single herb or a blend of them, each enchanted one by one.

1. The best way to start is by collecting herbs from the wild or those you have harvested from your garden. Speak aloud, "I am gathering these herbs for..." then place all of your

gathered herbs surrounding your mixing bowl on your altar, light the appropriate corresponding colored candles, and begin the visualization process.

2. Add your herbs to your mixing bowl and run your fingers several times through the herbs while softly and slowly chanting your intention, such as "petals of rose, petals of rose, bring to my life a love that grows."
3. Now enchanted, your herbs are ready for spellwork, or to be placed in spell jars to put around your home, etc. You can infuse edible herbs in boiling water, but it has to be in Pyrex, not metal. Keep the water covered so that no steam escapes. Let steep one teaspoon of herbs for every one cup of water, and then strain before using. You can also use a cheesecloth for bathing, making teas, and anointing your body.

Incense

Incense is a combination of any herb materials, which are then mixed together with charcoal. Burning aromatic resins and herbs is traditional around the world and has been for thousands of years. They not only smell good, but they are also used for healing ceremonies, purification, and for cleansing sacred areas. For magical purposes, incense is used in spellwork for its vibrations along with visualization, and can also be used for rituals and background vibrations during healing treatments. Ground your herbs in your mortar and pestle, light a charcoal block in your abalone shell, cauldron, or incense burner, and sprinkle small amounts of your herb incense onto the charcoal every couple of minutes while casting your spell.

Herbal Garden Incense Recipe from My Own Garden

This recipe, inspired by herbs I grew and harvested from my garden, is a blend of lemongrass, rosemary, and lavender.

What You'll Need:

- 1¾ teaspoon ground Salvia rosmarinus (rosemary)
- 1 tablespoon ground Cymbopogon citratus (lemongrass)
- 2 teaspoons ground Lavandula angustifolia (lavender)
- 1¼ tablespoon water

Steps

1. Grind the herbs into a powder.
2. Mix the powders.
3. Add 6 drops of water slowly, and each time mash the mixture with the back of a spoon, pressing them together, not stirring.
4. Eventually, a dough will form. You want it to be fairly dry, just moist enough to hold it together.
5. Once the dough is formed and holds together, pinch off a small amount and form it into a cone shape. (Make it skinny and tall).
6. Let your cones dry for at least one week on a flat surface. They have to be entirely dried out before they will burn. Light the tip of the cone with a flame and let it burn until it is smoking.
7. Place your cone on your incense burner!

Casting a Circle

Many modern-day witchcraft spells call for casting a circle. In its basic form, a circle is a sacred space visualized by the practitioner, their ritual tools, and their altar during spellcrafting. Most magicians think of the sacred circle as an energy container from within which they practice their craft. It is a spiritual protection shield from all things negative during the open emotional and vulnerable state necessary for spellwork. It is like an impenetrable invisible force field from which imbalance, disharmony, and negativity bounce off. Before you cast your circle, take a moment to clear all negative energy and then follow these steps:

How to Cast a Circle

1. Use one of your homemade incense to smoke the area where you will cast your circle.
2. Think carefully about your space and location. It can be as large or small as you desire. You can mentally and visually map out your circle with candles and crystals to mark the directions (N-S-E-W) and the corresponding Elements or directions.
3. Mark a pentacle if you include the Spirit Element in your pattern, otherwise using a cross pattern North (Earth), Air (East), Fire (South), and Water (West).
4. Start casting your circle by facing East and calling upon the Air Element. Moving clockwise, you will end up with the Earth element facing North.
5. North is where your ritual begins.

6. Start relaxing by using deep breathing techniques, center yourself, be calm and present.
7. Start visualizing the earth under your feet, earthing you, and chant, "I call upon you, Earth Element."
8. Moving clockwise (eastward), picture the wind swirling about you, "Element of Air, I call upon you."
9. Moving clockwise (southward), picture flames surrounding you and call upon the warming presence of the sun, "Element of Fire, I call upon you."
10. Turning westward, visualize waves, waterfalls, rivers, and streams, "Element of Water, I call upon you."
11. Moving back to the North spot of your circle, visualize your feet sending pillars of light deep down, all the way to the earth's core.
12. Pull the earth's energy from its core into your soul and throughout your body, creating a light flowing about you in a circle - "Under the spirit of the Earth, Wind, Water, and Fire, I cast this circle of protection below, above, and within."
13. Now your circle is sacred and ready for ritual.

Circle Tips

If you step out of your circle before you have finished your ritual, create a cut motion with your wand or blade across the circle's boundary and chant, "I open a door using my wand." The energy from your wand will direct you toward the open path. When you re-enter, use the same process to close the door.

Closing/Opening Your Circle

Closing or opening a sacred circle is a technique for showing gratitude to the Elements for helping you cast your intentions. Start the closing ritual by facing North and chant, "Farewell, Earth; I thank thee for thy energy." Next, release the water, facing westward, "Farewell, Water, I thank thee for thy energy." Turning southward, "Farewell, Fire, I thank thee for thy energy." Facing East, "Farewell, Air, I thank thee for thy energy." End back at the North point, "I bid you farewell, oh spirits of the world. I close this circle and send the energy back into the ground.

Jar and Bottle Magic

Without a doubt, there are zillions of ways to work and make magic. Magic practice takes many forms, running from a simple spoken charm to elaborately formulated rituals. This has been the way throughout the history of magic and across the various witchcraft traditions we have been taught. One historical and popular means of creative magic is the vessel, bottle, and jar spell. A vessel spell is a magical item created by the magician using some type of sealed bottle, jar, or other vessel, often with wax or a cork seal. These vessels are a part of many regional, folkloric, and cultural magical protocols and serve many different intentions.

Examples of bottle and jar charms are mentioned across Europe and the United States. They have been documented in grimoires, the Book of Shadows, and Black Books around the globe. Spell jars have survived in the folk customs of Hoodoo and continue to grow in popularity among magic practitioners of many modern-day spellcrafts. They are inexpensive to make with easy-to-find materials. They don't require much physical maintenance, and the spells continue to work for as long as the jar is sealed. It is a favorite practice among traditional practitioners, as the spells have remained mostly unchanged throughout the years. No longer are they just part of black and red magic. Many love spells, money spells, and others are performed as vessel rituals without any curses or hexes being involved, especially since herbs, crystals, oils, and vinegar meet the needs of so many magical goals.

Herbal Sachet Magic

While your herbal garden is good enough to eat and make potions, these wonderfully aromatic herbs can be tucked into sachets whose fragrance will carry you right back to the glory of your garden. You can use them to scent clothing in your dryer, a drawer, or even put one under your pillow. You don't have to be a seamstress either. You can purchase mesh bags, ready-made, and fill them with your dried herbs. Just tie them up and enjoy. On average, it only takes about 30-45 minutes to make your sachets. It all depends on how extravagant you want to get. Just gather your materials, and you will have gifts for the holidays and a family that smiles every time they open a drawer or retrieve their clothes from the dryer.

Follow the directions I gave you on how to dry your herbs and enjoy experimenting with them. It is essential to know when to harvest and dry out your herbs quickly to preserve their fragrance. Here are some easy steps for making your herbal sachets:

1. Blend enough of your herbs into the bag you have chosen for your sachet.
2. Place several drops of matching essential oils on your blend.
3. Fill your sachet with your blended herbs and essential oils.
4. Glue, sew or tie the sachet closed.
5. Wrap a nice string or ribbon around the sealed top of the sachet.
6. ENJOY!

Dressing Candles

When using herbs for candle dressing, start by thoroughly drying out the plant material. Otherwise, it can mildew and leave an awful scent. Finely crush your herbs in your mortar and pestle to release their aroma. You can also steep your ground herbs in heated wax for a few hours so that the herbal essence penetrates and becomes incorporated into the wax. Then strain the wax before you make your candle. Another way is to add the ground or chopped herbs as you pour your candle. This makes a beautiful design in your herbal candle projects, especially if they are colorful. At this point, you are probably thinking about the best herbs for dressing your candles. The same herbs used in aromatherapy evoke emotions and calmness and are also the most popular herbs for candles. The leaves and flowers are also used to dress the outside of your candles.

Lavender is one of the most popular candle herbs. Lavender reduces anxiety and elicits calm and relaxed feelings. Use the flowers to decorate the outside and infuse the grounded powder with your wax. Mint-scented candles, from spearmint to peppermint, make perfect gifts and centerpieces for holidays. Burn spearmint-infused candles year-round to cleanse your home of negativity and promote clarity of mind. Rosemary works well for its aroma and as a dressing design for your candles. Harvest the leaves or grow them in the same container you are going to make your candle in. Steep the leaves in a tight glass container, covered for three days. Chamomile has both decorative and aromatic values for candle-making. Lemon verbena is one of the most aromatic citrus-scented leaves there are. Place the leaves separately on screens and then store them in zippered bags. Keep all of your herbs in airtight containers.

Essential Oil Making

Coarsely chopped, dried herbs create soothing essential oil infusions. It is important to use dried herbs. The best choices for oils are olive and sunflower. The oil should be fresh so that the aromatic infusion will last the longest. Olive and sunflower oils are good choices. Be sure to use fresh oil so that the infusion will last longer.

What You'll Need:

- Canning jars or any glass jar with a lid works nicely.
- A cheesecloth, strainer, or a fine-weave towel.
- Amber glass makes your infusion last much longer because it blocks out light.

Herb-infused oil steps:

1. Make sure your jar is very dry and clean. Any water will spoil the oil.

2. Fill the jar to the top with herbs.
3. Slowly pour the oil over the herbs.
4. Move the herbs around slowly with a chopstick, making sure there are no air pockets.
5. Add enough oil to cover the herbs completely, fill the jar to the brim.
6. Cover the jar and shake it a couple of times.
7. Put your jar in a cool, dry place.
8. Every so often, shake your jar.
9. Your oil will be ready in about two months.
10. Strain the oil into your amber-colored storage bottles using a cheesecloth.
11. Squeeze the herbs over the cloth to get that last bit of herbal goodness.
12. Add one capsule of vitamin E to the oil.
13. Place a lid or cork on your bottles and label them. They will last up to two years.

PART 2:

THE SPELLS

In this section, spells will include all of the education provided in Part 1. From Love Spells to Health Spells, to Money Spells, to Protection Spells, herbs are healthy and magical to their very essence, and are beautiful. They are full of ways to practice healing and protection magic, as well as dressing candles, and do-it-yourself essential oil-making. They are the most ancient way to make your space sacred. But the most powerful way to use your herbs is by using them in your magic. Whether for love or healing, abundance or success, you can harness their natural energy for many of your mystical endeavors. Part 2 will fill your enquiring mind with spells from A to Z.

8

LOVE SPELLS

Long before movies, romance novels, and self-help books on how to attract that special someone, magical practitioners took matters into their own hands. The lovestruck, lovelorn, and the romantically loved turned to folk wisdom gathered from generations passed to keep and catch romance. Plants and herbs have been symbolizing devotion and love for centuries. The ancient Greeks wove marigolds and mint into wreaths and bridal garlands. Long ago in Italy, brides carried rosemary to be sure of the groom's fertility, and wheat for their own. During medieval times in Europe, brides carried chives and gals and other pungent herbs to ward off evil spirits that might try to disrupt their happiness. Furthermore, during the Victorian era, pansies, roses, marjoram, and lavender were combined for contentment and romantic success (aka love spells). Most love spells call for unique ingredients that have to be used in combination with specific sets of arcane words.

Love potions are documented as far as the Greeks of ancient times adding ground-up orchids to their wine for its aphrodisiac properties. They believed this potion would stimulate passionate love for whoever drank it. It was so popular among the Greeks that the sacred orchid became temporarily extinct. Versions of the Blister Beetle or Spanish Fly drink are still created today. Historically, true Spanish Fly was made from a substance called cantharidin, which is produced by blister beetles. When in contact with the skin, cantharidin caused blistering, hence the name. Spanish Fly has been traced back to an Empress in Rome, who used cantharidin for sexual purposes so she could then use the act for blackmail. It was also used for orgies by Roman gladiators. Unfortunately, what wasn't known by those unsuspecting lovers was that the warmth and swelling of the genitals was not stimulation but inflammation!

Magical textbooks in 16th century Europe also became increasingly popular. Once such book was entitled, *The Book of Secrets of Albertus Magnus: Of the Virtues of Herbs, Stones, and Certain Beasts.* One of his potions was made by mixing periwinkle with crushed earthworms, which was to stimulate affection between a married couple. Around that same time, animal products coupled with herbs also became common ingredients in love potions. Ingredients from snake fat, bat's blood, pigeon's heart, and sparrow heads were among them.

These spells don't require finding archaeological remains, and mine don't incorporate bat's blood or sparrow heads. One love spell asked the user to have a brass ring inscribed with the name of the Goddess of Love seated on a rooftop with a lotus in their hands chanting magical words at the moon. These spells do, however, require the tender loving care of your plants. Even if there is a blooming romance, love spells with all of their herbaceousness can influence the chemistry between you and your romantic partner in ways that create long-lasting fidelity, loyalty, and lust. I have made the following love spells to meet your specific circumstances, so take great care before you use them and consider your intentions carefully.

Bringing Love into Your Life Spell

Magical herbs are commonly used for creating love ties, often practiced by green witches. Sometimes, love ties are cast by blowing powdered herbs onto a candle's flame while performing ritual chants. Magnolia, Thyme, Rose, Rosemary, Verbena, Vanilla, and Violet are some of the herbs usually taking part in spells to bring love into your life.

HOW LONG IT TAKES:

1 hour

WHAT YOU'LL NEED:

- A basil plant you planted yourself in your living room
- Large pot
- Soil
- Dried basil leaves
- Dried leaves of lavender
- Red rose petals
- ½ teaspoon honey
- One red candle and lighter
- Rose essential oil
- A saucepan
- A small wooden stick or spoon
- A piece of paper
- A red ink pen or fine marker
- One piece of thin red ribbon
- A small clay bowl with a lid

- A thin red ribbon

STEPS:

1. Put your basil plant in the same room where you will be casting the spell.
2. On a large altar or spell table, light your red candle and ask the Sun Goddess or call upon the Element of Fire for its powers to bring love into your life.
3. Write your loved one's full name on the piece of paper, leaving room above it for your name. This way, the two of you will be joined with one on top of the other.
4. On the front of the paper, rewrite the two names all the way to the bottom.
5. On the back of the paper, neatly write: "I call upon the Element of Fire and the powers of animal magnetism to bind your heart as well as your feelings. Only me will you think of, and for only me will you feel love. The essence of each herb powered by the light of fire will be the fuel to our relationship as it will grow like the plant, always leafy and full of love. As it is and should be."
6. While the burning candle is doing its magic by the Element of Fire, start chopping the leaves of each herb, one at a time, and placing them in the saucepan.
7. Focus on the face of your love interest the entire time you are chopping herbs. Picture your future as if you are already living it. Picture making wonderful memories as you project your intention into the saucepan.

8. After all of the leaves of your herbs are chopped and in the saucepan, toss in your honey, hence keeping your love interest always sweet to you.
9. Place in your rose oil and mix with your wooden spoon.
10. Fold your spell written on the piece of paper and place it in the bottom of the clay pot.
11. Pour the mixture over the spell and cover the clay pot.
12. Tie the piece of red ribbon around the clay pot.
13. Bury your pot deep in the ground somewhere in your yard.
14. Once the spell has taken hold, and you are now with your loved one, or your present relationship has blossomed, dig up the clay pot and replace it with the basil plant you have been caring for from the start.
15. As your basil plant thrives, so will your relationship.
16. Thank the elements and the plant.

It's All About Loving Yourself Spell

It has to be about loving yourself first before the magic can be made at all. We live in a world of emotional struggles, comparisons, self-image, and societal pressures. If you have lost love and respect for yourself because of some emotional trauma, a failure, or a bad heart-break, this is the time for some self-love magic. Self-love spells can be the happiest and best magic there is for living a positive life. Too often, the focus is on loving others or wanting others to love us. Without self-love, it's impossible to show another person any real, true, or profound emotions. One of the most powerful ways to do this comes from nature, so this is one of my special herbs spells for self-love magic.

HOW LONG IT TAKES:

35 minutes

WHAT YOU'LL NEED:

- A mirror
- 3 pink candles
- 3 blue candles
- Lavender
- Rose petals
- Chamomile
- Mint

STEPS:

1. Place your mirror on your altar.
2. Place your candles around the mirror in a circle.
3. Put all of the herbs in your cupped hands and begin rubbing them between your fingers while feeling their energy.
4. Close your eyes and visualize yourself where you are sitting.
5. Imagine and picture in your mind a green ball of energy glowing in the middle of your chest.
6. Visualize the green light ball growing brighter and livelier and beginning to mix with the candle lights that are reflecting in the mirror and then against you.
7. Take several slow and deep breaths, exhaling.
8. While deep breathing, scatter the herbs onto the mirror and chant:

> *Love within, without a doubt*
> *All of my pain on its way out*
> *Heal my scars so that I may breathe*
> *No longer will I feel any thoughts that seethe*
> *As it is and should be*

Dreaming of Me Spell

The best way to use a spell about dreaming is to have the person wanting you with their free will. Magically getting a love interest or loved one to dream about you is not an easy feat. You have to free your mind of your own problems before you can influence another person's dreams. It also helps to put the thought of you into their mind before they go to sleep. Prior to your spellwork, some techniques are to call or text them before they go to sleep. Leave a picture of yourself near them at bedtime, burn incense familiar to you, or any other mystical ideas you can come up with to stir the unconscious of the person upon whom you are casting your spell.

HOW LONG IT TAKES:

40 minutes

WHAT YOU'LL NEED:

- Rosemary
- Lavender
- Cotton material
- Cotton
- Parchment paper
- Needle and thread

STEPS:

1. Cut two pieces of cotton fabric and sew them closed on three sides (you are making a dream pillow).

2. Stuff your pillow with cotton.
3. Add your herbs.
4. Sew the pillow closed.
5. Write the person's name and precisely what you want them to dream about on the parchment paper.
6. Prepare your altar with crystals and rosemary.
7. Cast a sacred circle (see casting a circle in the previous chapter) big enough for you and your altar to be in the middle.
8. Stand in the middle and place the parchment paper on top of the pillow.
9. Hold the pillow in your hands and chant:

> ***Blessed Earth, may this be***
> ***Send (person's name) dreams of me***
> ***Awaken their mind, as I hold the key***
> ***My voice, my heart, my soul, they can see***
> ***As it is and should be***

10. Place the pillow in the bedroom dresser drawer of the person upon whom you are casting the dream spell, where it can't be detected.

How Sweet Love is Spell (to Sweeten your Relationship)

The theory behind this honey jar spell is relatively simple. You use honey and a handwritten note that encourages both of you in a relationship to be more loving, kinder, and sweeter towards each other. The wonderful thing about jar magic is that it is very portable, meaning you can take your spell with you wherever you go if you are inclined to do so. Honey jar magic is a lovely example of sympathetic and gentle magic. It can also be used to sweeten any relationship, such as to make your boss sweeter, create a more loving relationship with family members, or even for a problematic neighbor.

HOW LONG IT TAKES:

1 hour

WHAT YOU'LL NEED:

I like to use a clear glass honey jar, but you can use pink too. Make sure the mouth of the jar is large enough for your ingredients. Pick a jar that you have meditated on while thinking about the person upon whom you are casting your spell. Make sure the lip can handle the heat of a candle.

- Honey or molasses
- Paper
- A pen
- Cardamom
- Lavender
- Rose

- Cinnamon
- Small red candle

STEPS:

1. Write the name of the person with whom you want to sweeten your relationship THREE times on your paper.
2. Rotate the paper 90 degrees.
3. Over the top of the person's name in a cross-type manner, since you rotated the paper, write your name THREE times. Your name will cross the other name like a grid.
4. Close your eyes and take 6 breaths in through your nose and out of your mouth, slowly.
5. With your eyes slowly opening, focus on the paper with the names. Think specifically about how you want the relationship to be sweeter (romantically, sexually, friendly, compassionate, etc.).
6. Focus strongly on your intention.
7. Using your pen, write your intention in a circle around the grid of names, making sure to connect the circle so it is sealed with the words (last word written to the first word written). I am not the best at writing in cursive, so don't worry if it looks messy, even if you write love in a circle over and over again.
8. You can add symbols or sigils; embellish your paper as you wish.
9. Fold the paper in half in the same direction as you wrote the other person's name.

10. Turn the paper 90 degrees and fold it in half again in the direction your name is written.
11. Anoint your parcel with drops of lavender oil.
12. Place your parcel in the jar and fill it with honey.
13. Add your herbs.
14. Stick your finger through the herbs and honey until you are touching your parcel and chant:

> ***Sacred honey from the bee,***
> ***Your sweetened powers, please lend to me***
> ***Just as this honey is sweet***
> ***So sweet shall (person's name) be with me***
> ***As it is and should be***

15. Touch your finger, covered in honey, to your lips.
16. Visualize the person's face as you lick the honey from your lips.
17. Close the jar with the heat-resistant lid.
18. Place your red candle on top of your jar.
19. Think about your spell with deep intention and light the candle.
20. Let the candle burn down all the way.
21. Leave the candle wax on the jar and store it in a safe place.
22. Go back to your jar frequently to look at it and thank it for its power.

I prefer to charge my spell jar twice a month, each time with a new candle. I rotate between red and white, restating my intention, so my spell stays strong. As you can tell, I am an herb-loving magical practitioner, and every time I write a spell for you or me, I learn something new.

Think of Me Spell

This is a simple but very effective spell and will help you keep your loved one connected with you! This magic ritual is effective and mighty, and once cast, there is no turning back, so be very clear about your intentions. Archangel Chamuel is the angle of nurturance in romantic love. He is often called upon for spells regarding relationships, restoring love, and understanding unconditional love. Ask yourself how strong you want your spell to be. Do you want someone obsessed and thinking non-stop about you? Do you want someone to start thinking about you more and more as each day passes? Do you have a crush and want thoughts of you to pop into your love interest's head? These are the questions you need to ask yourself before casting this spell.

HOW LONG IT TAKES:

15 minutes

WHAT YOU'LL NEED:

- A piece of white paper
- A red pen
- Basil
- Mint
- Lemon balm

STEPS:

1. Write the name of the person you are casting the spell on with a red pen.
2. Chop up your herbs.
3. Place them in the center of the paper.
4. Fold it into a parcel so that the herbs do not fall out.
5. Hold the parcel in your right hand and repeat the person's name three times.
6. Chant:

> **Help me, most powerful Archangel Chamuel to have (name of person) think of (your name) often. Through his powerful magic that only (your name) is the object of (person's name) thoughts of affection. To call me while lying down tonight and ask me to spend a life together. As it is and should be.**

7. Put the folded parcel under your pillow and repeat the person's name three times.
8. Do this for three nights and then hide it somewhere where it will not be disturbed.

Repair This Relationship Spell

Relationships are hopeful and made up of wonderful connections between a couple, family members, or friends. They are meant to be your personal love and protection support team. Whether meeting someone you are in a relationship with happened by chance or it was predetermined before this life cycle started, the timeline in every relationship always stands a chance of having separation, arguments, disagreements, or a rift between those involved. Sometimes, these rifts are learning lessons that help us grow and move forward in life, giving us lessons to take into the future. While these rifts can hurt at times, they don't have to be permanent. I created this spell to reconnect loved ones, friends, and family members who have let a rift make them forget what it feels like to have a sacred love connection.

HOW LONG IT TAKES:

30 minutes

WHAT YOU'LL NEED:

- Sage bundle for smudging
- Hawthorn dried and powdered (Crataegus spp.)
- Rose petals dried and powdered (Rosa rugosa)
- Motherwort dried and powdered (Leonurus cardiaca) or Lemon balm (Melissa officinalis)
- 1 white taper candle
- 1 pink candle
- Wooden toothpick
- Parchment paper

- Lighter

STEPS:

1. Clean your items and your sacred space by smudging them with sage.
2. Grind up your herbs into a powder.
3. Keeping the wick intact, break the white candle in half (if it is for two people, otherwise break it into sections according to how many people are involved in the rift.
4. With your wooden toothpick, scribe the name of each person into separate sections of the broken candle. While scribing, visualize the Earth grounding any negative energies of that person so they can return to their pure state.
5. Lay the broken white candle on the parchment paper and chant:

> **We have seen the bad weather**
> **Now it's time to come back together**

6. Light the pink candle.
7. Sprinkle one herb at a time into the candle flame and notice the beautiful sparks.
8. Drip the wax from the pink candle into the cracks of the white candle.
9. As the pink wax is repairing the cracks, picture in your mind's eye loving pink energy, and those involved being

connected by the wick, as the pink wax is strengthening the connection once again.

10. When the cracks are repaired, let the wax harden.

11. Visualize the white candle with a glowing and loving pink light surrounding it.

12. Visualize the person(s) you had the rift with surrounded by the same pink light.

13. Chant:

> *All is mended*
> *All is well*
> *Reunited we are*
> *My words do tell*
> *As it is and should be*

14. When you feel the spell is complete, light the candle and let it burn all the way down.

Relationship Passion Restoration Spell

Sometimes the spark in your relationship starts to dwindle or even feels lost. Rejuvenating the passion and restoring the romantic spark in your relationship is exactly what this spell was created to do. If things between you and your partner have been tough, you are not alone. One of the most challenging times that most long-term relationships face is a decline of passion and initial attraction. You can smooth this rough patch and get things back to hugs and kisses with my Passion Restoring Relationship spell.

HOW LONG IT TAKES:

Full moon overnight + 30 minutes

WHAT YOU'LL NEED:

- Full moon
- Cinnamon
- Vanilla
- 2 red candles
- 2 pink candles
- 2 white candles
- Red cellophane
- 1 elastic band
- 1 glass of water
- Lavender essence
- 1 red rose

STEPS:

1. Put your water in the center of your altar.
2. Place the red rose in the water.
3. Add your herbs.
4. Place the water with the rose and herbs under a full moon.
5. Put your bowl of water, rose petals, and herbs on your altar.
6. Light your candles in a circle around the bowl.
7. Focus on your candles and place three drops of lavender essence in the water while thinking of passionate love-making with your partner, and becoming one.
8. Do this for three minutes and then chant three times:

> *I call upon the passion of the moon*
> *Ignite the love between us two*
> *Together in love none too soon*
> *For romance, hugs, and kisses true*
> *As it is and should be*

Hands Off Spell (for removing unwanted affection)

The usage of garlic magnifies this Hands Off Spell tenfold! Sometimes it just happens. You want to be friends, but the other person wants more. They start clinging and constantly touching, even when they know it makes you uncomfortable. It is quite selfish, if you think about it. I remember when I was in school, I had a really nice friend. We would do our homework together, and talk about sports and psychology. Then he said to me that he wanted more from our friendship. I felt heartbroken. Darn, I knew I was going to lose my good friend. I told him I never wanted to take a chance on ruining our friendship. He said he accepted that but began moving closer and closer every chance he got. I could even smell his breath. I had to turn to my Black Book in the hopes of magic that would maintain our friendship without me ever having to smell his breath again or be uncomfortable from having him lean against my body every time he was about to leave.

HOW LONG IT TAKES:

10 minutes

WHAT YOU'LL NEED:

- Garlic oil
- Pen
- Paper
- Black candle
- Abalone shell

STEPS:

1. Write the name of the person producing the unwanted affection on a piece of white paper with a black pen.
2. Light your black candle.
3. Place three drops of garlic oil on the name written on the paper.
4. While smelling the garlic, think of how annoying this person's advances have become. Feel the aggravation and repulsion.
5. Hold the paper over the flame (being careful) until it lights on fire.
6. Drop it into your abalone shell.
7. Chant 10 times:

> *Friends we'll be*
> *Without you touching me*
> *So mote it be*

8. Let it burn until it goes out.
9. Drip the black wax over the ashes.
10. Dig a small hole in the dirt in your yard and dump the waxed ashes and cover it up.

Confidence of a Lion Spell

There are many reasons for a person to lack confidence. A bad experience, the way we were raised, being bullied. It is never your fault for why you are experiencing low self-confidence. The good news is that it is not a permanent state of being. This spell should be coupled with increased exercise (releases endorphins) and possibly a mani-pedi, which goes for both sexes.

HOW LONG IT TAKES:

35 minutes

WHAT YOU'LL NEED:

- Fennel seed
- Dogwood
- Curry
- Olive oil
- Small glass bowl
- Yellow candle
- Blue candle
- Mirror
- Pen and paper

STEPS:

1. Place your glass bowl in the center of your altar.
2. Rub the herbs in your hands until warm while smelling their aroma.

3. Place the herbs in the bowl and cover with olive oil (I like to use good regular olive oil for this spell, not virgin).
4. Put a candle on each side of the bowl.
5. Anoint your candles by touching the herbal olive oil and rubbing it on the sides of the candles.
6. Light both candles.
7. Write down five positive affirmations on the paper every ten minutes while the candles burn.
8. The spell is most powerful if you complete step 7 six times while looking in the mirror.
9. After reading the affirmations six times (after every ten minutes), snuff out your candles or let them burn down.
10. Lift the bowl gently, put the affirmations underneath the bowl, and let the herbs and oil magnify the words.
11. Leave it there until your confidence soars. You can make a small altar anywhere if you need to use your main altar and the bowl is in the way.

HEALTH SPELLS

The synchronicity between religion, magic, and medical practice becomes rather noticeable when one looks into ancient text and old scripts. Before the foundation of medical schools, monasteries and convents were the epicenters of medical practice and knowledge for thousands of years. Alongside the scientific development of medicine, which is rooted in the oldest of sciences, is the practice of folk medicine, most of all the herbal medicines, which are the original foundation and form of modern-day pharmacology. Recently, the number of people using herbal health practices, either in combination with others or alone, has risen dramatically. An herbal "renaissance" is occurring globally. The World Health Organization (WHO) reported that ¾ of the world's population use herbs for their basic health and wellness on a daily basis [1]. Furthermore, many pharmaceutical/conventional medicines distributed worldwide are made directly from both traditional remedies and nature. More than 50,000 species are used for herbal remedies, and some of these are facing extinction because of overexploitation.

Medicines such as morphine, quinine, and codeine all contain ingredients that are plant derivatives. These drugs, albeit synthetically manufactured, have become important to the lives of many of those who are sick and suffering. Isn't it wonderful to have nature on our side? Did you know that the ginkgo tree is appraised as a living fossil, with fossils found that are as old as 270 million years? The ginkgo tree can live to be 3000 years old. There is, however, a note of caution. Many herbs carry the same potential side effects and risks as manufactured drugs, and most are sold with unresearched promises. The good news here is that most teas and herbs offer many ways of improving our health, so do your homework about the effectiveness, safety issues, and potential interactions, especially for pregnant and breastfeeding mothers, as well as infants and children.

Herbs' magical and spiritual power has been documented for thousands of years through observation and use. These herbal allies' purposes and magical properties have been cherished more and more as people have learned about their growing conditions and natural habitats, how they are used for healing, and by analyzing their colors, scents, and flavors. Throughout millennia and experience, magicians and others have attributed specific qualities and energies to specific herbs. Both modern and ancient cultures have used herbs to repel negative energy and attract the positive. Magical crafters hang charms and poppets, make amulets, create perfumes and incense, blend potions and elixirs, and provide offerings to deities. From incense to smudging, witches have learned how to harness the power of herbs for health and wellness, protection and wisdom, and any imaginable purpose.

Bad Vibes Begone Spell (for releasing negative energy)

Each of us draws energy from a variety of sources to nourish our emotional needs. This is also how we power up the cells in our bodies, raise our cortisol levels, and metabolize cells, depending on emotional triggers. There are herbs specific to this process that have been used for centuries, and their frequencies directly impact transforming and deflecting negative energies. The worrisome thing about negativity is that you can only feel it; you can't see it. The good news is that you can eliminate it! Negativity can bring disharmony, lower your self-confidence, create emotional turmoil, and ruin peacefulness.

HOW LONG IT TAKES:

15 minutes

WHAT YOU'LL NEED:

- Basil
- Black pepper
- Cayenne
- Black tourmaline crystal
- Smoky quartz crystal
- Black onyx crystal
- White candle

STEPS:

1. Keeping a basil plant or plants will help you form stronger connections with the spirit world.

2. Place the crystals near your front door entrance on a shelf or small table.
3. Sprinkle black pepper on your doorstep at dusk to keep out unwanted intruders.
4. Light a white candle on your altar and sprinkle cayenne into the flame.
5. Clap three times.
6. Snuff out the candle.

Bad Habit No More Spell

Are you trying to rid yourself of a bad habit, like smoking or your carb intake? At some point in our lives, all of us conclude that certain behaviors, when repetitive, no longer serve us and become unhealthy. They usually begin as innocent activities, but then with time, they take over places in our lives where they were never intended to be. The longer we take to break the cycle, the more the bad habit becomes entrenched within us. By the time you realize how destructive this habit has become in your life, ridding yourself of it can seem insurmountable. Let me help you dig your way out of this problem with my Bad Habit No More Spell.

HOW LONG IT TAKES:

2 weeks

WHAT YOU'LL NEED:

- Full moon
- One box
- Paper and pen
- 2 rosemary sprigs
- 1 garlic clove
- One handful of graveyard dirt
- 1 roll of pennies
- 4-6 nails and a hammer
- 1 example or symbol of your bad habit (could be a cigarette, a twinkie, wine bottle cork, or a cuss word written down)
- Shovel

STEPS:

1. This spell requires commitment, as quitting any pattern in life does. It is very powerful but can also be quite tedious.
2. Meditate on your certainty about quitting your bad habit. It requires that you are positive and you wish to quit.
3. On the paper, write a list of reasons for wanting to stop. Keep it close by for reflection.
4. Decorate your box with a skull and bones and project your intent into it.
5. Leave your box outside under a full moon overnight to charge it.
6. Place it on your altar the following day.
7. You do not have to quit immediately. However, each time your bad habit tempts you, drop a penny in the box. If you are not at home, drop your penny or pennies in your box as soon as you arrive home.
8. Do this for two weeks. In the first few days, you will probably be dropping a lot of pennies in the box, but by the end of the two weeks, the number of pennies will significantly decrease.
9. Following the full moon, on night one of the waning moon, add your garlic clove and rosemary to your box.
10. Hold your bad habit symbol cupped in both hands. It may be matches, a candy wrapper, a dollhouse rocking chair, or a potato (to banish laziness). Get creative.
11. Take five minutes to grieve over your symbol. After all, it is like getting rid of a good friend.

12. Place your symbol in your box and seal your box with nails.
13. Take your box, shovel, nails, hammer, and graveyard dirt away from your home.
14. Dig a hole and put your box in the hole.
15. Throw your graveyard dirt on top.
16. Walk away without ever looking back.
17. Consider this as having had a funeral for your bad habit.

Restore Energy with a Peaceful Sleep Spell

Sometimes, even with enough sleep, we still feel like the energy is zapped from our bodies. Once in a while, I can get a good six to seven hours of sleep at night, and I exercise at the gym twice a week and do yoga at least three times a week, but somehow I still feel lethargic during the day. I wondered what was zapping my energy and what I should do about it. This spell worked wonders for me, but even better when I combined it with my Now I Lay Me Down To Sleep Spell, which is in my last book, *The Crystal Magic Spell Book*. I will put another spell I crafted to pair with this spell here because the two go hand in hand with the added power of peaceful dreams for energy magic.

HOW LONG IT TAKES:

20 minutes

WHAT YOU'LL NEED:

- Same rose quartz
- Chamomile tea
- 3 dried lavender stems

STEPS:

1. Sit in your bed in a comfortable position.
2. Prepare your chamomile tea.
3. With your eyes closed, gently move the rose quartz crystal around in your hands until you feel it warming. Let its

energy pass through your hands and throughout your whole body.
4. Stir your tea with the lavender stems 9 times in a sunwise (clockwise) direction.
5. Start sipping your tea.
6. Send this warming and sedating energy down to your stomach, all the way to your toes.
7. Allow your mind to settle into a peaceful state.
8. After a moment, quietly chant:

> *Calming peace come to me*
> *For tomorrow, it is the energy I need*
> *Grant restful sleep tonight*
> *Tomorrow I will be full of fight*
> *As it is and should be*

Give Me Energy, Give Me Strength Spell

This spell is for the day after the Restore My Energy with a Peaceful Sleep Spell.

HOW LONG IT TAKES:

15 - 30 minutes

WHAT YOU'LL NEED:

- Rose quartz crystal
- Dried vervain (Verbena officinalis)
- Your favorite music or song

STEPS:

1. Light the vervain.
2. Place your crystal next to it.
3. Turn up the music.
4. Start moving around and lose yourself in the music for as long as you feel, but not less than 6 minutes.

Creatively Creative Spell

Artfulness comes in many forms. Creating something wonderful that started as a tiny spec of an idea is truly magical. Creative thinking is manifestation at its deepest level. I'm not just referring to making a scrapbook or sculpting a clay pot - all creativity is a magical manifestation. Being creative can be a bit tricky, as it seems to come and go. Sometimes our creativity seems to come out of left field when we didn't know we had a creative purpose at that very moment, like when I am sitting at a stoplight. I love this spell, but it does take time, care, and nurturing. With each passing day, your creativity will grow.

HOW LONG IT TAKES:

1 month

WHAT YOU'LL NEED:

- Small piece of paper
- Seed of your choice
- Garden pot

STEPS:

1. Write your intended result for your creative project or plan on a piece of paper. Write these words when you feel filled with excitement over your plan. Use first-person and present tense, as if it has already manifested.
2. Prepare your garden pot with rich soil.
3. Dig a hole in the center of the soil.

4. Fold up your paper and stick it in the hole.
5. Place your seed next to the paper in the hole.
6. Cover your intention and the seed with rich potting soil.
7. Every time you water the plant, speak aloud your intention.
8. The manifestation will grow stronger as the plant begins to grow, until your desired result is achieved.
9. If your results are not what you expected, trust that it is for your highest good, and only good will come out of this spell.

Away with Illness Potion Spell

We are a culture that thrives on every technique, strategy, method, and motivation to ward off illness. Preventative medicine, a modern term, has been around since the beginning of time. "An apple a day keeps the doctor away." We take our vitamins every day, exercise, and stay hydrated. Some of our loved ones are too young or too old to keep up with a daily regimen of health and wellness activities, so a bit of magic goes a long way. I keep a constant supply of this magical potion, and it has worked wonders for my family and me for decades, especially during the cold and flu seasons.

HOW LONG IT TAKES:

20 minutes

WHAT YOU'LL NEED:

- 2 tablespoons grated ginger
- 2 tablespoons thyme
- Pinch of cayenne
- 2 tablespoons rosemary
- 1 teaspoon turmeric
- 2 tablespoons oregano
- Juice of 1 lemon
- 13 drops dragon's oil
- 1 teaspoon honey
- Water

STEPS:

1. Add ginger, turmeric, cayenne, rosemary, thyme, and oregano to a small saucepan.
2. Cover with water.
3. Boil for 10 minutes until the water is darkened.
4. Strain the potion.
5. Add the juice of one lemon.
6. Add honey.
7. Add 25 drops of dragon's blood.
8. Stir to mix.
9. Store in the refrigerator and take one shot per day to ward off illness.

New Friends on the Block Spell

Making new friends is always exciting but can also be somewhat anxiety-provoking, as the process of establishing trust begins. For most of us, our friendships are a big part of our lives. They are the people with whom we share and make memories, and who go through our pain and joys with us. I wouldn't be who I am without my friends, and I am sure you feel the same. When meeting a new friend or wishing to make new friends, work this spell and enjoy its results. I will not steer you wrong.

HOW LONG IT TAKES:

24 hours

WHAT YOU'LL NEED:

- 1 bowl or dish of spring water
- 3 rose petals
- Lemon
- 3 sunflower petals
- Rose oil
- Vanilla ice cream

STEPS:

1. In a dish on your altar, float your rose and sunflower petals in some spring water with two drops of rose oil and let it soak until evening. Or, if you plan on meeting people in the evening, wait until you are ready to go to bed.

2. Before setting off for work in the morning, drink a glass of spring water with squeezed lemon.
3. Visualize the lemony light enveloping you from the inside and illuminating out of your eyes and onto your face.
4. When you are in a social environment, envision the light of the lemon coming out of your eyes and notice how much more alive and interested you feel.
5. Make plans with your new friend(s) to enjoy some vanilla ice cream together to solidify the friendship.

Cleanse My Spirit Spell

Burning or smudging herbs is a sacred ritual in many ceremonies held for healing and shamanic traditions. It is a way to cleanse your spirit of negative energies, influences, and vibrations. Burning sacred herbs allows access to the plants' powers, and their aromas release high levels of vibrational energies to protect your spiritual and physical bodies. The sacred herbs are tied into a bundle and then set to dry, making a "smudge bundle." Treat your bundles with respect.

HOW LONG IT TAKES:

10 days

WHAT YOU'LL NEED:

- String
- Lavender
- Sage
- Sweetgrass
- Cedar
- Palo Santo
- Copal
- Abalone Shell

STEPS:

1. Each one or a combination of the above ingredients will create your bundle. Feel free to add a bit of lavender to each bundle.

2. Tie each group of herbs at the base with string in a secure knot.
3. Beginning in the center, start wrapping the string toward the top of the bundle and then crisscross the string back to the base.
4. Do not crush the herbs when tying your bundle.
5. Cut off the excess string.
6. Hang your bundles upside down for ten days or more in a cool, dry place.
7. Hold your stick over your abalone shell and evenly light one end. Let it burn for a few moments, and then blow out the flame.
8. Set your intention to cleanse your spirit.
9. Smudge your body from your feet to over your head.

Anxiety Begone Spell

Feelings of anxiety can be so overwhelming that sometimes you have to lie down. It is a necessary defense mechanism, as it warns us of impending danger and triggers hormones necessary for us to fight. Sometimes, we experience anxiety over a simple thought or irrational fear of impending doom. This spell is to rid you of the unhealthy type of anxiety that can be so crippling that it interferes with your quality of life. I thought at one time in my life that I was going to suffer chronic anxiety attacks forever. Not the case! With some exercise, meditation, rituals, and spells, I now live comfortably in my own skin.

HOW LONG IT TAKES:

11 days

WHAT YOU'LL NEED:

- Chamomile
- Honey
- Lavender oil
- White candle
- Wooden toothpick

STEPS:

1. Prepare for yourself a cup of chamomile tea with honey.
2. In the center of your altar, place your white candle and anoint it with lavender oil.
3. Light your candle and meditate while sipping your tea,

drawing upon its white light for calmness and relief from anxiety.

4. Sit your tea on your altar next to the candle and chant:

> *I draw upon my power so strong*
> *With it, all anxiety is gone!*
> *No worries, no fear*
> *For peace is now here*
> *As it is and should be*

5. Let the candle burn for five minutes and then snuff it out.
6. Repeat the chant with a cup of tea and a lighted candle for eleven days.

Another Serving of Psychic Intuition, Please Spell

Psychic ability, much like the five senses, gives us information about our surroundings on an energetic and spiritual level. As a witch, I believe that increasing my psychic intuitions is what moves me forward in my spiritual journey.

HOW LONG IT TAKES:

20 minutes

WHAT YOU'LL NEED:

- A spell jar (You can use a regular jar with a lid or a colored jar - it becomes a spell jar after you place your intention upon it.)
- Water
- Salt
- Mint
- Aloe
- Goldenrod
- 1 quarter
- 1 clear quartz crystal
- 1 oxtail bone

STEPS:

1. Place all of your ingredients except the crystal, quarter, and oxtail bone in the bottle.

2. Place your quarter, oxtail bone, and clear quartz crystal in a triangle shape around your spell jar.
3. Imagine silver lights swirling up, down, and around your jar.
4. Focus all of your senses and intentions on enhancing your psychic abilities.
5. Let your energy fill your spell jar.
6. Leave it on your altar overnight to charge.
7. Place it with you wherever you spend time in your house.
8. Place it back on your altar once a week with the bone, quarter, and crystal to recharge.

WEALTH SPELLS

Most people are interested in money, especially when struggling to make ends meet. After love magic, money magic is the most common spellwork asked about, and the most commonly practiced after healing spells. As usual, all spells are powered by your intention. A wise witch once told me that while a person's happiness cannot be bought, not having financial burdens certainly makes life easier. I agree that having money also helps us escape many constraints on our energy and time. Time and energy are much better spent on enlightened spiritual pursuits instead of the constant anxieties of finances. Money gives us the autonomy to make decisions about how we choose to live our lives. This chapter will provide you with practical, insightful, and clever spells for changing insubstantial patterns in life to plentiful life patterns in any way you wish to apply your intention. If you find yourself struggling to make it to the end of each month, it is only because you have not yet learned how to attract money. These spells will help you to do just that.

For Richer or Richer Spell

Harnessing moon power is an effective way to attract prosperity. When moon magic and herbal magic work together, it is a recipe for financial success. Basil is often called the abundance herb, and cinnamon the "sweet money herb." Clove, along with cinnamon and basil, raises your spiritual vibrations and amplifies moon magic. This spell is one of my "feel good" spells, too!

HOW LONG IT TAKES:

30 minutes

WHAT YOU'LL NEED:

- Full moon
- Sachet bag
- Cinnamon
- Clove
- Dried basil

STEPS:

1. Cast this spell during a full moon.
2. Place all of the herbs in a sachet bag.
3. Run a warm bath and place the satchet bag into the tub.
4. As you soak in this water during a full moon, envision your spiritual energies rising.
5. As you soak, know, and meditate on your wallet as it fills with money and all of your bills are satisfied.

6. As the water cools, drain your bath.
7. Quickly bury the sachet in the earth under the full moon.

Want Ads New Job Spell

There is always something so exciting yet frightening about looking for a new job. "What if they don't like me?" "Did I do well in the interview?" "Will I have to relocate?" Seeing a job is exciting because it gives rise to new opportunities, widens your network, builds up your resume, and helps you learn new skills. It is the change that is so intimidating. If you want or need a new job and you have anxiety, you're not alone. Anxiety about finding a new job is common but conquerable.

HOW LONG IT TAKES:

50 minutes

WHAT YOU'LL NEED:

- Green fabric
- Needle and green thread
- Pen and paper
- A dollar bill
- Clear quartz crystal (small)
- Allspice
- Cinnamon
- Mint
- Rosemary

STEPS:

1. Using your green fabric, sew together three sides of the sachet.
2. Write down your dream job and some general circumstances for the job you are looking for. Trust in the universe to know what is best. Some examples include "a good salary, good teamwork, use of my creativity."
3. Place into the sachet the herbs, and your paper folded up into a parcel.
4. Add your clear quartz crystal and the dollar bill.
5. Sew your sachet closed.
6. Smudge with sage and chant:

> *A new job, a good job, is for me*
> *Finding it is as easy as 1, 2, 3*
> *This new job will make me happy as can be*
> *So mote it be*

7. Look for the largest tree near your home and bury the sachet near its roots.
8. While you are searching for your job, periodically stop by and water the tree.
9. Happy job hunting and good luck!

Good First Impression Spell

Everyone wants to be remembered. However nice it is to make a good first impression, it also takes some effort on your end. Our need to make a good first impression dates back to prehistoric times, and serves as a defense mechanism by processing information about facial patterns a person exhibits during a first meeting. Our first impression provides us with our feelings about how trustworthy, friendly, honest, and morally sound is the person we are meeting.

HOW LONG IT TAKES:

45 minutes

WHAT YOU'LL NEED:

- 1 whole orange
- 4 tablespoons vanilla extract
- 8 rose petals
- 1½ teaspoons bay leaves
- ½ teaspoon spearmint
- ½ teaspoon peppermint
- ½ teaspoon thyme

STEPS:

1. Draw a warm bath.
2. Place all of the herbs, the rose petals, and vanilla in the water.
3. Cut the orange in half and put it in a bowl next to the tub.

4. Get in the water.

5. Squeeze the juice of ½ the orange into the water.

6. Chant:

> *The first time you meet me, who will I be*
> *A great first impression you will have of me*
> *The day we first meet, I'm sure you will see*
> *You will from now on think highly of me*
> *As it is and should be*

7. Suck the orange out of the other half.

8. Float the orange halves in the water until it starts to cool.

9. Drain the tub and collect the wet ingredients.

10. Scatter them about your yard for the earth and animals to enjoy!

You're Promoted Spell

My first time being promoted felt really good. I felt a sense of worth rooted in hard work. I felt validation for the time and effort I had been putting in. It motivated me by appealing to my ambition. It made me want to achieve even more, and I knew if I added magic to my ambition and motivation, I would work my way to the top. And I did. You can, too, if you set your intentions to match your ambition.

HOW LONG IT TAKES:

10 minutes each morning

WHAT YOU'LL NEED:

- 1 handheld bell
- Ginger
- Patchouli bundle
- Cinnamon sticks
- Clove spice
- Mint (½ cup)
- Gold glitter
- Olive oil (1 cup)
- Frankincense

STEPS:

1. Cleanse your kitchen by smoking the patchouli bundle.
2. Next, add all of the dry ingredients except the gold glitter to a small pot.

3. Add olive oil.

4. Simmer as a potpourri.

5. Each morning sprinkle a pinch of gold glitter in your pot, ring your bell three times, and chant:

> *I work hard, I stay in motion*
> *This week, I will be granted a promotion*
> *Those up the ladder will now notice me*
> *As it is and as it should be!*

6. Do this every day until you receive your promotion.

Debt Free for Me Spell

Have you ever asked yourself, "How did I get here?" Have you found yourself in bondage to your bills? When you get your first loan or credit card, you don't plan on the interest or even making payments. Most people say to themselves, "I am just going to pay it at the end of every month."

HOW LONG IT TAKES:

5+ days

WHAT YOU'LL NEED:

- 1 jar with lid
- Small coins
- Medium-sized coins
- Large coins
- 5 tablespoons flour
- 5 cinnamon sticks
- 5 teaspoons cayenne pepper
- 5 whole pecans

STEPS:

1. Fill up the jar with all the ingredients.
2. Cap it tightly.
3. Shake it and chant:

> *With the power of these herbs*
> *and the powers that be*
> *My future and now will be debt-free*
> *As it is and should be*

4. For the first five days, put the jar in the southwest corner of your kitchen.

5. Then carry the jar with you in a velvet sack wherever you go.

Money on the Spot Spell

When I first began my business, I really needed some extra cash. I believed in myself, and I believe in magic, so I started a money bowl. As my business grew, so did my bowl. My goal was to turn a profit within six months of starting it. I hit that goal in two months. Once again, place your intention into each item before putting it in your bowl.

HOW LONG IT TAKES:

One week to one month

WHAT YOU'LL NEED:

- 1 roll of dimes
- Allspice
- Basil
- Wine cork
- Dollar bill
- Money clip
- Old wallet
- Cloves
- Sage
- Green gem
- Green tea candle
- Green cloth
- Anything green and natural

STEPS:

1. Add one dime per day to the bowl.
2. Each day put one ingredient in the bowl along with another dime.
3. Continue this process every day.
4. Your money will grow.

Happy Retirement Spell

Have you ever worried about retirement? How much money do you need? Most people share that boat with you. Depending on their financial status, people retire at all different ages, though most are in their 60's. Some people don't wish to retire until they are unable to work. Perhaps they have not imagined the spiritual journey that retirement affords us. It is by no means for me to judge what a person chooses to do. If you love your job, you never have to work a day in your life. However, for many, they have certainly put in their time and hopefully can look forward to their later years with vibrancy, magic, and much left to learn.

HOW LONG IT TAKES:

Once a month

WHAT YOU'LL NEED:

- Ashwagandha (Winter cherry)
- Turmeric
- Ginseng
- Allspice
- Cumin
- Garlic
- Basil
- 1 silver-colored object
- 1 gold-colored object
- 1 lock of your hair
- 1 jar with lid

STEPS:

1. Prepare your spell jar with the listed ingredients and seal it tightly.
2. On the day of the new moon, take your spell jar with you to a park.
3. Sit on a park bench.
4. Take off your shoes.
5. Start earthing (review chapter six).
6. Chant:

> *I thank the Goddesses*
> *I thank the Gods*
> *I thank myself for working hard*
> *I thank the Elements*
> *I thank the herbs*
> *For giving me the quality of life I deserve*
> *It's not about riches*
> *It's all about love*
> *Love for everyone below and above*
> *In this year now and years to come*
> *I will cherish my garden for giving me love*
> *As it is and should be*

7. Once a month, find a peaceful place for earthing while holding your spell jar. Feel the grass of a golf course, the sand on the beach, the snow on a mountain, anything that represents things you want to experience when you retire joyfully.

8. Repeat the chant at each place, and it will become sacred and represent a future of retirement beyond your wildest dreams. Believe, as it is and should be.

End My Bad Luck Spell (to banish bad luck)

Have you found yourself chipping a tooth, dropping something heavy on your foot, running out of ink when you just replaced it? I have been there and done that, and it was time to end that string of bad luck. Whether you feel you have just had a string of bad energy or that you may be cursed, this wonderful spell will banish the bad luck you may be experiencing. Before I do this spell, I always take a ritual bath, cleanse, clean and bless my home and myself. I also promise always to follow my intuition and respect my personal signs and intentions.

HOW LONG IT TAKES:

5 hours

WHAT YOU'LL NEED:

- 10" square piece of paper
- Black pen
- Abalone shell
- White candle
- Sage
- Allspice
- Bay leaves

STEPS:

1. In your sacred space, write "BAD LUCK" on a piece of white paper.

2. Under those words, write how bad luck has influenced your life.

3. Draw a large red **X** over each circumstance or experience you wrote about, X-ing them out of your life forever.

4. Imagine yourself safe from harm.

5. Draw a large red **X** over each letter in "BAD LUCK," manifesting your string of bad luck to be banished.

6. Place the herbs in an abalone shell and place the candle on top.

7. Light the candle, light the piece of paper on fire, and drop it into the abalone shell.

8. As the fire burns chant three times:

> *Dark hours, burning fire, my luck improves by the hour*

9. Once your ingredients have cooled, take ¼ of the ash and scatter it in your toilet, and chant three times:

> *Water on earth running free*
> *I flush this bad luck away from me*

10. Take ¼ more of the ash and throw it in the wind, and chant:

> *Ash in the wind on this dark night*
> *Take my bad luck, and all will be right*

11. Take ¼ more of the ashes and bury them in your garden, and chant:

> **Earth transforms and does not hesitate**
> **Remove my bad luck, for I do not relate**

12. Carry the last ¼ of the ash in a baggie and empty it out of the window of a car when you are as far from your house as possible and chant:

> **As it is and should be**

A Path to New Opportunities Spell

I hate to be the one to tell you, but new opportunities don't just land in your lap. They require you to find ways to attract them into your life. Along with your magic, you have to put yourself out there. Being open-minded and in touch with your energy will empower your magic to open your eyes to opportunities when they arise. They can come in many forms. They may be small opportunities like lending a helping hand or big opportunities like a new job. Or huge opportunities, like getting to take a ride on a space shuttle. After you cast this spell, you just have to notice them, and it will seem like they fell into your lap.

HOW LONG IT TAKES:

30 minutes

WHAT YOU'LL NEED:

- Fire-safe bowl
- Matches
- Charcoal
- Feather
- 1 tablespoon crushed camomile leaves
- 1 teaspoon cinnamon
- ½ teaspoon ginger
- ½ teaspoon bay leaves

STEPS:

1. Mix all of the ingredients in the fire-safe bowl.
2. Close your eyes and envision yourself walking down a hallway of an ancient house to a very old door. The old door represents any obstacles or anything blocking you from new opportunities.
3. Imagine yourself opening the door, and a brilliant light flows in and covers you.
4. Meditate on the freedom you feel facing a world of new opportunities and chant:

> **Opportunities are new**
> **Coming out of the blue**
> **Sacred brilliant light**
> **Has removed all of my fright**
> **Onward I march without any fear**
> **I thank my herbs, and hold them dear.**

5. Place the charcoal atop the herbs and light it.
6. Fan yourself with the smoke using a feather and chant:

> **As it is and should be**

Shamrock Good Luck Spell

The luck of the shamrock dates back to Celtic priests known as the Druids in the early times of Ireland. They believed that carrying a shamrock, or three-leaf clover enabled them to foresee evil spirits, providing them time to escape. For the Celtics, by 1620, four-leaf clovers were thought of as magical charms to keep away bad luck. During the middle ages, children believed they would see fairies if they were to carry a four-leaf clover. This discussion first appeared in a text by Sir. John Melton in 1620, in which he suggested they bring good fortune[1]. I believe those children saw fairies because they intended to see fairies and believed in fairies. Good luck has to be believed in for this spell to work. Intention has to be truthful for any spell to work.

HOW LONG IT TAKES:

30-45 minutes

WHAT YOU'LL NEED:

- A shiny new penny
- A white candle
- Abalone shell
- A drawing of a four leaf clover
- Spearmint or mint leaves

STEPS:

1. Cleanse your altar.
2. Light the white candle.
3. Place your mint leaves in your abalone shell.
4. Flip the penny onto your altar until it lands on heads three times in a row. It may take a while, but eventually, it happens.
5. Burn your drawing atop your herbs in your abalone shell and chant:

> *Luck of the shamrock, send luck to me*
> *With this offering*
> *As it is and should be*

6. Let the candle burn all the way down.

FINAL THOUGHTS

If you are new to spellcrafting with herbs, know this: spells are cast, and rituals are performed every day by many people. Understanding how important it is to have positive energy is vital to raising your spiritual vibrations. You have made a connection with each herb by learning everything you can about them. The more confidence you have in your spells, the more powerful they become and the faster your results. Herbal magic takes time, patience, love, and understanding. So, there is a bit more to green magic than one may practice with candles or crystals. All three together make for powerful, strong magic, and you do not have to grow your candles or water your crystals. I love it because the watering, feeding, providing the right amount of sunlight and knowing when to harvest their leaves, roots, stems, flowers, and their essences all create a bond that is much like the one I have with my closest friends. Tapping into your inner strength for empowerment is essential to magic-making. Learning the techniques of herbal magic will enable you to master your spellcraft and fulfill your destiny of becoming a skilled practitioner! Your effort and patience will greatly reward you if you focus your intention, believe in your spell, and keep your focus during the session. Focus, intent, and belief are the core ingredients to all spells.

Detailed in this book are herbs' magical history, folklore, recipes, elixirs, jar spells, bathing rituals, and much more. Pagan Sabbats or holidays are set to the earth's natural rhythms and seasons. The Sabbats detailed in this book celebrate the earth's journey around the sun, known as the Wheel of the Year, and the celebrations commemorating the Sabbats are referred to as Turning the Wheel. Also provided is a step-by-step guide for casting a sacred circle. In its fundamental form, a sacred circle can be a space visualized by you or can be designed with your ritual tools and created within and around your altar, outside, or anywhere you cast it for spellcrafting. Most magical workers believe their sacred circle is an energy container, and they practice their craft from within it. It is a spiritual shield protecting you from all negativity during the deeply emotional and vulnerable state you have to be in for your spells to work. It is like an invisible, impenetrable force field, from which negativity, imbalance, and disharmony bounce off.

In this book, you are provided with powerful love spells that so many people have come to me for. When people come to me for love magic, they are full of the power of positive thinking and trust in the process. I hope you feel the same. Practicing love spells is about - you guessed it - Love! Here is the deal; love spells work much more efficiently if the energy is already there and headed in a specific direction. Therefore, if the feelings budding are mutual, magic helps to accelerate the feelings, emotions, vibrations, and energies between the two people involved. It works like a magnetic force field pulling two people together. It is about attracting rather than making someone love you. Keep an open heart and mind while casting love spells. Sometimes they deliver more than you bargained for, but in a good way.

The money spells provided to you are designed to meet your specific individual needs, whether you are job hunting, need to improve your finances, preparing for retirement, or even to nudge along a business transaction. I shared these particular spells intending to help those looking for magical resources, and you may want to adjust them to meet your individual needs. Herbs have been used for centuries to amplify money spells. Money in its basic form is a tool you use for the trade of services or goods. However, it does contain energy, as in "the flow of money." The only time money becomes a problem in life is when you do not have enough of it to meet your needs or when you start hoarding it instead of saving it. When you become so worried about spending a penny, you are basically shouting out to the universe that you don't trust that it has your back. Hence, you block the energy flow of money.

To know thyself is the first rule of witchcraft. That includes understanding your relationship with money, how it developed, and which herbs work best for you in your prosperity spells. This book contains detailed information on the correspondence between money and basil, clove, rosemary, ginger, sage, and others, which have been used in spellwork and for trade throughout history. Remember, some herbs are not edible, so err on the side of caution. You can make powders by grinding up herbs with your mortar and pestle and then making magical blends. Roll your candles in herbs, add them to your money jar or mojo bag, add a stick of cinnamon or some basil in your coin purse or wallet for a bit of daily money magic.

Herbs have been a part of healing magic from the Stone Age and ancient societies all the way up to modern times. Western medicine's origins lie in the early healing lore of sedentary farmers, Paleolithic hunters and gathers, and herding nomads, rather than in traditional academically-based pharmacists and doctors. Healing with herbs is an integral aspect of this book and the many ways people from ancient times and today have used herbs in their surrounding environment. Traditions and knowledge that have been handed down to treat various conditions and ailments encountered in our daily lives are a priceless part of the magic kingdom. In writing this book, I realized the truest magic in all worlds is the opportunity to make a difference in someone's life. I hope this knowledge and these spells do that for you!

NOTES

1. THE MAGIC OF HERBS

1. The World Health Organization. WHO Traditional Medicine Strategy: 2014–23. 2013. 6 August 2018. http://apps.who.int/medicinedocs/en/m/abstract/Js21201en/

4. ESSENTIAL HERBS

1. https://garden.org/ideas/view/Sharon/982/Looking-for-Magic-Cayenne-Pepper/
2. https://www.thespruceeats.com/history-of-cinnamon-1807584
3. https://www.bowerandbranch.com/the-legend-of-the-dogwood/#:~:text=A%20-dogwood.,again%20be%20used%20in%20crucifixion

9. HEALTH SPELLS

1. https://www.ncbi.nlm.nih.gov/pmc/articles/PMC4020364/

10. WEALTH SPELLS

1. https://sctlandtrust.org/2020/03/17/history-of-the-four-leaf-clover-clover-crafts/#:~:text=The%20Druids%20(Celtic%20-priests)%2C,and%20ward%20off%20bad%20luck.

SPECIAL OFFER FROM HENTOPAN PUBLISHING

Get this additional book free just for joining the Hentopan Launch Squad.

If you want insider access, plus this free book, all you have to do is scan the code below with your phone!

www.ingramcontent.com/pod-product-compliance
Lightning Source LLC
Chambersburg PA
CBHW071800080526
44589CB00012B/630